Items should be returned on or before the last date shown below. Items not already requested by other borrowers may be renewed in person, in writing or by telephone. To renew, please quote the number on the barcode label. To renew online a PIN is required. This can be requested at your local library.
Renew online @ **www.dublincitypubliclibraries.ie**
Fines charged for overdue items will include postage incurred in recovery. Damage to or loss of items will be charged to the borrower.

Leabharlanna Poiblí Chathair Bhaile Átha Cliath
Dublin City Public Libraries

Baile Átha Cliath
Dublin City

Date Due	Date Due	Date Due

D1422571

CONTENTS

First published 2008
by Teagasc, Oak Park, Carlow, Ireland.

ISBN: 1-84170-515-2
Price: €30

Photographs are reproduced with kind permission of An Foras Talúntais,
Teagasc and other Library Sources.

Printed by GPS Colour Graphics Ltd.

AGRICULTURE AND FOOD DEVELOPMENT AUTHORITY
www.teagasc.ie

EDITOR

Michael Miley has more than 30 years experience in broadcasting, journalism and communications and is former head of public relations with ACOT and Teagasc. He is now working with Pembroke Communications.

PRODUCTION EDITOR

Mark Moore, Publications Manager, Teagasc.

DESIGN

Eamon Sinnott & Partners, Naas.

CONTRIBUTORS

Professor Gerry Boyle is director of Teagasc.

Brian Gilsenan is former head of publications in AFT.

Brendan Kearney is an economics consultant and former head of the AFT economics and rural welfare research centre.

Tom Kirley is director of administration in Teagasc.

Brendan Lynch is head of the pig production development unit in Teagasc.

Joe Murray is a broadcaster and journalist.

Dr Nuala Ní Fhlaithbheartaigh is head of the forestry development unit in Teagasc.

Dr David O'Connor is former head of education in Teagasc.

Dr Tom O'Dwyer is chairman of Teagasc.

Cormac Ó'Gráda is a professor in the School of Economics, University College Dublin. His latest book is *Ireland in the Age of Joyce: A Socio-economic History* (Princeton University Press, 2006). *Famine: A Short History* (also from Princeton UP) is due to be published in autumn 2008.

Lorcan O'Toole is head of the horticulture development unit in Teagasc.

Paddy Smith is a journalist, broadcaster and writer.

ACKNOWLEDGMENTS

I would like to thank all the people who generously gave up their time to talk to me and the other contributors and for making available manuscripts and historical documents. Their recollections and reminiscences made our task so much easier and added to the enjoyment of the exercise. Particular thanks must go to Pierce Ryan and Liam Downey, former directors of AFT, ACOT and Teagasc. I am also indebted to Reddy Day, Paddy O'Keeffe and T K Whitaker for their invaluable insights.

A special word of thanks is due to Olive Daly, Michael Butler, Paddy Geoghegan, Bernard Lewis and Pat Markey for their stories about the early years of AFT and to John Callaghan and Michael Galvin for guidance on developments in the advisory service. I am grateful to Ned Culleton, Noel Culleton, Gary Fleming, John Lee and Willie Murphy for their assistance in compiling the chapter on the highlights of research at Johnstown Castle, to Larry Doyle for memorabilia on Dr Tom Walsh and to Denis Conniffe for sharing his memories of the statistics service.

The help of the following former and current staff in compiling the section on beef is gratefully acknowledged – Paddy Cunningham, Roger McCarrick, Joe Harte, Vincent Flynn, Gerry Santry, Paddy Kelly, Elizabeth Cronly, Michael Diskin, Michael Drennan, Gerry Keane, Pádraig O'Kiely, Edward O'Riordan and Sinéad Waters. Seamus Hanrahan, Seán Flanagan, Vivian Timon, Tom Nolan and Frank Young provided vital support and advice for the section on sheep.

Thanks are also due to former and current Moorepark staff for their memories and views on dairying research. They include Michael Walshe, Dan Browne, Pat Gleeson, Jerry O'Shea, Michael Fleming, Pat McFeely, Kevin O'Farrell, Mick Reidy, John Palmer, Pat Dillon, Pádraig French, John Walsh and Margie Egan. Donal Cashman was, as always, ever supportive. The story on tillage research could not have been written without the help of Tom Thomas, Michael Conry, Harry Kehoe, Brendan Dunne, Dermot Forristal, Bernard Rice, Tom Kennedy and especially Jimmy Burke.

We drew on the expertise and support of the following former and current staff at Moorepark and Ashtown in charting developments in food research – Liam Donnelly, Vivian Tarrant, Michael Carroll, Tim Cogan, Barry Connolly, Tom Beresford, Geraldine Duffy, Ronan Gormley, Phil Kelly, Declan Troy, Vincent McLoughlin, Michael O'Keeffe, Paul Ross, Sean Tuohy, Michael Mulcahy, Joe Phelan and Frank O'Connor.

Aidan Conway is deserving of special mention for his unstinting support, calming influence and wise counsel at all stages. I want to thank Ultan Shanahan for making available his extensive memoirs and Charlie Godson for assistance with pictures. Appreciation is also extended to Máire Caffrey, Teagasc librarian, and Mary Doyle, librarian in the Department of Agriculture, for their help and courtesy during research. Thanks also to Ray Ryan of the Irish Examiner for access to his personal files and to Joanne Banks for making available extracts from interviews conducted for her thesis on the history of the advisory service.

In addition to the contributors listed on page (i), with whom it was a pleasure to work, I want to thank Ted Alter, Matt Dempsey and John Shirley for their reflections on important aspects of the period. I am very grateful to Gerry Boyle and Tom Kirley for their confidence, encouragement and professional guidance, to Teagasc chairman Tom O'Dwyer for his continuous support and to Teagasc authority members, Jimmy Brett, Patrick Fottrell, Stephen Flynn and Margaret Sweeney for reading a draft of the book and making valuable suggestions. Sincere thanks to Mark Moore for his professionalism, persistence and patience in ensuring that the book was published on schedule and for input into designing the overall look of the book and organising the extensive range of visuals that appear throughout. Finally, thanks to Alison Maloney for her help in organising the material.

The following references are also gratefully acknowledged:
Daly, Mary E. 2002. *The First Department: A History of the Department of Agriculture*. Dublin: IPA.
Rouse, Paul 2000. *Ireland's Own Soil: Government and Agriculture in Ireland, 1945 to 1965*. Dublin: Irish Farmers Journal.
Boyle, Gerry et al 2002. *The Costs and Benefits of Agricultural Research in Ireland*. Cork: Oak Tree Press.
Neenan, Michael. *A Popular History of Irish Agriculture 1879-1972*. Unpublished.

Michael Miley

PREFACE

The establishment of An Foras Talúntais (AFT) in 1958 marked a watershed for the Irish agriculture and food industry. This book is a celebration of the work of the early professionals and their successors in AFT and Teagasc and charts the contribution of research and innovation to the transformation of the agriculture and food industry during the last half-century.

Ireland in the late-1950s was in the depths of a prolonged depression. Agriculture was characterised by extremely low productivity. Yet, it dominated the economy and accounted for well over half of total exports, an indication of the poor state of the overall economy. The vision of Dr Tom Walsh, the first director of AFT, in developing a world-class research institute and the pioneering work of the cohort of young scientists he recruited were central in shaping the sophisticated food industry and rural society of today.

It is a story of national partnership in developing, disseminating and implementing new technologies and improved methods of producing, processing and marketing food and enhancing the fabric of rural Ireland. Advisers, first with the county committees of agriculture and later under ACOT and Teagasc, played a pivotal role in promoting and transferring the new technologies to farmers. Innovating farmers, who had the courage to adopt the technologies, were beacons on the road to a better way of life for all. The revolutionary changes could not have happened without the wholehearted support of the Department of Agriculture, the farming organisations, the wider agriculture and food industry and the media. The agricultural media, especially the Farmers Journal, is deserving of special recognition for transmitting new knowledge in a highly accessible form to farmers.

The establishment of AFT opened up a whole new world of opportunity for graduates at a time when employment prospects in Ireland were very limited. The current chairman of Teagasc, Dr Tom O'Dwyer, recalls as an under-graduate in UCD, hearing on a radio news bulletin the announcement by An Taoiseach Éamon de Valera of the imminent formation of the new body. Later that day, he informed his classmates that the new research institute was where he was going to work.

He did and later went on to play a central role in the development and implementation of EU agricultural policy. Many of the early recruits gave a lifetime of service to research while others, like Tom O'Dwyer, went on to play leading roles in other areas of the food industry and the economy.

This book is not intended to be an exhaustive account of all activity over the five decades since the foundation of AFT. It merely offers a glimpse of some of the key achievements and the people behind them. Many innovations have had to be omitted and this should not be interpreted as meaning that these were of lesser value or that the people involved did not make an equally important contribution to research and development. Research is a team effort and the successes of AFT and Teagasc owe an enormous amount to the dedication of technicians, administrative and farm staff throughout the organisation. This book is a tribute to their professionalism as much as it is to the achievements of the higher profile scientists.

Advisory and training services in agriculture have a much longer history than research. Separate chapters are devoted to the evolution and development of both services and their crucial role in disseminating the results of research is interwoven throughout the book.

I hope this publication provides an informative and enjoyable account of the development and evolution of research, advisory and training services in agriculture and food during an important period in Irish history as well as acting as a useful reference on the role of science and technology in the development of a modern industry.

I would like to fulsomely acknowledge the role of Michael Miley as editor. Quite simply, the production of this book would not have been possible without his wholehearted involvement, dedication and enthusiasm at all stages of its publication.

Professor Gerry Boyle
Director Teagasc

KEY MILESTONES

1945 – Department of Agriculture establishes research centre at Johnstown Castle following donation of the castle and estate to the state.

1949 – Head of Marshall Aid office, Joseph Carrigan, proposes establishment of an agricultural research institute.

1958 – An Foras Talúntais (AFT) - the new agricultural research institute - established.

1975 – Government White Paper proposes establishment of National Agricultural Authority, merging AFT with advisory and training services.

| 1945 | 1948 | 1949 | 1954 | 1958 | 1959/60 | 1964 | 1975 | 1977 |

1977 – National Agricultural Authority (NAA) established, but did not come into effect.

1948 – Soil testing laboratories opened at Johnstown Castle.

1954 – Agreement with US on £1.84 million funding for new research institute.

1959/60 – AFT establishes centres for research on dairying, beef, sheep, tillage, horticulture, soils, economics and food.

1964 – AFT operating from 21 research centres/farms with over 4,500 acres.

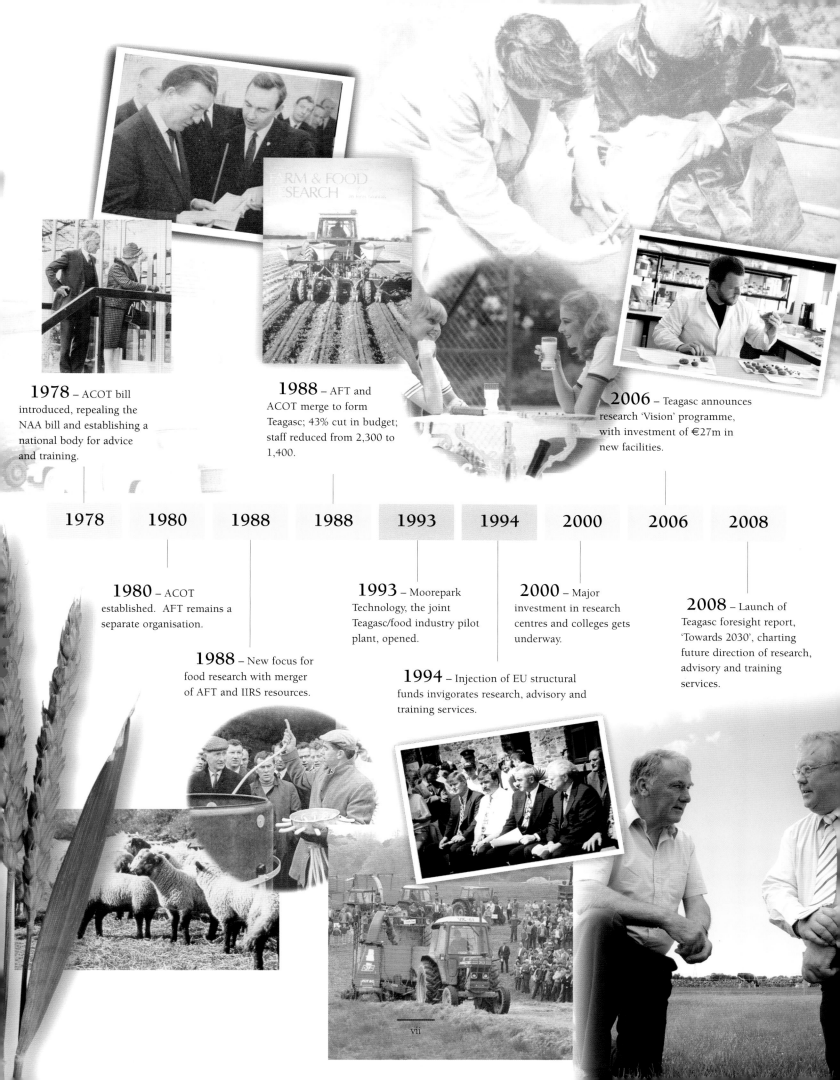

1978 – ACOT bill introduced, repealing the NAA bill and establishing a national body for advice and training.

1988 – AFT and ACOT merge to form Teagasc; 43% cut in budget; staff reduced from 2,300 to 1,400.

2006 – Teagasc announces research 'Vision' programme, with investment of €27m in new facilities.

| 1978 | 1980 | 1988 | 1988 | 1993 | 1994 | 2000 | 2006 | 2008 |

1980 – ACOT established. AFT remains a separate organisation.

1993 – Moorepark Technology, the joint Teagasc/food industry pilot plant, opened.

2000 – Major investment in research centres and colleges gets underway.

2008 – Launch of Teagasc foresight report, 'Towards 2030', charting future direction of research, advisory and training services.

1988 – New focus for food research with merger of AFT and IIRS resources.

1994 – Injection of EU structural funds invigorates research, advisory and training services.

CHAPTER 1
IRELAND IN THE 1950s

Cormac Ó Gráda

An Foras Talúntais, was born at a time of economic gloom and crisis. Towards the end of the same year when 'an institute for agricultural research to be known as An Foras Talúntais' was established, a key public policy document noted that *'a sense of anxiety'* about Ireland's economic prospects was indeed justified; *'after 35 years of native government people are asking whether we can achieve an acceptable degree of economic progress'*.[1] Almost simultaneously, in late 1958 the Irish Banking Review lamented that *'Ireland (had) been suffering from a mood of pessimism in recent years. Expressions of despair about the future…are heard on all sides'.*

The economy's dismal performance in
the 1950's was mainly, though not entirely,
the product of poor economic policies.

Two years earlier, the cover of the July 1956 issue of Dublin Opinion, capturing the despondency that ruled the Irish Republic in the mid-1950s, had borne a cartoon showing a map of Ireland with the caption, 'Shortly Available: Underdeveloped Country: Unrivalled Opportunities: Magnificent Views, Political and Otherwise: Owners Going Abroad'.

The widespread belief in the 1950s that Ireland's economy was under-performing is borne out by Figure 1, which describes the ratio of Irish to UK Gross Domestic Product (GDP) per head between 1938 and 1965. Even before the outbreak of Word War II that ratio was almost certainly less than it had been at independence in 1921/2. The impact of the war, which drove the ratio down to 0.4 in 1943, is striking. The Emergency, as World War II was known in Ireland, proved conclusively that no economy is an island. Then, after a short-lived post-war recovery, in 1958 the ratio reached a new low point. The huge fall in the ratio of Irish to British share prices between 1950 and 1958 also captures the dominant mood of economic pessimism.

Given its relative backwardness, there was a presumption that the Irish economy should have grown faster than the British: standard growth theory argues for the conditional convergence of GDPs per head.[2] However, tables 1 and 2, derived from economist Angus Maddison's historical national accounts database, describe the growth in GDP and in GDP per head in Ireland and a selection of other countries between 1939 and 1958.[3] The first block of economies in both tables was directly involved in World War II, while the second remained neutral. Since Ireland, uniquely, lost population over this period, it fared better over the period as a whole in Table 2 than in Table 1. Considering the sub-periods, Ireland fared worst of the neutral economies in 1939-45 and only Franco's Spain fared worse in 1945-50. And Ireland fared worst of all economies in 1950-58, both in terms of GDP growth and GDP per capita growth.

Table 1: GDP GROWTH RATES (% per annum), 1939-58				
Country	**1939-45**	**1945-50**	**1950-58**	**1939-58**
Austria	-14.1	15.7	5.9	2.2
Belgium	-3.0	5.3	2.6	1.6
Denmark	-1.8	7.4	2.6	2.5
Finland	0.5	5.5	4.2	3.4
France	-11.3	15.4	4.4	2.3
Italy	-9.5	12.7	5.9	2.8
Netherlands	-11.2	17.8	4.0	2.9
Norway	-1.1	7.3	3.5	3.1
Greece	-16.9	14.9	6.4	1.3
United Kingdom	2.4	0.0	2.1	1.7
Ireland	*-0.0*	*2.8*	*0.9*	*1.1*
Sweden	2.5	4.9	3.0	3.3
Switzerland	4.1	4.4	4.0	4.1
Portugal	1.5	3.9	3.7	3.1
Spain	2.4	1.7	5.4	3.5

Table 2: GDP PER CAPITA GROWTH RATES (% per annum), 1939-58				
Country	**1939-45**	**1945-50**	**1950-58**	**1939-58**
Austria	-14.4	15.3	5.8	1.9
Belgium	-2.9	4.6	2.1	1.2
Denmark	-2.8	6.3	1.9	1.6
Finland	0.2	4.2	3.2	2.5
France	-10.4	1.4	3.5	2.0
Italy	-10.1	1.2	5.3	2.2
Netherlands	-12.1	16.1	2.8	1.6
Norway	-1.8	6.2	2.5	2.1
Greece	-17.2	14.3	5.5	0.6
United Kingdom	2.0	-0.0	1.7	1.3
Ireland	*-0.1*	*2.7*	*1.4*	*1.2*
Sweden	1.7	3.8	2.3	2.5
Switzerland	3.3	3.1	2.7	3.0
Portugal	0.5	2.9	3.1	2.2
Spain	1.6	0.8	4.5	2.6

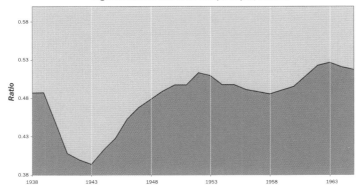

Figure 1. Ratio of Irish to UK GDP per Capita, 1938-65

Dismal Performance

The economy's dismal performance in the 1950s was mainly, though not entirely, the product of poor economic policies. The lack of attractive foreign outlets for agricultural produce hurt, both during World War II and later. However, two other factors mattered more.

First, the strategy of import-substituting industrialisation (ISI) practiced by all Irish administrations since the early 1930s had simply not worked. Instead of generating an expanding, self-sustaining economy, less reliant on the land, it had resulted in an inefficient, highly protected manufacturing sector that produced a small range of products in small plants with short production runs.

An admittedly extreme example is the 'best kip boots' for men, still produced in 1959 by Hilliard & Palmer for 56 shillings per pair, although there was only one worker left who could make them. The boots weighed three kilos per pair.[4]

Many firms simply produced or assembled foreign goods under license, without giving a thought to exports. And as for exports, it is symptomatic that at a time when whiskey and linen accounted for the bulk of Irish manufactured exports to the United States, a senior member of the Marshall Plan mission to Ireland saw tourism and *'smoked salmon, Belleek, special linen products, unusually [sic] printed books and cards'* as the only other potential prospects for earning scarce dollars.[5]

Second, short-run macroeconomic management in the post-war period was poor. In retrospect, it is striking how heavily - nay, obsessively - economic commentary and policy focused on the balance of trade. Thus, according to the *New York Times*, which in those days contained surprisingly frequent reports of Irish economic conditions, *'Ireland betters position in trade'* (January 6th, 1953); *'the balance of payments has reached so dangerous a state of disequilibrium that we are within sight of national bankruptcy'* (July 29th, 1956, citing an Irish Times editorial); *'Irish austerity balances trade: Dublin cuts imports'* (January 7th, 1958).

An undue, neo-mercantilist focus on the gap between imports and exports led to a succession of stop-go measures that stifled the growth potential of the economy. The disastrous budget of 1952 was the work of Fianna Fáil's Seán McEntee. In 1956 Fine Gael's Gerard Sweetman ushered through two deflationary budgets, the second of which, among other measures, increased levies on a wide range of 'luxuries' to a preferential rate of 40 per cent on imports from the United Kingdom and 60 per cent on imports from most other countries. The ensuing decline in consumption was drastic enough to restore the balance of payments. Both McEntee and Sweetman, following the conventional economic wisdom of the day, underestimated the ability of the macroeconomy and the balance of payments to self-correct.[6]

The Vanishing Irish

The Republic's population reached its post-famine nadir in 1961 at just over 2.8 million. Emigration, which had fluctuated considerably since independence, was largely responsible for the decline. Economic depression and the Second World War had reduced the rate of emigration since the early 1930s, but emigration took off again in the wake of World War II. So much so that it prompted the Catholic hierarchy to express its alarm in public and to express in a private resolution sent to An Taoiseach its worries about *'foreign agents [being] allowed to enter the country to attract girls abroad with promises of lucrative employment, the fulfilment of which no one in this country could control'.*[7]

During the second half of the 1950s, the net outflow reached levels not matched in proportionate terms since the 1880s. Most of those who left headed for Britain.[9] Most, male and female, were literate but otherwise poorly skilled workers from rural backgrounds. Still, the significant emigration of skilled, better educated emigrants in this period - doctors, engineers, architects, nurses - is a reminder that while high levels of education may have been a necessary condition for economic growth, they were no guarantee of it. In the late 1950s, Irish medical schools were producing 'about 360' new physicians, of whom only about one-third could be absorbed in Ireland. This may mean that Ireland was over-investing in third-level education in the 1950s, in the sense that the benefits were being reaped where people emigrated, not in Ireland.[10]

Much has changed in the interim. In an address to Irish fund-raisers in late 2007, former Coca-Cola president Donald Keough warned of the costs of Ireland becoming more 'mentally distant' for Irish-America.[11] This seems inevitable, given that the virtual embargo on Irish immigration to the US between 1931 and 1945, followed by a restrictive immigration regime thereafter, forced most Irish emigrants to head east rather than west. Still, emigration to the US resumed on a modest scale after the war and in the 1950s Irish politicians, desperate for foreign exchange, sought to tap the American market for nostalgia. In 2007, Keough spoke of Ireland's 70 million-strong diaspora. In 1955, William Norton, Minister for Industry and Commerce in the inter-party government, spoke more modestly of *'the 20,000,000 people of Irish stock in the United States (who) might be induced to buy even a pounds worth (or $2.80) of Irish goods on a St. Patrick's Day, or during that week (as) a practical way…of helping the Irish economy to the tune of £20,000,000 a year'.*[12]

In fact, the scale of such operations was exaggerated, but the emigration of adolescents, particularly girls, would continue to worry the bishops and others. The creation of a commission to inquire into 'emigration and other population problems' in 1948 was in part a response to such commentary. The experts produced no panacea, however, and their much-delayed report, which did not appear until 1956, was very short on policy recommendations.[8]

Foreign Investment

The success of the Celtic Tiger between the late-1980s and the mid-2000s has been linked, plausibly, to the enticements offered by Ireland's business-friendly tax regime to foreign, and particularly US, multinational corporations. Without access to foreign markets provided by the European Economic Community, which Ireland joined in 1973, and the Single European Act (1986) such a strategy would not have worked so well. However, the switch from a policy of penalising importers to one of subsidising exporters dates back to the 1950s.

In the 1950s, few Irish manufacturers focused on export markets. Those who did so were overwhelmingly dependent on the British market. From the early-1950s on, as the failure of the domestic market to deliver sustainable growth became increasingly obvious, policy shifted cautiously away from import-substituting industrialisation. The focus on export-oriented subsidiaries of multinationals was politically attractive, since it did not threaten existing indigenous firms directly. By 1955, Irish delegations were visiting Sweden, Germany and the US seeking foreign investment.

The package of incentives they offered was remarkably similar to that already available in Northern Ireland since the early post-war period. The shift towards reliance on foreign capital in the Republic was thus not merely a question of soul-searching based on experience since the 1930s. The authorities in the mid-1950s cannot but have been aware of Northern Ireland's relative success in attracting foreign investment and of the relative buoyancy of the Northern economy.

Northern policy, directed through the Northern Ireland Development Council (NIDC), sought to compensate for employment losses from the decline of traditional industries and to diversify the Northern Ireland economy. It offered aspiring investors grants and loans for premises, plant and machinery.

An aggressive marketing campaign included a series of large advertisements in the *London Times* in 1957 and repeated press announcements of new firms and expansion schemes. By late-1957, Northern Ireland could boast 130 new industrial establishments since 1945, most British, six American.[13] In late-1958, NIDC announced that it had aided 22 new firms and seven expansion schemes in the previous three years, projects which, when fully operational, would employ 6,500 men and 900 women. In October 1958, it announced the subsidiary of the eighth American firm to establish a base in Northern Ireland, a Texas company producing valves for oil wells in Carnmoney, near Belfast, which would employ about 60 males and export to *'all the oil-producing areas of the world except the United States'.*[14] If the South would later steal a march on the North with its policy of low taxes on corporate profits, then Northern industrial development policy was the more innovative in the 1950s.

William Norton was a vigorous proponent of the new approach. Both he and his successor, Seán Lemass, envisaged export-oriented manufacturing industries servicing a European free trade area from bases in Ireland as the way forward.[15] Thus, on March 11th 1958, Lemass announced new incentives for industrial investment - a five year exemption from taxation on all profits derived from exports, plus complete freedom to repatriate profits - and the expansion of free trade operations at Shannon - low rent on sites, construction grants, no tariffs on imports of raw materials. The success of such measures was predicated on expected Irish membership of a broader European free trade area. It would take some years for this policy shift to bear fruit.

Agriculture

Today, agriculture accounts for only 2 per cent of GDP and 5 per cent of the labour force. Half a century ago, the figures were about 25 and 35 per cent, respectively. Farming offered full-time employment to over 0.4 million males in 1957/58, not to mention the number of full-time female equivalents, while live animals and food products accounted for over half of the revenue generated by exports. Farming mattered then but its poor record affected the economy at large. Part of the problem was that, since the 1930s, farmers in the Republic had lacked the advantages in terms of market access and subsidisation available to their Northern neighbours. The growing divergence between the composition of agricultural output in the two Irelands between the 1930s and the 1960s and its subsequent convergence in the wake of EEC membership is significant in this respect.[16]

In addition, World War II had prevented Irish agriculture from fully exploiting its comparative advantage in dairying and meat exports, and had left it badly undercapitalised. An expert from New Zealand employed by Agriculture Minister, James Dillon, produced a report indicating that *'there is no area of comparable size in the northern hemisphere which has such marvellous potentialities for pasture production',*[17] but that potential was compromised by soil exhaustion and the under-use of lime and phosphates in the wake of the Emergency.

In Dillon's picturesque assessment, Irish grass *'would fill a cow's stomach and yet let her die of starvation where she stood'.* The Irish Grassland Association, founded in 1946, was born of such concerns. It anticipated the kind of co-operation between farmers and researchers associated with Johnstown Castle, acquired by the Department of Agriculture in 1945 and handed over to AFT in 1960. Ireland's fertiliser deficiency backlog, a major policy preoccupation in the 1950s, would take a long time to eliminate, but the consumption of lime and fertilisers rose by almost two-fifths between 1957 and 1962.

Farm Incomes

A pioneering survey carried out by the Central Statistics Office, with the *'wholehearted co-operation'* of farmers, in the mid-1950s confirmed the low incomes earned by a majority of farmers at that time (Table 3). At the same time, it implied, after leaving out of account mini-holdings of less than five acres, an average farm family income of nearly £500, at a time when the average industrial worker earned £350-£450 a year. Inequality on the land was considerable. Applying the Central Statistics Office's estimates of family income to official data on the size distribution of holdings suggests that one-tenth of farmers with holdings of 100 acres or more accounted for nearly one-quarter of family income.

In the mid-1950s, as noted earlier, agriculture accounted for the bulk of Irish exports. However, competition from Argentina and the UK system of deficiency payments, which kept UK prices below world levels for consumers but compensated UK farmers accordingly, militated against production and exports.

Table 3: FARM INCOMES IN THE 1950's			
Farm size (acres) in survey	No. of farms	Income per farm (£ in country	No.of holdings (1955)
5-15	108	209	59,066
15-30	265	332	83,896
30-50	287	464	63,080
50-100	284	697	52,270
100-200	151	1,034	21,930
200 +	79	1,425	7,152
Total	**1,174**		**287,394**

Source: Ó Gráda 1997: 161

Agriculture also naturally played a major role in Dr T K Whitaker's Economic Development. Eight of its twenty-four chapters were devoted to agriculture, which also featured prominently in several other chapters. Given manifold constraints, including the lack of markets, underinvestment, the high average age and poor education of farmers, and the large number of uneconomic holdings, Whitaker declared that it would not be easy 'to break out of the vicious circle of low production at high cost'. In a stinging critique of the role played by the universities, Economic Development declared that in view of the need of An Foras Talúntais to hire trained staff, the time had come to reassess the role of UCD's Faculty of Agriculture. The ensuing Programme for Economic Expansion (1959-62) expected very modest growth from the farm sector.

Between mid-1955 and mid-1956, the price of prime bullocks dropped from £9 to £6 per cwt, while Irish bacon was being priced out of the British market.[18] Between 1949/51 and 1959/61, net agricultural output, including turf, rose by 17.7 per cent. Nevertheless, the productivity of Irish agriculture in these years remained low relative to both Northern Ireland and Great Britain. Tens of thousands of farms remained uneconomic. The average farmer was poorly educated. Policy, as already noted, diverted farmers away from their comparative advantage in milk and beef and much of the land was in poor condition. The sector's underperformance was the stimulus for both Joseph Johnston's Irish Agriculture in Transition (1951) and Raymond Crotty's Irish Agricultural Production (1966).

It is significant too that today's two main farming organisations were founded in the 1950s. The National Farmer's Association, later to become the IFA, held its inaugural meeting on January 6th 1955, followed by a formal dinner at the Royal Hibernian Hotel, an event far removed from the everyday lives of most farmers of the day. Within a few years, angered at gains made by public sector workers, the NFA was claiming that it would take £83 million, presumably in transfers from the rest of the community, for farmers to regain the relative status they had in 1953. This claim prompted Taoiseach Seán Lemass to warn of *'the futility of relying on a statistical approach to the problem'.*[19] The NFA's main rival, the Irish Creamery Milk Suppliers' Association, had been formed five years earlier. As its name implies, it was strongest in the dairying areas, and so its council held its inaugural meeting in Cruises Hotel, Limerick. Formed in response to Agriculture Minister, James Dillon's decision to cut the price of milk back from 14d to 12d per gallon, (approx one cent per litre in today's terms!) it too acquired a reputation for militancy. A third farming organisation, Macra na Feirme, had been founded in 1944 as an instrument for educating young farmers in a social setting.

Looking Ahead

For all the gloom and doom, there were signs too in 1957/58 that change was afoot. On August 8th 1957, Ireland joined both the International Monetary Fund and the World Bank. In July 1958, the Industrial Development (Encouragement of External Investment) Act removed many of the remaining restrictions of the Control of Manufactures Acts, which had discriminated against foreign capital since the 1930s. Three years later, Ireland applied for full membership of the European Economic Community.

In the late 1950s, something changed in the economy and Ireland entered a period of economic growth that would last for several years. Motor vehicle registrations, one plausible proxy for consumer confidence, suggest widespread gloom between early 1956 and mid-1957. Car sales then began to rise and were 40 per cent higher in 1960 than in 1959 and annual sales would continue to rise for several years thereafter. A comparison of the percentage change in ordinary share values in Ireland and the UK indicates that Irish investors began to show clear signs of greater 'bullishness' from early-1960 on. Net emigration, a sensitive marker of economic performance, would be lower between 1961 and 1966 than during any inter-census period since independence.

There is still no consensus as to why the shift happened. Writing in 1971, the late F S L Lyons claimed that the Department of Finance's Economic Development was crucial: *'it is hardly too much to say…that even today it can be seen as a watershed in the modern economic history of the country'.*[20] T K Whitaker, main author of Economic Development and the ensuing Programme for Economic Expansion, held that *'objective students of our past philosophy and performance'* would find it hard to dismiss the *'psychological stimulus of planning between 1958 and 1963'.*[21]

Although accorded an important role in Irish accounts,[22] it is curious how the foreign press made little or nothing of Economic Development or the Programme for Economic Expansion. In retrospect, the focus on agriculture and tourism in those documents seems excessive, but their insistence on the need for, and possibility of, even modest economic growth was significant. Other factors posited include the election as Taoiseach of Seán Lemass in June 1959; investments made in social overhead capital during the 1950s beginning to bear fruit; the rapid growth of Ireland's trading partners and a commitment to trade liberalisation giving the fillip to growth at home. Or perhaps all of these changes helped.

Bibliography:

- Chubb, Basil and Patrick Lynch. 1969. Economic Development and Planning. Dublin: IPA.

- Crotty, Raymond D. 1966. Irish Agricultural Production: Its Volume and Structure. Cork: Cork University Press.

- Daly, Mary E. 2002. The First Department: A History of the Department of Agriculture. Dublin: IPA.

- Daly, Mary E. 2006. The Slow Failure: Population Decline and Independent Ireland, 1920-1973. Madison: University of Wisconsin Press.

- Delaney, Enda. 2007. The Irish in Post-war Britain. Oxford: Oxford University Press.

- Department of Finance. 1958. Economic Development [Pr. 4803]. Dublin: Stationary Office.

- Flanagan, Sean. 2006. 'Irish Grassland Association 1946-2006: delivering the benefits from grassland'.

- Holmes, G.A. 1948. Report on the Present State and Methods of Improvement of Irish Land. Dublin.

- Honohan, P. and C. Ó Gráda. 1998. 'The Irish Macroeconomic Crisis of 1955-56: How Much Was Due to Monetary Policy'. Irish Economic & Social History, vol. 24: 52-80.

- Horgan, John. 1998. Seán Lemass: The Enigmatic Patriot. Dublin: Gill & Macmillan.

- Lyons, F.S.L. 1971. Ireland since the Famine. London: Weidenfeld & Nicholson.

- McCarthy, John F. 1990. Planning Ireland's Future: the Legacy of T.K. Whitaker. Dublin: Glendale Press.

- Ó Gráda, C. 1997. A Rocky Road: the Irish Economy since the 1920s. Manchester: MUP.

- Ó Gráda, C. 2000. 'From 'frugal comfort' to ten thousand a year: trade and growth in the Irish economy'. In Ray Ryan, ed. Writing the Republic, London: Palgrave Macmillan, pp. 263-82.

- Ó Gráda, C. and K.H. O'Rourke. 1996. 'Irish economic growth since 1945', in N.F.R. Crafts and G. Toniolo, eds. European Economic Growth. Cambridge: Cambridge University Press, pp. 388-426.

Footnotes:

[1] Department of Finance 1958: 5.
[2] Ó Gráda and O'Rourke 1996.
[3] Maddison's data may be downloaded at http://www.ggdc.net/maddison/. They are also the source for Figure 1.
[4] Ó Gráda 1997: 52; Ó Gráda 2000.
[5] Cited in Ó Gráda 2000: 267.
[6] Honohan and Ó Gráda 1998.
[7] Ó Gráda 1997: 212.
[8] Daly 2006: 172-79.
[9] The best account is Delaney 2007.
[10] NYT, July 7th 1957.
[11] Irish Times, November 8th 2007.
[12] NYT, Aug 28 1955.
[13] NYT, Nov 27th 1957.
[14] The Times, Nov 11th 1958; NYT, Oct 9th 1958.
[15] Horgan 1998: 167-68.
[16] Ó Gráda 2000: 275-76.
[17] Holmes 1948: 8.
[18] NYT, July 29, 1956.
[19] Cited in Ó Gráda 1997: 159; see also Daly 2002: 372-85.
[20] Lyons 1971: 628.
[21] Cited in Chubb and Lynch 1969: 300.
[22] E.g. McCarthy 1990.

The head office and some of the buildings at Drinagh Co-op, Co. Cork.

The President, Seán T O'Kelly, presiding at the AFT foundation ceremony on May 19th 1959. Also included is the Lord Mayor of Dublin, Mary Byrne, Dr Tom Walsh and AFT Chairman, John Litton.

Security was tight for the large number of national and international dignitaries attending the foundation ceremony. Among the many politicians in attendance were, front row, from left: Micheál Ó Móráin, Minister for Lands; Dr James Ryan, Minister for Finance; Frank Aiken, Minister for External Affairs; John A Costello, former Taoiseach and William Norton, former Tánaiste.

CHAPTER 2

ESTABLISHMENT AND EVOLUTION OF AN FORAS TALÚNTAIS

Michael Miley

The nature and extent of agriculture and food research in Ireland over the past 50 years could have been very different without the pivotal role of an American scientist and American money. An Foras Talúntais (AFT) was the brainchild of Joseph Carrigan, the first head of the Irish office of the European Recovery Programme (ERP), popularly known as the Marshall Plan. The ERP, which was established in 1947, involved the donation of US money for re-building Europe following the devastation of World War II. While Ireland had remained neutral in the war, our pivotal position as a food exporter, particularly to the UK, made us eligible for funding.

The President, Seán T O'Kelly, unveiled a plaque, expressing gratitude to the US for its funding of AFT, during the foundation ceremony. Also included are Scott McLeod, former US ambassador, Joseph Carrigan, former head of the ERP office in Ireland and James Dillon, former Minister for Agriculture. The plaque which bears the AFT coat of arms and the national emblems of the US and Ireland, is now in the Teagasc head office in Oak Park, Carlow.

Carrigan, who was the dean of agriculture in the University of Vermont, came to Ireland in 1948 as head of the Economic Co-operation Administration (ECA) office in Dublin, which had responsibility for administering the recovery programme. He assessed the state of Irish agriculture and decided that the establishment of a research institute was a top priority. In 1949, he recommended to James Dillon, the Minister for Agriculture, the establishment of an autonomous research institute. Following a gestation period of nine years, the new institute was established in 1958 with funding of £1.84 million from the US.

The body that emerged was dramatically different to that envisaged by Carrigan. His recommendation was for an all-embracing institute that would bring agricultural and veterinary research, university teaching and advisory services into a single national organisation. It was based on the US model, the 'Land Grant College' system, which Carrigan had played a major role in developing in his home state of Vermont. The adoption of the model in Ireland would have resulted in advisory services (then provided by 27 county committees of agriculture) being transferred to the new institute, which would also take over all research carried out by the Department of Agriculture and the universities, as well as dramatically expanding the level of research.

It would also have meant that students in agriculture, veterinary medicine and dairy science at UCD, Trinity College and UCC would complete the final two years of their degree programmes at the headquarters of the new institute. A potential site had been earmarked at Brownsbarn, Clondalkin, in west Dublin.

The Long Debate

The Carrigan proposal led to divisive and rancourous debate over much of the following nine years. In the early stages, James Dillon decided that the advisory services would not be brought under the new institute. He had already launched the famous but ill-fated Parish Plan, where an adviser appointed by the Department of Agriculture and separate to those employed by the county committees of agriculture would be assigned to every three parishes. The experiment, which is covered in some detail in Chapter 13, was short-lived and was terminated in 1958. Dillon's insistence on excluding the advisory service from the new body was strongly opposed by Paul Miller, who succeeded Joseph Carrigan as head of the ERP office in Ireland in 1950. Miller had served as director of advisory services in the state of Minnesota for the previous 12 years and was a strong advocate of integrating research and advisory services within the one organisation.

Dillon tried to persuade the universities to join the new national institute and soon realised that when it came to raw politics the academics could teach the party politicians a lesson or two. The opposition was led by UCC president Dr Alfred O'Rahilly and by Dr Michael Tierney, the president of UCD, who saw the new institute resulting in a diminution of the status of their universities. Tierney was a former Cumann na nGaedheal TD, having been elected for the North Mayo constituency in 1925, and he had also served in the Seanad. O'Rahilly was also a former member of the Seanad and, following the death of his wife, was ordained a priest in 1955 and later became a monsignor.

*Architects of the Marshall Plan:
President Harry S Truman, Secretary of State,
George C Marshall, Administrator Paul G Hoffman
and special representative in Europe Averell Harriman.*

The Catholic hierarchy also voiced strong opposition to the new over-arching institute. The archbishop of Dublin, John Charles McQuaid, in an obvious reference to the inclusion of Trinity College, complained about the dangers of mixed education removed from a Catholic atmosphere. The bishop of Cork, Cornelius Lucey, well known for his sermons at the annual confirmation ceremonies on the immorality of artificial insemination and other cattle breeding developments, was concerned about the impact the absence of a chaplain would have on the students at the new institute headquarters at Clondalkin. He described Trinity as "if not wholly Protestant, then is free thinking or indifferent as regards religion." The Bishop of Galway, Michael Browne, also got in on the act. Rather than bringing all university education into a central campus, he wanted a separate faculty of agriculture in University College Galway.

Americans Get Impatient

By the time the inter-party government left office in May 1951, there was little progress on the establishment of the new agricultural institute. The US authorities were getting impatient. The Mutual Security Act (MSA) had replaced the ECA and, as Ireland was not a member of NATO, there would be no MSA office in Ireland so negotiations would have to take place with officials in Washington. The Taoiseach, Éamon de Valera, and members of the cabinet visited the Department of Agriculture research centre at Johnstown Castle in Wexford to see the research that was being carried out and to get a feel for the type of work this proposed new research institute would undertake. A sub-committee of the cabinet, made up of Minister for Agriculture Thomas Walsh and two former ministers, Dr James Ryan and Paddy Smith, was established and it came up with the following recommendation: the new institute would not be responsible for the advisory services and it would not be located on a central campus; however, it would have responsibility for third-level education as well as for all research. This was ratified by the cabinet and became government policy in January 1953. The opposition from the universities continued and there was also continuing debate on how the governing body of the new institute should be appointed.

Throughout all of this, there was little comment from the Department of Agriculture, which was clearly opposed to the loss of many of its functions. The one organisation that supported the Carrigan proposal from the beginning was the Agricultural Science Association (ASA), which was established in 1942 to represent the interests of graduates in agriculture. It regarded the merging of the advisory and education services and an enhanced research service into a single authority as an imperative for progress.

Little progress was made during 1953 or during the early months of 1954. The inter-party government regained office at the general election in May 1954 and Dillon was back as Minister for Agriculture. An agreement was signed with the US authorities on the funding of the new agricultural institute to the tune of £1.84 million, from what was now called the Grant Counterpart Fund. In addition to the institute, funding was also provided for a ground limestone transport scheme (£1.75m), bovine TB eradication (£0.7m) and pasteurisation of separated milk (£0.5m) as well as support for exchange of research workers, students and teachers between Ireland and the US. The US also provided substantial loans to finance a number of agricultural projects under a scheme called the Loan Counterpart Fund.

Farmers Enter the Fray

Now that the level of US support for the institute was agreed, opposition by the universities intensified. But Dillon persisted and a White Paper published by him in 1955 envisaged that, as well as being responsible for research, the institute would provide all higher agricultural education and that degrees would be awarded by the National University or Trinity College. This meant that the original Carrigan proposal of the institute taking over the faculties of agriculture in UCD and Trinity and the dairy science faculty in UCC still stood. The newly-formed National Farmer's Association (NFA), now the Irish Farmer's Association (IFA), entered the fray and with Macra na Feirme came out in opposition to the new body controlling third-level education. Dillon and the Taoiseach, John A Costello, decided that the opposition to any interference with university structures was too great.

The US authorities agreed and, after almost eight years of debate, the drafting of a bill to set up an institute with responsibility for agricultural research got underway. The new body would have no control over the universities.

Dillon introduced the Agricultural Institute Bill to the Dáil on December 5th 1956 and the second stage was scheduled for debate on February 13th 1957. In the meantime, the Dáil was dissolved and Fianna Fail returned to power following the March 1957 election. A 'new' bill was introduced the following November by Minister for Agriculture Seán Moylan. It was the same as that produced by Dillon a year earlier, with just two changes. The Dillon bill had stated that the chairman and director should be one and the same person. This was changed by Moylan, who made provision for a full-time director and a part-time chairman. The title of the bill was also changed from the Agricultural Institute to the Agriculture (An Foras Talúntais) bill. Moylan died soon after introducing the bill and its passage was shepherded through the various stages in the Dáil and Seanad by Frank Aiken, the acting Minister for Agriculture and by Paddy Smith, who succeeded Moylan as Minister for Agriculture, and by the Taoiseach, Éamon de Valera. The bill passed all stages on February 12th 1958. Protracted debate had resulted in a delay of nine years in setting up the new body and this would have a serious impact on the development and growth of Irish agriculture over the following decades.

Joe McGough, Bord Bainne (second from right) sharing a platform with AFT scientists, Tom O'Dwyer, Michael Walshe, Michael Mulcahy and Tony O'Sullivan at a meeting on milk production in 1966. Below: A section of the large audience.

US Funding for AFT

AFT was established with an 'endowment fund' of £1 million and a 'capital fund' of £840,000, both coming from the US Grant Counterpart Fund and worth around €25 million at 2008 values. The endowment fund could not be touched but AFT could use the interest on the investment to fund its day-to-day operations. The capital fund was to be used to cover the cost of land, buildings, laboratories and offices, which would be needed by the new organisation. In the early years, investment income from the endowment fund and the unspent portions of the capital fund exceeded £100,000 per annum and this was an important component of the AFT budget.

The endowment fund continued until 1980 when agreement was reached between the Irish and US governments on releasing the fund and AFT benefited from a once-off £1 million windfall.

Joseph Carrigan, who in 1949 proposed the establishment of the research institute, was the recipient of many commendations in the Dáil and elsewhere. Paying tribute to him in the Dáil in February 1958, James Dillon went as far as suggesting the new body should be called the 'Carrigan Institute'. The first decision of the AFT Council at its inaugural meeting in August 1958 was to 'send a message of greetings to Dr. Carrigan'. He was also a guest at the AFT foundation ceremony, which was performed by the President, Seán T O'Kelly, in May 1959. The ceremony was also attended by Taoiseach Éamon de Valera and by Scott McLeod, US Ambassador to Ireland. Although now in opposition, James Dillon was also a prominent guest, in recognition of his role in the establishment of the new body.

Talúntais

The origin of the word 'Talúntais' in the title of the new body sparked the following exchange between the former Minister, James Dillon, and the Taoiseach, Éamon de Valera, during the final day of the Dáil debate on February 12th, 1958.

Dillon: Would anyone be kind enough to tell me where did the word "talúntais" come from?

Taoiseach: The idea was that when you have an Irish word it should, if possible, be a word easily understood and pronounced. "Talmhaíocht" is the alternative and I think the Deputy will admit that, for a person who does not know the language, it is not the easiest word to pronounce. There is an adjective "talúnta" and "talúntas" is an abstract noun formed from that adjective. It is an easy word to pronounce according to the way it is spelled.

Dillon: I am no purist, but are we going to start inventing words? I do not believe any living creature has seen in print or heard from the lips of man the word "talúntas" before.

Taoiseach: It came from the adjective.

Dillon: I suspect it came out of the fertile mind of the Taoiseach himself. I know he likes to look upon himself as the father of his people and, in a sense, from time to time feel that he begot us all. I speak, of course, in a purely mystical or spiritual sense, but I must call a halt if he is now arrogating to himself the function of rewriting the whole Irish language. That is going further than his most ardent admirers would be prepared to concede, that if he gets a notion that he does not like the look of an Irish word, that the sound is not euphonious in his ear or that he feels some future generation may find it difficult to pronounce a word, there is conferred upon him a sovereign right to abstract out of the air a completely new word and say: "If you cannot sound the other one, sound that and it will do as well." That is going too far

Taoiseach: … I did not, of course, invent the word. I asked if we could get a word that could be easily pronounced in accordance with the spelling. This was the word that was suggested and I accepted it. It is common in most languages to form abstract nouns from adjectives and that is what was done in this case. It seems to me there is a lot of nonsense talked about it.

Guests at the AFT inauguration dinner, Gresham Hotel, May 19th, 1959

Getting Up and Running

The functions of the new research institute were to 'review, facilitate, encourage, assist, co-ordinate, promote and undertake agricultural research.' It was to be governed by a council consisting of a chairman, who would be appointed by the President, and 12 'ordinary' members. Four council members were to be nominated by the universities, one each from Trinity, UCC, UCD and UCG. A further five were to be nominated through a complicated electoral system involving 25 farming, industry and rural organisations. The final three members would be appointed directly by the government. The legislation also provided for the appointment of a director as the chief officer.

Dr Tom Walsh, who had been responsible for research and specialist advisory services on soils and grassland in the Department of Agriculture, was appointed by the government as the first director of AFT. The first chairman was John Litton, a prominent Wicklow farmer, who had completed a degree in agriculture in UCD but did not graduate because he refused on principle to pay the graduation fee. Litton was one of the founding members of Macra na Feirme and had played an important role in establishing the Farmers Journal and the NFA, now the IFA. Walsh's starting salary as director was £2,750 per annum while Litton was paid a fee of £1,000 per annum as chairman. In addition to the US capital fund and the interest from the endowment fund, AFT received a state grant of £146,000 to cover staff and running costs in its first year.

The first meeting of the council took place on August 19th 1958 in the Institute of Advanced Studies in Merrion Square, Dublin. Walsh, or the 'Doc' as he became affectionately known, moved into temporary accommodation in Earlsfort Terrace and work began on assembling staff and developing a structure. The first two recruits were Michael O'Sullivan and Rena Grace, who were seconded from the Department of Agriculture. O'Sullivan was appointed head of the secretariat and remained with AFT for the next 30 years, eventually becoming a deputy director. Rena Grace became personal secretary to the 'Doc' and remained with him throughout his period in AFT and in ACOT until both retired in late 1982. In December 1958, Olive Daly joined from the RDS and was given responsibility for library and information services. She went on to play a major role as public relations officer with AFT for the following 30 years. Pat Markey came from the Department of Agriculture to take charge of personnel and finance. A former Louth footballer, Markey remained with AFT until 1980 when he moved to ACOT as director of administration.

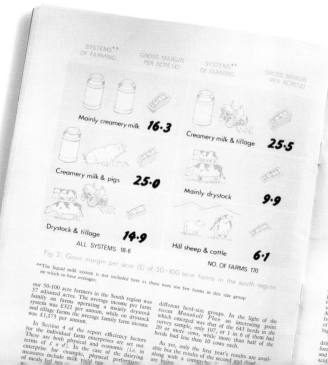

New Structures and Staff

A permanent headquarters was established at 33 Merrion Road, beside the RDS, and the 'Doc' began to recruit staff and establish research centres at whirlwind speed. A structure was established involving five research divisions – animal production, plant sciences and crop husbandry, soils, horticulture and forestry, and rural economy. Over the following months, a chief of division was appointed to lead the five research programmes.

Larry O'Moore, who had worked with the Department of Agriculture at Johnstown Castle, was appointed chief of the animal production division, based initially at Thorndale and later at Dunsinea in Dublin. Pat Ryan, who had also worked in Johnstown Castle, became the chief of the soils division at Johnstown Castle. Bernard Crombie, who was head of plant breeding with the Irish Sugar Company, was appointed chief of the plant sciences and crop husbandry division, initially based at Thurles. Jim Byrne was appointed head of the rural economy division, which was based initially in Shrewsbury Road, Dublin and later established its headquarters on a green field site at Sandymount Avenue, Dublin. Professor E J Clarke of UCD acted as adviser to the horticulture and forestry division until David Robinson was appointed as chief of the division, which was established at Kinsealy in north Dublin.

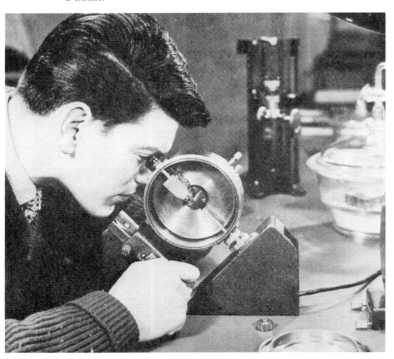

John Kilroy, who had worked as a research scientist under the 'Doc' at Johnstown Castle, was appointed as scientific aide with responsibility for developing and co-ordinating the research programme. The quiet, unassuming Roscommon man played a crucial role in the evolution of AFT over the following decades. A massive programme of staff recruitment got underway, involving the transfer of staff who had worked in research with the Department of Agriculture and the hiring of new scientists, many of whom were recent young graduates, with others who were employed in industry and universities at home and abroad being encouraged to apply for jobs in the exciting new venture. There was hectic activity in advertising of posts, organising interview boards, conducting interviews and making appointments, all overseen by Pat Markey and his new staff in the personnel section.

By the time the AFT foundation ceremony took place on May 19th 1959, more than 40 research scientists had been appointed as well as a large number of technicians and key support staff. Recruitment continued at a frenetic pace over the following years and in March 1964 total research staff had reached 173. There were 291 technicians, 70 administrative staff and 350 farm workers, giving a total staff of 884. In March 1968, 10 years after AFT was established, staff numbers had increased to 1,077, made up of 222 research, 342 technicians, 93 administrative and 420 farm staff.

Research Centres and Facilities

Side-by-side with staff recruitment, land and buildings were acquired and state-of-the-art research facilities developed at break-neck speed. In early 1959, the 600-acre farm at Grange, Co Meath, owned by the Department of Agriculture since 1949, was handed over to AFT for research on beef. The blanket peat research centre at Glenamoy in Mayo was also handed over by the Department as were farms at Clonsast in Laois and Derrybrennan, Lullymore, in Kildare. With the development of new buildings and facilities, these latter two farms became the Lullymore peatland research centre.

Within the space of 12 months, close on 2,000 acres of land were acquired and research facilities developed at eight centres throughout the country. This included 100 acres at Kinsealy in Dublin, which was purchased for £12,000 for research on glasshouse crops and vegetables. (Legend has it that the 'Doc' bought the Kinsealy land and paid the deposit with a personal cheque.) A farm at Clonroche in Wexford was also acquired and this became the centre for research on soft fruit and beekeeping. A research facility for apple growing was established on land owned by the co-operative fruit growers' society at Dungarvan. Mayo County Council offered to sell the former sanatorium and 316 acres at Creagh, outside Ballinrobe.

A price of £7,000 was agreed and Creagh became the national centre for research on sheep. At that stage, a large number of estates were in the possession of the Land Commission. One of these was at Moorepark, outside Fermoy, and AFT acquired 350 acres of the estate as the national centre for research on dairying. Another estate at Oak Park, on the outskirts of Carlow, was seen as the ideal location for tillage research. The estate of 850 acres and a stately home was purchased from the Land Commission and it became the national research centre on plant sciences and crop husbandry in early-1960. Meanwhile, the legislation governing the gift of Johnstown Castle and the 1,000-acre estate to the Department of Agriculture in 1945 was amended and the estate was handed over to AFT in January 1960, becoming the national centre for soils and grassland research. A farm of 33 acres was also purchased at Ballinamore in Leitrim for research on impeded soils and the 'Doc' got sanction from the council 'to purchase whatever additional land was necessary.'

Within two years of its establishment, AFT had established a national research infrastructure involving offices, laboratories and farms. After five years, the organisation was operating from 21 research centres and satellite demonstration farms with a total land area of over 4,500 acres. It was a remarkable achievement and demonstrated the energy, ingenuity and vision of the 'Doc' and the support he received from John Litton and the council.

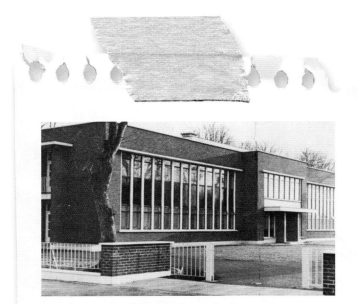

Rural Economy Division Headquarters,
Sandymount Avenue, 1967.

Home for the Embassy

By the early-1970s, conditions were getting crowded for staff at the AFT head office in Merrion Road. They moved to a new building on ground beside the economics and rural welfare centre just around the corner in Sandymount Avenue.

The British embassy in Merrion Square was burned down during the riots following Bloody Sunday in January 1972 and a new embassy was needed. Matt Dempsey, then working in RTE, met Gerry White, agricultural attaché in the embassy who enquired if Matt knew of anything likely to come up for sale that would be further away from the emotional GPO and more easily secured than Merrion Square. "I mentioned the AFT building; he said he would follow it up and so it happened," said Dempsey.

Sandymount Avenue continued as the AFT and Teagasc head office until 2004 when Teagasc relocated to Oak Park in Carlow. The building was then demolished and a luxury apartment complex is now built in its place.

Finances in the Early Years

The dramatic growth in staff numbers during the early years led to AFT becoming an expensive organisation to finance. This and, as we will see later, other issues became a source of contention between AFT and the Department of Agriculture. The state grant of £146,000 provided by the government for current expenditure in 1958/59 had increased to £400,000 in 1960/61 (the financial year at that time ran from April 1st to March 31st). Also, in March 1960, Michael Barry, then assistant secretary in the Department of Agriculture, informed AFT that it could expect a state grant of £450,000 for the following year and it should formulate its expenditure plans accordingly. The council was not pleased and passed the following motion: *"That the Director should write to the Department of Agriculture stating that the council cannot accept a situation where the state grant for 1961/62 is arbitrarily determined at this stage without examination of the research programme for the year."*

The AFT central library in Dublin.

Notwithstanding the Department's letter, the council sought a grant of £647,000 for 1961/62 and, following lengthy discussions, including a meeting with the Taoiseach, Seán Lemass - it received £500,000. It sought £889,000 for 1962/63 and received £650,000. Always a strong believer in 'raising the bar', the 'Doc' got the council to sanction a request for £1.13 million for 1963/64. He received £850,000. The allocation for 1965/66 was £1.3 million, rising to almost £1.4 million in 1967/68. Differences between the level of grant sought and the amount allocated by the government were regularly referred to in the AFT annual report. A typical reference was in the report for 1962/63: *"the disparity necessitated curtailments in the programme and deferment of development work at research centres."* These references were a continuing source of displeasure to the Department of Agriculture.

The cost of acquiring land and developing research facilities was covered by the £840,000 capital fund provided by the US Grant Counterpart Fund. However, this money was spent by 1964 and AFT sought an annual capital allocation from the government. It received £125,000 in 1965 and around £100,000 in the following years. So, after 10 years in operation, AFT was costing the state £1.5 million a year, about €20 million at 2008 values. While this was very low compared with expenditure on research by other comparable countries, it was far higher than what was envisaged by the Department of Agriculture when AFT was established in 1958.

The Eight Chairmen

AFT and Teagasc had eight chairmen during the past 50 years. The first five were appointed by the President, under the terms of the AFT Act, while the last three were appointed by the government, under the terms of the Teagasc legislation.

Wicklow farmer John Litton served as first chairman, from 1958 until 1967. The other seven chairmen were: Dr Tadhg Ó'Tuama, Irish Sugar Company; Paddy O'Keeffe, editor and chief executive, Irish Farmers Journal; Rory Murphy, Bunclody Co-op; Matt Dempsey, editor and chief executive, Irish Farmers Journal; Joe Rea, former IFA president; Dan Browne, managing director, Dawn Meats, and the current chairman, Dr Tom O'Dwyer, former senior official in the European Commission.

The last two were former research scientists – Browne, who started his career in Moorepark, and O'Dwyer, one of the early recruits to the rural economy division. Also, two of the 15 Ministers for Agriculture who served during the past 50 years started their careers in AFT – Dr Michael Woods, one of the first scientists to be recruited to Kinsealy research centre, and Joe Walsh, who worked in dairy processing research in Moorepark.

Professor Patrick Fottrell holds the distinction of being the longest serving member of the governing bodies of AFT and Teagasc. He first joined the council of AFT in 1973 and served until 1988 when Teagasc was established. He has served on the Teagasc authority since 1988 and was re-appointed for a further five-year term in 2007. He started his career as a research scientist in Johnstown Castle and went on to become president of NUI Galway and has held many key positions in the educational and scientific spheres.

Paddy Cunningham is another former scientist to reach the pinnacle of the scientific profession. He joined the AFT animal breeding and genetics department in 1962 and went on to become a deputy director of AFT. He was later appointed professor of animal genetics at Trinity College Dublin and served in senior positions with the FAO. He is now chief scientific adviser to the Irish government.

| John Litton | Dr Tadhg Ó'Tuama, | Paddy O'Keeffe | Rory Murphy | Matt Dempsey | Joe Rea | Dan Browne | Dr Tom O' Dwyer |

Michael Butler, who joined in 1959 and was later secretary to the AFT council for many years, is of the view that the department regarded the new institute as a body that would donate grants for research to universities and would do a small amount of research itself. *"They never imagined that it would develop into a massive institution,"* said Butler. There was no better man than the 'Doc' to use the legislation to shape a research organisation of international standing and to withstand all efforts by the department to row him back. The department had the additional problem that, although the government had the power to directly appoint three council members, it had no representative on the first council. It was therefore hearing about decisions long after they were made. From 1961, when the first term of office of the council ended, the department did have a representative on the council but by then many of the critical decisions on staffing and structures had been made.

Difficulties with the Department

Relations with the Department of Agriculture were, to say the least, difficult during the years following the establishment of AFT. The almost complete lack of planning on what the new body was to be given responsibility for, the rapid increase in the cost of the new organisation, previous difficult relationships between the 'Doc' and senior department staff combined with what the department saw as overly attractive terms for AFT staff all contributed to a stormy period that required the mediation of successive Taoisigh and Ministers for Agriculture on a number of occasions. The views of the Attorney General on the legal interpretation of the AFT Act were also required. Details of a number of these episodes are covered in detail in Mary Daly's book, *The First Department,* and in Paul Rouse's *Ireland's Own Soil.*

The department's unhappiness with the route the new research body was taking stemmed to a large degree from the legislation, which gave the council and director of AFT complete control over the number of staff they could hire, the pay and conditions of the staff and the number of centres they set up. James Dillon encapsulated the approach of politicians to the independence of AFT when, during the Dáil debate on the legislation in November 1957, he said: *"Dáil Éireann cannot run this institute; the Department of Agriculture cannot run it. If you err at all, err on the side of giving its director and council too wide a scope. Whatever you do, do not err on the side of hemming them in."*

One of the first sources of contention was the level of pay for research staff. On the recommendation of the 'Doc', the council set research staff salaries at about 10% higher than equivalent salaries in the civil service. The first indication of department disapproval came at the February 1959 council meeting when the chairman, John Litton, informed the meeting of *"the contents of a confidential letter (of 17 February 1959) from the Minister for Agriculture, Paddy Smith, on the subject of salaries of professional staff, and his reply. The council unanimously expressed complete agreement with the Chairman's action."* In other words, the chairman informed the minister of the council's statutory right to set salaries at a level it saw fit for the calibre of people employed by it.

Joe Harte addressing farmers at the Grange open day in March 1966.

A Subservient Body

However, later at that February '59 meeting, it emerged that difficulties with the department were not just confined to staff salaries when the chairman and director informed the meeting of *"a number of instances in which the Department of Agriculture disputed the authority of AFT to discharge its statutory functions as the national body for agricultural research."* There followed a full discussion *"during which the Council strongly voiced its unwillingness to become a body subservient to the Department of Agriculture…"*. The meeting decided to adjourn pending a decision by the government on the functions, work and responsibilities of AFT. The chairman wrote directly to the Taoiseach, Éamon de Valera, seeking a meeting.

The Taoiseach sought position papers from both sides and the meeting took place on March 25th, 1959. The outcome, as reported to the reconvened AFT council meeting on April 7th, was a decree by the Taoiseach that the legislation *"did not specifically entrust AFT with responsibility for the actual carrying out of agricultural research on a national level but it was a specific and sole responsibility of the council to co-ordinate all agricultural research at that level."* The meeting may have cleared the air but a ceasefire was still a long way off.

Rosaleen Keane and Máiréad Lennox analysing blood samples in the Dunsinea laboratory in 1964.

The department opposition to the higher salaries continued and surfaced during discussions on the annual AFT state grant. Pat Markey remembers efforts to base the state grant on professional salary scales that applied in the Department of Agriculture and not on the higher AFT scales. The opposition re-emerged when the department put its own representative on the AFT council in 1961. The first example of this was at the November 1961 council meeting when it was agreed to implement revised salary scales for all staff. Michael Barry, assistant secretary of the department, proposed an amendment that the new scales should not be implemented until government approval was obtained. He was supported by James B Ruane, professor of agriculture in UCD, who had also joined the council a few months earlier and had a frosty relationship with the 'Doc'. The amendment was lost by six votes to two.

Dr Tom Walsh presents the Chairman Tadhg Ó'Tuama with the first issue of the Irish Journal of Agricultural Economics and Rural Sociology in 1967.

The issue arose again in January 1962 when a further increase in the salary for the chiefs of the research divisions was agreed. Barry proposed that the maximum of the scale should be reduced from £2,900 to £2,800, presumably to bring it into line with salaries of assistant secretaries in the department. His motion was not seconded. At the same meeting, Barry was the sole dissenter on a motion that *"the general conditions of service of staff shall not be altered."*

Conference of nominating organisations

"The people who have the day-to-day practical problems in agriculture should have a right to a say in agricultural research." With this statement, which contained in a nutshell the reasons for calling such a meeting, the Chairman of the Council of the Agricultural Institute, Mr. John G. Litton, opened the conference of Nominating Organizations to the Council, at Oakpark, Carlow, last July.

Of the Institute's 12-member Council 5 are nominated by 25 farming and rural organisations. Along with government and university nominees, this furnishes the governing authority of the Institute with ready-made machinery for consultation on the broadest national basis. The July conference brought some 60 delegates from these organisations together to consult with the Chairman, Director, Council and research staff on the entire research programme.

The Chairman pointed out that every group had what it considered the most urgent possible problem. It was, he said, the Council's job to sort these out in order of priority and see which problems needed to be tackled from the national point of view and which were important to the largest possible number of people.

Director's address

The Director, Dr. T. Walsh, stressed the fact that investment in research was investment in growth. Describing the various processes by which the national agricultural research programme had been developed, he said that it was now systematically geared to meet the needs of economic expansion. This aspect of the Institute's work had received especially favourable comment from outside experts visiting the country. Both the short range and long range requirements had to be met.

Dr. Walsh placed particular emphasis on the work which was designed to secure a more rational use of our land resources under intensive management systems. As part of this work a geochemical survey lin... National Soil Survey was under way.

New techniques of grassland manag... ...ial attention was being given...

The Soils and Grassland study group in session at the conference of nominating organisations.

Professor E. J. Clarke addresses the Horticulture study group at the conference.

At Loggerheads

While staff and finance issues were a continuing source of tension, the most serious rows arose over the respective responsibilities of the department and AFT for research. Starting with the de Valera 'mediation' in March 1959, these continued throughout the 1960s during which the 'Doc' and the secretary of the department, John Nagle, were regularly at loggerheads. The biggest difficulty arose over the breeding of cereal varieties, which was carried out by the department up to 1958 under the direction of John Brady, an accomplished plant breeder. When the 'Doc' joined the department in 1945 as soils advisory officer, Brady was his superior and personality clashes quickly emerged. The arguments between the two over the research programme, which was established by the department at Johnstown Castle in 1946, are legendary.

Reddy Day, who worked in Johnstown Castle as an experimental officer at the time, recalled that: *"Tom Walsh saw Johnstown as his institute for research on soils and grassland while John Brady saw it as an extension of his plant breeding programme."* In 1952, the 'Doc' was promoted by his namesake, Thomas Walsh, the Minister for Agriculture, to head a new department unit on research and advisory services on soils and grassland and the tensions with Brady eased. The department also bought a farm at Backweston, near Lucan, for cereal breeding, which also helped in keeping the two apart.

Brady had the opportunity to join AFT in 1958 and earn a bigger salary but the fact that the 'Doc' would then be his boss seemed to have been a step too far. He stayed with the department and insisted that cereal breeding stay with him. The stand-off, which created a lot of tension between the two bodies, was one of the direct consequences of the nine years of vacillation and delay in setting up AFT. Ironically, in 1952, the department regarded cereal breeding as one of the key areas of research for the new institute. In 1959, because of entrenched positions, it was seen as a critical function of the department. Despite many proposals during the past 50 years that it move to AFT, and its successor Teagasc, it still remains a function of the department.

There were also conflicts over veterinary research. This was first discussed by the AFT council at its second meeting in September 1958, when the chairman, John Litton, said that: *"discretion and a diplomatic approach was very advisable."* After much debate, the department wrote to AFT in March 1960 stating that the government did not intend that veterinary science should be covered by the AFT legislation. The controversy eased after that and AFT went on to play a crucial role in research on animal health while the department confined itself to the statutory side of disease control.

Meat research was also the subject of unnecessary friction. Although AFT established a department of meat research in 1960, the department started discussions with the meat industry on setting up a separate unit independent of AFT. The new unit was included as a proposal in the Second Programme for Economic Expansion, published in 1963, much to the annoyance of the 'Doc' and the AFT council. The separate meat research unit was never established. Both sides eventually learned to live with each other and effective working arrangements and liaison systems were built up. It must also be stated that even during the most argumentative periods there were cordial relationships between department officials and AFT research scientists. Members of the department's specialist advisory service, which was established in the 1960s, worked very closely with scientists in the various research centres in ensuring that the results of research were disseminated to the county advisory services and to farmers.

Contacts and Communications

From the beginning, huge emphasis was placed on developing international scientific linkages and in establishing the most effective strategies for communicating the results of research to farmers and industry and to the international scientific community. Olive Daly's first job at the end of 1958 was to make contact with every research institute in Europe, America, Australia, New Zealand and even Russia, alerting them to the establishment of AFT and seeking their scientific publications. Hundreds of books and scientific papers came flooding in. She also travelled to a number of the leading UK research institutes to learn about their systems for disseminating research results.

Bernard Lewis, who had worked for 10 years with Potash Ltd and had developed an effective system for transferring technical information to advisers and farmers, was appointed agricultural aide in 1961 with responsibility for ensuring that the results of research were communicated to all end-users. He was joined by Paul Broughan, an adviser in Athy, and Eamon McCormick, a dairy scientist who had been deputy secretary of the Creamery Managers Association, and the trio developed a systematic programme that linked research with advisers, farmers, agri-business and the food industry.

One of the highlights was the development of 'research bulletins' that contained practical, usable information from each research project. The bulletins were coloured green for agriculture, blue for horticulture and yellow for dairy processing and these were sent to advisers working with the county committees of agriculture and later ACOT, to advisers working with input suppliers and to creamery managers and dairy scientists working in the food industry. They became a vital part of the armoury for advisers in assisting farmers to adopt new and better management practices and for professionals working in the dairy processing industry. Another early innovation was the production of a quarterly magazine, *Farm Research News*, which kept leading farmers, policy-makers and industry executives in touch with the major innovations emanating from the research centres. As the volume of food research increased, the title of the magazine changed to *Farm and Food Research*. Launched in 1960, its consistent high quality over almost 30 years was a tribute to the professionalism of its editors, Brendan Clarke and Brian Gilsenan (one of the contributors to this book).

The reputation of a scientist and a research institute is determined by the excellence of its scientific publications. Prior to his appointment as director of AFT, the 'Doc' had almost 60 scientific papers of his own published in international scientific journals. He was adamant that the new AFT scientists should have access to an Irish scientific publication and one of his earliest initiatives was the establishment of the *Irish Journal of Agricultural Research,* the first issue of which was published in 1960.

Paddy Geoghegan, who edited the journal as well as managing the extensive range of AFT publications for more than 25 years, is convinced that the journal put AFT and Irish research on the international stage. Some of the leading scientists in the world were enlisted as 'referees' so that the scientific excellence of the publication was beyond reproach. Three issues of the journal were published every year, an indication of the amount of high quality research that was being produced by the new institute. Indeed, before the end of the 1960s an additional outlet had to be found for research emanating from the rural economy division and the *Irish Journal of Economics and Rural Sociology* was launched with Brian Gilsenan as editor.

In 1977, *the Irish Journal of Food Science and Technology* was developed to cater for the scientific output from the food research programme at Moorepark and Ashtown, with Ned Culleton as editor. In more recent years, scientific output is concentrated in a single publication, the *Irish Journal of Agricultural and Food Research,* with Seamus Hanrahan as senior editor.

In addition to the scientific journals, annual reports were published on all research programmes carried out by AFT and a wide range of manuals for farmers and industry was produced on key components of the research programme. A massive programme of in-service training was undertaken to ensure that advisers and other professionals in industry were continually updated on new technologies coming from research. Special conferences were run for representatives of the 25 organisations that had the right to nominate members to the AFT council and a comprehensive programme of national seminars was organised each year where scientists presented the results of their work. Combined with the excellent work carried out by Olive Daly on developing a strong profile for the organisation in national and local media, all of this activity ensured that AFT was regarded as a central force in the development of a modern agricultural industry.

The Minister for Agriculture, Charles Haughey, with Michael Woods at Kinsealy, 1965.

Changing Structures

The 1960s was a period of buoyancy and excitement for the fledgling AFT. The young and enthusiastic group of scientists and technicians were treading on new ground. Many of the new recruits had the opportunity to go to the US, UK and New Zealand on post-graduate programmes and they returned with new ideas and a zeal for change. The structures developed in 1958 involving five research divisions had worked well. However, the major research centres had rapidly developed into forces of change and it was felt that changes in the research management structure could enhance the operation and impact of these centres. In 1970, a Canadian expert, Dr Andel Anderson, was invited to examine the structures and make recommendations.

He recommended that the research programme should be structured on the major research centres and a deputy director should be appointed at head office. Pierce Ryan, who had been head of the national soil survey since 1959, was appointed deputy director and posts of assistant director were established to manage the research programme in each of the major research centres. Pat Ryan, who had been chief of the soils division, was appointed assistant director at Johnstown Castle. Simon Curran, who was head of the livestock husbandry department in the early years, became assistant director in charge of the Grange and Dunsinea centres. Tomás Breathnach, who was chief of the rural economy division since 1961, was appointed assistant director of the renamed economics and rural welfare centre.

P J O'Hare moved from the Glenamoy peatland centre to become assistant director of the Oak Park tillage research centre and David Robinson, who had been chief of the horticulture and forestry division, was appointed assistant director in charge of the horticultural and forestry research centre at Kinsealy. Michael Mulcahy, who had been in charge of dairy processing research at Moorepark, was appointed the assistant director in charge of the Moorepark dairy research centre while Michael Walshe, who had been the officer in charge of the Moorepark research centre, was offered the post of assistant director in charge of the western research centre at Creagh, Ballinrobe. It was this latter offer that led to the first major upheaval in AFT.

Walshe was the first scientist appointed to Moorepark and had built a big reputation as a leader and innovator in dairy research. He was the odds-on favourite for the assistant director post at Moorepark and he expected it. The event was the subject of much coverage and comment in the media, especially in the Farmers Journal and RTE. The 'Doc' insisted that the offer of the post in the west, where a person of exceptional calibre was required, was recognition of Walshe's huge abilities - but not everyone was convinced. Walshe turned down the western job and Vivian Timon was subsequently appointed assistant director at Creagh. Walshe resigned from AFT in early-1971 and joined the World Bank in Washington.

National Agricultural Authority and ACOT

Entry into the EEC in 1973 led to a huge lift in confidence in farming and farmers looked to AFT for the technologies that would enable them to capitalise on the new opportunities. It was a boom period for farmers and research scientists. But there were major concerns about the capacity of the advisory service to disseminate the new technologies to farmers. The structure had not changed since its establishment by Horace Plunkett in 1900. It was being run by 27 county committees of agriculture with some specialist support from the Department of Agriculture, while education in the colleges was controlled by the department with the county committees involved in providing local courses for young and adult farmers.

In April 1975, a government White Paper was published which proposed the merging of AFT and the advisory and education services provided by the county committees and the department into a national organisation called the National Agricultural Advisory, Education and Research Authority (NAAERA).

This led to the publication in late-1976 of the NAAERA bill by Mark Clinton, Minister for Agriculture in the Fine Gael-Labour coalition government. It became known as the National Agricultural Authority (NAA). The advisers gave a warm welcome to the bill, seeing it as an opportunity to improve their employment conditions and deliver long-sought promotions. It also received general approval from the farming organisations. However, it was vehemently opposed by research staff in AFT who saw it as a complete erosion of the independence of research. Through their union, they mounted a major campaign against the NAA.

When the bill was first debated in the Dáil on February 9th 1977, Jim Gibbons, Fianna Fáil spokesman on agriculture, announced that his party was completely opposed to the NAA. It led to a divisive, vitriolic debate, in stark contrast to the almost total harmony between government and opposition that characterised the passage of the AFT bill almost 20 years earlier. Gibbons' opposition was centred on the negative impact the new bill would have on AFT. *"Farmers view with the most incredulous dismay this wanton destruction of the institute (AFT) for base political reasons,"* he told the Dáil. He pledged that Fianna Fáil would repeal the legislation when it got back into government.

Whether Gibbons was fundamentally opposed to the inclusion of AFT in the new national organisation or Fianna Fáil was playing opposition politics is open to debate. But the opposition was a godsend to the AFT research staff. The bill was passed by the Oireachtas on May 11th 1977 and the Dáil was dissolved two weeks

later. The June election saw Jack Lynch return to power with a landslide 20 seats majority. During the interregnum between the election and the formation of the new government, Mark Clinton appointed the 'Doc' as director of the NAA and Paddy O'Keeffe, editor of the Farmers Journal, who was then chairman of the AFT council, as the new chairman. A number of the 24-member council were also appointed and the board held a couple of meetings. However, when Gibbons was appointed Minister for Agriculture he made it clear that his threat to repeal the legislation was not an idle one so the NAA never got off the ground.

A big casualty in the whole saga was Harry Spain, the senior civil servant who was the chief architect of the NAA bill. Spain was centrally involved in the ill-fated Parish Plan during the late-1940s and 1950s and, by 1977, had risen up the ranks to become deputy secretary of the department. Gibbons had taken a dislike to Spain and committed the indiscretion of naming him in the Dáil during the debate on the NAA. When he returned as minister, he froze out Spain, who decided to take early retirement a few months later. In an interview in 2006 with Joanne Banks for her PhD thesis on the advisory service, Spain said: *"I left at the end of March next year, 1978. (After Gibbons was appointed) our paths never crossed despite the fact that my room door was opposite his room door on the fifth floor in the Department of Agriculture. He didn't want anything to do with me despite the fact that I was deputy secretary. Anything he wanted to know in my area, he got through others. So it was time for me to depart."*

The Agriculture (An Comhairle Oiliúna Talmhaíochta) Bill was introduced by Gibbons to the Dáil on May 23rd 1978. In his opening speech, he said: *"The main purpose is to detach from the operation of the National Agricultural Authority the agricultural research function."* The bill was enacted on April 26th 1979, leading to the development of the national agricultural advisory and training body, which became known as ACOT. The 'Doc' was appointed the first director of ACOT after 22 eventful years at the helm in AFT. Pierce Ryan took over as director of AFT, which was to remain a separate body at least for a few more years.

At the opening of the new meat industry development plant at Dunsinea in 1978, from left: Simon Curran, Assistant Director, Dr Tom Walsh, Director; Paddy O'Keeffe, Chairman; Frank Cantwell, architect and Jim Gibbons, Minister for Agriculture.

The Minister for Agriculture, Michael O'Kennedy and Joe Rea, the first chairman of Teagasc (both in the foreground) with Dr Pierce Ryan the first director (right), and members of the authority at the first meeting of the Teagasc authority in September 1988.

The Cashman Report

From the late-1970s, the Irish economy went into a tailspin with high employment, high inflation and huge pressure on public finances. By the mid-1980s, the Department of Finance was looking at every opportunity to cut public expenditure and attention was focused on two separate bodies for research and advisory/training services in agriculture. During 1984, the National Planning Board recommended the merger of AFT and ACOT. In April 1985, the Minister for Agriculture, Austin Deasy, established a review group to review the operations of AFT and ACOT with a view to establishing the fullest possible degree of co-ordination between the services. It was chaired by Donal Cashman, former IFA president, and had five members – Flor Riordan, former president of Macra na Feirme, Dan McCarthy of the ICMSA, Philip Lynch, chief executive of the IAWS, Bart Brady from the Department of Finance and Paddy Power from the Department of Agriculture.

The group's report, published in April 1986, recommended that AFT and ACOT should retain their separate identities but stated that a further review should be carried out after five years and *"if appropriate reforms have not taken place, the creation of a unified body should be considered."* It advocated the establishment of a single board to govern both bodies and a series of actions that would bring greater co-ordination to their work.

The report also examined staff trends and the age profile of staff in both organisations. Staff numbers in AFT had reached a peak in 1980 of 1,345 of which 255 were research and 436 were technicians. By 1985, staff numbers had dropped to 1,201 due to closures of some centres and budgetary pressures. The number of research staff and technicians then stood at 236 and 394, respectively. The review group highlighted the ageing structure of research staff, noting that 61 percent were over 45 years of age and 40 per cent over 50 years of age. Just 17 per cent of researchers were less than 35 years old. This was a reflection of the massive recruitment during the 1960s. Research is a 'game' for young people and the lack of 'new blood' had now become a problem for AFT. The report also referred to the 34 senior research staff located in the AFT head office, describing the figure as *"excessive, anomalous and unnecessary."*

The number of staff in ACOT in 1985 was 1,116 and the age structure of professional staff was more balanced than in AFT, with 42 per cent of advisers and teachers over 45 years.

The Budget Bombshell

As the Cashman report was being examined by the two organisations, the economy and public finances continued to become more precarious. The general election in February 1987 led to the formation of a Fianna Fáil government with Charles Haughey as Taoiseach, Ray MacSharry as Minister for Finance and Michael O'Kennedy as Minister for Agriculture. In September, O'Kennedy indicated in a speech in Portlaoise that AFT and ACOT were to be merged and, in his subsequent budget statement, MacSharry announced the merger and a cut of 43 per cent in the budget of both organisations. A voluntary early retirement scheme, aimed at dramatically reducing staff numbers in both organisations, was also introduced. Both organisations decided to operate an indiscriminate retirement scheme; no one was going to be refused. This resulted in a mass exodus of staff, especially from AFT where a large number of senior scientists opted to leave. Almost the entire research management structure was lost with deputy director Paddy Cunningham and assistant directors such as Aidan Conway in Johnstown Castle, Jim O'Grady in Grange, Brendan Kearney in economics and rural welfare and David Robinson in Kinsealy leaving. The two organisations had a total staff of 2,300 in December 1987. Eighteen months later, the merged organisation had a staff of just over 1,400.

Liam Downey, who was director of ACOT when the merger was announced and became director of Teagasc in 1994, described the *"unplanned nature of the marriage as irresponsible and seriously damaging to both organisations."* He said *"the impact on the research programme in particular took the bones of 10 years to recover from."*

Formation of Teagasc

The legislation to establish Teagasc was introduced in the Dáil on February 16th 1988. During the debate, Michael O'Kennedy said the 43 per cent cut in the budget, amounting to £15 million, reflected the need for the two organisations to generate more income as well as the reduction in staff numbers resulting from the early retirement scheme. He announced that 350 staff had left in the previous six weeks and a further 120 were expected to go over the following months. The opposition castigated the government on the unplanned nature of the merger and used every opportunity to recall Fianna Fáil's opposition to the NAA bill 11 years earlier. Austin Deasy, the former Minister for Agriculture, made reference to the ageing research staff, saying that: *"people got old together in AFT."* The bill was enacted on June 22nd and Teagasc was established the following September. It was to be governed by an authority consisting of a chairman and 10 members.

Pierce Ryan, who had joined AFT in 1959 and had been director since 1980, was appointed the first director of Teagasc and he and the 11-member authority had the difficult task of uniting two organisations and developing integrated services against the background of a massive cut in budget. The first chairman was Joe Rea, the former president of the IFA. An effective farm leader, Rea's five years as chairman of Teagasc would not be regarded as the most spectacular period in his career.

THE MEN AT THE HELM

Dr Tom Walsh was director of AFT for its first 22 years, serving from its establishment in 1958 until 1980. He was followed by Dr Pierce Ryan, who was director of AFT from 1980 until 1988, and was the first director of Teagasc from 1988 until 1994. The mantle was then passed to Dr Liam Downey who directed Teagasc from 1994 until 2002. Jim Flanagan was then appointed director and, following his retirement in 2006, Tom Kirley served as acting director until the appointed of the current director, Professor Gerry Boyle in late-2007.

ACOT had two directors during the eight years it operated as a separate national organisation for advisory and training services – Tom Walsh from 1980 to 1982 and Liam Downey from 1983 to 1988 when it was merged with AFT to form Teagasc. Four of the five directors of AFT, ACOT and Teagasc cut their teeth in research – Walsh with UCD and the Department of Agriculture; Ryan at Johnstown Castle as head of the national soil survey; Downey as a food scientist in Moorepark and Boyle in the economics and rural welfare research centre in Dublin. Jim Flanagan worked with the Department of Agriculture for 30 years and was the department's chief inspector before his appointment as director of Teagasc.

Michael Butler, who was secretary to the Teagasc authority in the early years and had experience of observing chairmen in AFT, regarded Rea as very clever but felt he never fully understood his role as chairman of a major semi-state body. *"He thought the job was the same as being president of the IFA,"* said Butler.

Teagasc operated under enormous financial constraints in the early years and ran up a big financial deficit. At one point, AIB, which was the organisation's banker, got concerned about the size of the deficit and held a crunch meeting with senior management. Eventually, the deficit was wiped out through a series of supplementary grants from the government, the biggest of which was £8 million provided at the end of 1989. The skill of Liam Downey, in securing substantial money for research, advice and training under EU structural funds in the first half of the 1990s was a major boost and underpinned the revitalisation of the organisation, particularly in research. These developments, which are covered in some detail in other sections of this book, have brought Teagasc to the forefront of research in some key areas of agriculture and food. That the organisation could recover from such a difficult birth is a tribute to the professionalism of its current staff in the same way as the pioneering work of the early scientists put Ireland on the world scientific stage.

Reflections of a Chairman

Matt Dempsey

I was honoured to accept an invitation from the Minister for Agriculture, Austin Deasy, in 1985 to be chairman of AFT. As the chairman was formally appointed by the President, the trip was undertaken with the then director, Pierce Ryan, to meet President Patrick Hillery.

While the milk quota had been introduced in 1984, there was still no realisation that we were in for a long period of falling real prices as the European Community introduced a successive range of measures to curtail surpluses. AFT had a formidable range of assets grouped around the major research centres. Some of the work being undertaken was ground breaking in international terms. Aspects of research had great potential that was never realised, some was ahead of its time and some made a fundamental difference to Irish farming productivity.

Looking back 20 years on with the full benefit of hindsight, what were the lasting achievements from the Irish research effort? We became world leaders in wheat yields and mushroom production. Grass and potato breeding were of a world standard. Moorepark was still recovering from the Michael Walshe traumas of the early-1970s but the higher milk prices following the introduction of quotas meant that milk production from grass grew in profitability compared with every other enterprise.

With unemployment at almost 20% in the 1980s, full-time, small-scale dairying on very difficult land such as Ballinamore in Leitrim was seen as a valid research programme. Despite the eventual closure of the station, there was fundamental work done on gravel filled mole drains and baled silage which revolutionised fodder conservation. The expertise built up by the likes of the late John Mulqueen was world class and he put it freely at farmers' disposal.

Beef was advancing on two fronts. Significant resources were going into a twinning programme based at Belclare in Co Galway. Efforts to base the unit at Grange were unsuccessful and, partially as a result, Grange never built up the critical mass that was in Moorepark. Nevertheless, the growing use of the then legal hormones in beef production underpinned an intensive winter finishing sector and a research programme to service it.

It is only now, after more than 20 years, that the essential underpinning of the knowledge of soils and their chemistry is again being recognised and rejuvenated. The county soil classifications were still being done in remarkable detail but budgetary pressures were beginning to seriously bite. It was partly because of these budgetary pressures that the decision to merge ACOT and AFT was undertaken. I was flattered to be asked to chair ACOT in parallel with AFT. The two directors, Pierce Ryan and Liam Downey, were very different. The core of both organisations was retained but their traditions were fundamentally different. The county committees of agriculture were still in existence, though their role following the formation of ACOT was essentially redundant and they were abolished when Teagasc was established.

AFT was less than 30 years in existence when I became chairman. During that time, it had built up world-class facilities, scientists and analytical capacity. Its farm income survey became a model for others to emulate. It was a unique privilege to get to know men like David Robinson, former head of Kinsealy, now sadly deceased.

I will always be grateful for the opportunity to see so much that was worthwhile and meet so many with such capacity. One can only hope that the new agricultural confidence will cement its contribution into the future as it builds on such a worthwhile past.

*Matt Dempsey is Editor and Chief Executive
of the Irish Farmers Journal*

The Marshall Plan – A US Perspective
Theodore Alter*

The Marshall Plan, known also as the European Recovery Programme (ERP), was conceived in June 1947 by US Secretary of State, George C Marshall, as a US initiative for economic recovery in Europe. It was designed to use economic and financial incentives and new institutional structures to promote reconstruction, recovery and prosperity in Western Europe, thereby countering expansionist tendencies of domestic communist parties and Soviet troops in Eastern Europe. Under the plan, the United States transferred $13 billion to the war-torn economies of Europe between 1948 and 1951. It was hailed as one of the great foreign economic policy achievements following the end of World War II and essentially revived the European economy.

Because of its neutral stance during World War II, participation by Ireland in the ERP was not readily approved in either Washington or London. However, Ireland's geographical location played a crucial role in United States, British and West European defence planning. Also, Ireland and Britain were economically and financially interdependent. Excluding Ireland from the ERP would have hurt the British economy indirectly. It was therefore decided that isolating Ireland due to its wartime neutral stance would only jeopardise ideological security in the long run.

Ireland participated in the ERP from 1947 to 1952 while still continuing its non-aligned neutral status. In 1951, Ireland was given the opportunity to align itself with the US in a defence arrangement in exchange for continued economic aid. However, the Irish government was unable to do so as it had already declined to align itself with the North Atlantic Treaty Organisation (NATO) in February 1949. James Dillon, the Minister for Agriculture from 1948 to 1951 was the sole parliamentarian who vehemently disagreed with Irish neutrality. He was committed to fight against communism around the world and drafted a plan to establish a global federal structure to thwart communism. Ireland's Department of External Affairs was at that time headed by Frederick Boland, who was supportive of James Dillon and welcomed the opportunity to improve Ireland's international reputation by discarding neutrality.

As detailed elsewhere in this chapter, the establishment of an agricultural institute was first mooted in 1949 in order to address the educational, research and mechanical deficiencies of the Irish agricultural sector. The sector was continuing to decline in the wake of the failure of pro-tillage policies. In October 1949, the outline of a scheme was sent to the American authorities for approval but as already outlined a protracted debate took place among the various interests in Ireland about the structure of the new research institute. Following Dillon's return as Minister for Agriculture in 1954, agreement was reached on funding of £1.84 million from the Marshall Plan, or what was then called the Grant Counterpart Fund, to establish the agricultural institute. This money had a direct impact on the formation, four years later, of what became known as An Foras Talúntais.

**General
George C Marshall**

*Theodore (Ted) R Alter is Professor of Agricultural, Environmental and Regional Economics in the College of Agricultural Sciences at Pennsylvania State University

Dr Tom Walsh – the 'Doc' – a career in agriculture
that spanned 45 years, from 1937 to 1982.

With Martin Cranley, (front row, fourth from left) director general of the
Institute for Industrial Research and Standards (IIRS) and senior staff from
AFT and IIRS at a meeting in the mid-1970s to discuss research collaboration.

With the President, Éamon de Valera,
Michael Gardiner, AFT national soil
survey and Professor Myles Dillon,
president of the Royal Irish Academy
at a scientific meeting in the academy.

DESTINED FOR HIGH OFFICE
- A PROFILE OF THE 'DOC'

Tom O'Dwyer

Dr Tom Walsh, or the 'Doc' as we who had the privilege of working with him in An Foras Talúntais (AFT) came to know him, was the single most influential figure in the development of an internationally renowned research infrastructure in Ireland which shaped the modern agriculture and food industry of today This history of the first 50 years of research would probably have a very different complexion without his vision, drive, energy and enormous scientific brain,

The 'Doc's' career in the public service spanned 45 years, starting as a graduate in agricultural science from UCD in 1937 and ending on his retirement as director of ACOT, the national agricultural advisory and training body, at the age of 68 in 1982. Twenty-two of these eventful years were spent as director of AFT.

He was always destined for high office. Even as a young graduate, he stood out as a leader and innovator. He was a highly accomplished scientist, building up a big reputation nationally and internationally. His research on soil fertility and trace elements in UCD with professors Paddy Gallagher and E J Clarke and later with the Department of Agriculture at Johnstown Castle was central in putting a scientific foundation under Irish agriculture. He had an enviable record in scientific publication. He published almost 60 scientific papers between 1941 and 1958 together with managing a sizeable research programme during much of this period. He was one of an elite group of scientists to receive a doctorate of science, DSc, a coveted accolade in the scientific world and awarded strictly on the basis of the volume and quality of scientific output.

He had come to national notice as early as 1943. This is evidenced in a letter from the Wexford county manager, T D Sinnott, to the Minister for Agriculture, Dr James Ryan, urging the government to purchase the Johnstown Castle estate and use it as an agricultural college and research centre. The letter, dated September 10th 1943, referring to a meeting between Sinnott and the bishop of Wexford the previous day, stated: *"I could see the whole project take shape yesterday evening … with Walsh installed as research director."* The 'Doc was then working in UCD and was just 29.

The Obvious Choice

He was extraordinarily popular throughout the country among advisers, farmers and people in industry, both during his period in UCD and, from 1945 onwards, when he joined the Department of Agriculture. He led the campaign on tackling soil fertility, provided advisers with vital support and was always available to speak at meetings anywhere in the country. He was elected president of the Agricultural Science Association (ASA) on two occasions – in 1952/53 and 1959/60 – the only person to achieve that honour in the 66-year history of the association. This was an indication of the esteem in which he was held among his professional colleagues

He would have been a target for universities and research institutes overseas, because of his strong scientific reputation. The Irish Independent carried a story, which was not denied by the 'Doc', that he had an offer of an associate professorship in a university in the US mid west in 1952. The seriousness of the offer or the 'Doc's' interest in accepting it has never been fully established. However, it was a factor in his promotion in 1952 to the position of senior inspector in the department with responsibility for a new unit on research and advisory services on soils and grassland.

When AFT was eventually established in 1958, after 10 years of protracted debate, the 'Doc' was the obvious choice as director. His huge personal standing in the country, his reputation as a scientist and the relationships he had built with senior politicians in all parties gave him all the credentials. Reddy Day, who worked with him in the Department of Agriculture, is convinced there was never the slightest doubt that he would get the job. A year earlier, he had been a candidate for the professorship of farm management in UCD and had lost out to James B Ruane. When it came to the AFT job, he had covered all the angles.

Humble Beginnings

Ironically, he was born not far from the gates of the 1,000-acre Johnstown Castle estate in Wexford, the place that would become his research base during the 1940s and 1950s and would form the nucleus of the national research infrastructure after AFT was established in 1958. Pierce Ryan, who worked with him from the early-1950s and succeeded him as director of AFT, recalls him reminiscing about looking in the gates of the castle as a small boy and wondering what went on inside. Little did he know that he would eventually become the big chief.

He came from a very small farm; his father worked for the local priest, an unusual background for a university graduate of that period. His vision of agriculture and rural development arose from his humble beginnings and gave him a common touch. Irrespective of their role, everyone was treated with the same dignity and respect and made to feel that their job was of vital importance. The story is told that the first time he went to Johnstown Castle in 1945 after it was acquired by the Department of Agriculture, he was met at Wexford railway station by William Breslin, who was chauffeur with the original owners and had transferred to the department. *"You're very welcome sir,"* said Breslin. The 'Doc' replied: *"Billy, those days are gone forever."*

Eugene Grennan addressing the 'Doc' and members of the AFT Council during their visit to the Glenamoy research station in 1967.

'A Breath of Fresh Air'

"A moving spirit and a man with a mission" is how T K Whitaker, distinguished civil servant and the man dubbed the father of the modern Irish economy, described the 'Doc' in an interview for this book in March 2008. Both Whitaker and the 'Doc' passionately believed in the need to abandon the self-sufficiency ideal and, in the case of agriculture, to focus on exploiting the advantages of producing food from grass rather than the failed tillage policy of previous decades. There was a huge concentration on agriculture in the First Programme for Economic Expansion, published in 1958. This reflected the huge importance of agriculture to the economy at the time. While the 'Doc' was not directly involved in writing the section on agriculture, Whitaker remembers having many discussions with him about it. *"I remember being very impressed by Tom Walsh's charisma – yes, he had that quality – and he was a real stimulus to me and my colleagues. He was a breath of fresh air in a rather staid civil service,"* said Whitaker.

Paddy O'Keeffe, the former editor of the Farmers Journal and chairman of AFT for six years in the 1970s, remembers the 'Doc' as having energy way beyond normal and having a capacity to manipulate the political system everywhere he could. His passion and enthusiasm to advance the cause of the industry earned him respect with senior politicians and he was particularly close to Dr James Ryan, a fellow Wexford man who was Minister for Finance during the early years of AFT.

London 1965; the 'Doc' is awarded the Francis New Memorial Medal.

He was friendly with Frank Aiken, the Minister for External Affairs. These contacts proved very important during difficulties over the AFT annual budget when the telephone call or private meeting between the 'Doc' and a senior minister made all the difference.

'Down the Chimney'
He was highly regarded by James Dillon, the Minister for Agriculture in the 1948/51 and 1954/57 inter-party governments. Olive Daly, who worked closely with the 'Doc' during all of his 22 years as director of AFT, recalls hearing the following back-handed tribute by Dillon to his commitment and persistence: *"You would have a meeting with Tom Walsh; he would have left the room and you'd expect to be at peace but here he is again – down the chimney."*

While there were differences, particularly in the early years, with senior civil servants over functions and finances, there was never less than full respect for his intellect and commitment. In 1977, when AFT and ACOT were merged into the National Agricultural Authority (NAA), the 'Doc' was appointed its first director.

He was deeply committed to the concept of a unified research, advisory and training organisation and the failure of the NAA to get off the ground was a source of great disappointment to him. Three years later, when ACOT, the national advisory and training organisation, was formed, he was the obvious choice as its first director notwithstanding his 65 years. These and numerous other appointments to public bodies, many outside the sphere of agriculture and food, are evidence of the esteem in which he was held.

'A Unique Vision'
The breath-taking speed at which the 'Doc' developed research centres and recruited staff has already been covered. What makes his achievement all the more remarkable is the unique vision he brought to the research programme of the fledgling organisation. Disciplines such as rural sociology and socio-economics were included from the beginning. He expounded on balanced rural development and gave it a research focus more than two decades before it appeared on the national or European agenda and he highlighted environmental sustainability long before it became an important policy issue. He was talking about 'mission statements' in the 1960s, a concept that did not enter the vocabulary of the public and private sectors until the late-1980s and 1990s.

He had an amazing breadth of international linkages and a global vision of agriculture, which was of enormous benefit to the developing AFT research programme. He was personally responsible for enabling a large number of young scientists to undertake post-graduate studies at research institutes and universities in the US, New Zealand, UK and mainland Europe throughout the 1960s. The experience and knowledge they gained played an important part in building world-class scientific expertise in AFT. In later years, many AFT staff played a key role in the development of research services and in the establishment of agricultural development programmes in Africa, Asia and the Mediterranean region, working on projects funded by the World Bank and other international development agencies.

*Receiving a research donation from Bill O'Connell,
Albatros Fertilisers in 1973 also pictured is Mrs O'Connell.*

*With Pierce Ryan, Conor McGann and Tom O'Dwyer in
Moorepark in 1969.*

Infectious Enthusiasm

His infectious enthusiasm was perhaps his most outstanding
attribute. As a young lecturer in UCD, Reddy Day remembers
that while he may have lacked some of the finer skills in
communication he more than compensated in enthusiasm
and motivational skills. *"He was selfless in the time he devoted
to students,"* said Day. Those who worked with him in AFT,
including myself, can testify to his phenomenal motivational
skills. After a meeting with him, you felt that the research
you were conducting was absolutely vital to the future of
the industry and you went away feeling very important and
invigorated. His real interest was in science and research
and in bringing the results therof to the practitioners in the
food and agricultural industry. Reddy Day tells the lovely
story of the 'Doc' being invited to open an art exhibition
and within five minutes warming to the subject of the
research needs in the world of art! He was, even sometimes
to a fault, totally protective of his staff and defended them
against attacks from all sides.

When he started a 'new' career in 1980 as director of ACOT
at the age of 65, he displayed the same level of enthusiasm,
energy and innovation to developing a national structure
for advisory and training services. John Callaghan, who
worked with him as director of development in ACOT, is
still amazed at the enormous contacts he had in ADAS, the
English research and advisory services and in the Scottish
Agricultural Colleges and across Europe and these opened
important doors to the new organisation as it charted a
new course for advice and training.

One of his biggest achievements during his short period as
director of ACOT was the establishment of structures that
led to the development of the 'green cert', which transformed
training of young farmers. While he continued to regard
the scientists in AFT as his children, once he joined ACOT
his loyalties switched totally to advisory and training staff.
This was exemplified when ACOT developed a corps of
regional specialist advisers. The decision met with intense
opposition from some senior scientists in AFT, who felt
that they were the real specialist advisers. The 'Doc' pushed
ahead, insisting that the job of the scientists was to develop
the technologies and the role of advisers was to transfer
it to farmers. Ironically, almost 20 years earlier, he had
vehemently opposed the establishment of specialist
advisers by the Department of Agriculture, insisting that
such work was the preserve of AFT scientists. Tom Walsh
was indeed a giant figure in Irish agriculture for almost half
a century and he did the state extraordinary service.

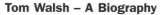

Bill Carroll, Co-operative Pig Producers presenting a cheque to support pig research.

Tom Walsh – A Biography

Tom Walsh was born in Piercestown, Co Wexford in 1914, the youngest of four sons of Pat and Mary (nee Hall) Walsh. He was educated at Piercestown national school and Wexford CBS. He studied agricultural science in UCD, qualifying with a BAgrSc in 1937. He was awarded the MAgrSc in 1938, the PhD in 1941 and the DSc in 1947. He married Mimi (nee Caffrey), daughter of Professor Michael Caffrey of UCD, in 1940 and the couple had three children.

Following graduation, he worked for a short period as an experimental officer with Imperial Chemical Industries (ICI) and as adviser in north Tipperary before joining UCD as a lecturer in soil science in 1938. In 1945, he was appointed soils advisory officer with the Department of Agriculture with responsibility for research and advisory work on soils and fertiliser use. In 1948, he set up the soil testing laboratories at Johnstown Castle. In 1952, he was promoted to senior inspector in the department, in charge of a technical group concerned with research and specialist advisory services on soils and grassland.

He was appointed the first director of AFT in 1958, where he remained until 1980 when he was appointed director of ACOT, the new national advisory and training authority. He retired from ACOT in 1982.

He was the recipient of many awards including honorary degrees from the National University of Ireland and Trinity College Dublin, a Boyle medal from the Royal Dublin Society, the Francis New memorial medal, a fellowship of the American Association for the Advancement of Science, a fellowship of the Institute of Food Science and Technology and the medal from the French Society of Soil Science. He was a member of the Royal Irish Academy and was senior vice-president as well as serving as secretary of the academy for seven years. In 1979, he was made a freeman of Wexford and in 1987 the Teagasc soil laboratories at Johnstown Castle were dedicated to him.

He was a founding member of the Agricultural Science Association (ASA) and president of the association on two occasions. He was a founding member and president of the Fertiliser Association of Ireland. He served as president of the Irish Grassland Association and was a member of the board of the Irish Agricultural Organisation Society (IAOS). Outside of agriculture and food, he served on many statutory and voluntary organisations including chairman of the National Council for Educational Awards (NCEA), chairman of the Garda Training Review Body and chairman of the Advisory Council on Development Co-operation (DEVCO) and its successor, the Association for Professional Services Overseas (APSO). He was a board or council member of a range of other bodies including the Economic and Social Research Institute (ESRI), the Institute of Public Administration (IPA), the School of Ecumenics, the Commission on Higher Education, the Commission for Justice and Peace, the Nuclear Energy Board and Thomond College Limerick.

At international level, his involvements included chairman of a number of high-level FAO committees, head of the Irish delegation on the EU Standing Committee on Agricultural Research (SCAR), vice-president of the International Institute for Co-operation in Agricultural Research (CICRA) and visiting professor at the university of Madrid. He died in 1988. In 1992, with support from a large number of organisations and companies, his collection of some 75 scientific and technical publications were published in two large volumes and presented to his wife and family. At the same time, Teagasc director Liam Downey established the Walsh Fellowships, within which to date over 1,000 students have attained masters and PhD degrees in a collaborative exercise between Teagasc and the universities.

Roadside glimpse at soils map at Croaghmuckross
in the West Donegal Resource Survey area.

Gerry Foley (centre), chief agricultural officer in Meath
discussing the soil map for the county with members of the soil
survey team, Michael Gardiner (left) and Toddy Radford.

CHAPTER 3

SOILS, GRASS AND ENVIRONMENTAL RESEARCH AT JOHNSTOWN CASTLE

Michael Miley

Prior to the establishment of AFT in 1958, Johnstown Castle had already acquired a national profile for its early research on soil fertility and grassland. This work, which was conducted at Johnstown Castle by the Department of Agriculture from 1946, provided the scientific basis for priming the transformation of the post-war subsistence agriculture on to a new commercial footing. This early research, combined with the soil testing service, which was established in 1948, had a particular impact on the build-up of soil fertility from the depressingly low post-war levels.

Dr Tom Walsh with delegates attending the International Potash Institute conference at Johnstown Castle in 1963.

An indication of the poor state of Irish grassland in the post-war years can be seen from a report in 1949 by G A Holmes, the New Zealand government's agricultural attaché in London. Holmes, who was asked by the Minister for Agriculture, James Dillon, to prepare a report on Irish grasslands, wrote: *"I saw hundreds of fields which are growing just as little as it is physically possible for the land to grow under an Irish sky. This statement is not intended as a criticism of the competence of the farmers, or of the policy of any government, but it is a commentary on the circumstances which have combined to bring about such a state – more than thirty years of political and economic instability, some sixteen years of hopelessly inadequate fertiliser supply, with the nine years just past during which the compulsory tillage was superimposed upon a desperate famine for fertiliser. It is a miracle that some of the land is able to grow grass at all."*

Dr Tom Walsh, the first director of AFT, was appointed by the Department of Agriculture as head of research and specialist advisory services on soils and grasslands in 1952 and, under his direction, research concentrated on demonstrating the benefits of lime, phosphorus and potash and the strategic use of trace elements for grassland and tillage crops. This research was led by Pat Ryan, John Kilroy, Pat McDonnell, Gary Fleming and Brendan Golden, all of whom went on to join AFT in Johnstown Castle and elsewhere. Others, such as Michael Neenan, Aidan Conway, Roger McCarrick, Michael Walshe and Willie Murphy, who became household names in AFT research in the 1960s and 1970s, also joined the research staff at Johnstown Castle when it was under the control of the Department of Agriculture.

Others who were recruited as young graduates to Johnstown Castle and became prominent in the industry include Seamus Sheehy, the leading agricultural economist, Reddy Day, who headed the Pigs and Bacon Commission for many years, Pat Fottrell who subsequently became President of NUIG and Tom Raftery, who had a distinguished career in UCC and also served as a member of the European Parliament. After the formation of AFT, Johnstown Castle became a sort of a 'mother house' where new recruits were sent to learn the basics in research practice before they were assigned to the other centres that were established for livestock and crops research.

The Early Pioneers

The work of these early researchers meant that when AFT took over the Johnstown Castle centre from the Department of Agriculture in January 1960 a fair amount of scientific information had already been built up on grassland and soil fertility. The principles of experimental design and statistical analysis, spearheaded by the early Department researchers, Joe Prendergast and John Brady, were also firmly in place. Neither of these two early scientists joined AFT. Prendergast went on to become a grassland specialist with the Department of Agriculture and in 1980 became director of operations with the new national advisory and training body, ACOT. Brady, an accomplished cereal breeder, continued to run the Department's cereal breeding activities and later became chief inspector.

Pat Ryan, who was in charge of Johnstown Castle when it was run by the Department of Agriculture, was appointed head of the new AFT soils division. As well as Johnstown Castle, he also had responsibility for research on blanket peat at Glenamoy in north west Mayo, on cutover bog at Lullymore, Co Kildare and on drumlin soils at Ballinamore, Co Leitrim. Under the leadership of Jim Brogan, Gary Fleming and Willie Murphy, major advances were made in understanding soil fertility and in devising prescriptions for fertiliser use on grassland and tillage farms.

Fertiliser usage increased significantly resulting in a 20 per cent increase in cattle numbers and more than a 50 per cent increase in yields of tillage crops during the 1960s. The work at Johnstown Castle also provided the basis for much of the research carried out in the 1960s by AFT scientists working on dairying, beef, sheep and tillage. For example, the classic farmlet scale work on stocking rates for dairying carried out by Michael Walshe and Dan Browne at Moorepark and on beef and sheep by Aidan Conway at Grange drew heavily on the soil fertility research that emanated from Johnstown Castle.

Discussing the report on the soils of Limerick with President Éamon de Valera in Áras an Uachtaráin in 1966 were Dr Tom Walsh, Chairman John Litton and Pierce Ryan, head of the national soil survey.

The head of the EEC directorate general for agriculture,
Mr J van Lierde and his wife on a visit to Johnstown Castle in 1969.

Johnstown Castle - A Brief History

The Johnstown Castle estate, situated near Wexford town, comprises 400 hectares of farmland, woodlands, lakes, gardens and ornamental grounds. The ancestral seat of the Esmondes, it was established in the late 12th century during the reign of Henry II. In the mid-1600s, Cromwell confiscated the estate from the Esmondes and gave it to Lieut. Col. Overstreet in lieu of unpaid wages. It passed from Overstreet's widow to John and Mary Reynolds, Wexford merchants, and one of their three daughters married a local man, John Grogan, who took over the estate in 1692.

The property remained in the hands of the Grogan family and their descendants until 1945, except for about 12 years after the 1798 rebellion when the then owner, Cornelius Grogan, was court marshalled and hanged on Wexford bridge by the British forces. The last private owner was Captain M. V. Lakin, a descendant of the Grogans who inherited the estate from his grandmother in 1942. Captain Lakin made a gift of the estate to the Irish nation in 1945. It was used by the Department of Agriculture as a research centre and horticultural college until January 1960 when it was taken over by the newly established AFT as a research centre.

The castle is a fine example of 19th century 'Gothic revival' architecture. The earlier structure, built around 1500, was a plain fortified tower house.

A second tower was added around 1700. The castle that exists today was built after the estate was returned to the Grogan family in 1810.

As well as being the centre for soils and environmental research in Teagasc and for advisory and training services in Wexford, Johnstown Castle demesne is now also the headquarters of the Environmental Protection Agency (EPA) and more than 300 staff of the Department of Agriculture, Fisheries and Food are also located there. It is also the home of the Irish Agricultural Museum, which is located in restored farm buildings, built around 1810. The museum contains a large display of farm and household equipment and tools. It also houses the impressive famine exhibit, which was developed by Teagasc in 1995 to mark the 150th anniversary of the Great Famine. The establishment of the museum owes much to the dedication of many staff at Johnstown Castle and elsewhere, including in particular Austin O'Sullivan, the first curator, and T J Maher, former IFA president and MEP, who was the first chairman.

Michael Ryan demonstrating soil survey techniques to
Department of Agriculture land project officers in 1965.

*Members of the AFT technical advisory committee on
soils at their first meeting in Johnstown Castle in 1962;
seated: G P Campbell, chief inspector, Department of
Lands; Dr Tom Walsh; G F Mitchell, registrar Trinity
College; M V O'Brien, director Geological Survey.
Standing: O V Mooney, forestry division, Department of
Lands; J Corkery, director Land Rehabilitation Project;
P Kavanagh, CAO Laois and William Brickley, UCD.*

The Soil Fertility Crisis

An indication of the level of soil impoverishment can
be seen in a scientific paper published by Tom Walsh,
Pat Ryan and John Kilroy in the 1950s. This showed that
over 90 per cent of soil samples tested in the Johnstown
Castle laboratories in 1950 were very, or moderately
deficient in phosphorus, over 50 per cent were deficient
in potash and over 50 per cent had less than satisfactory
levels of lime. A further analysis carried out in 1957
showed little or no improvement.

The first benchmark study on the state of grassland
management was carried out by Michael Neenan,
Aidan Conway and Willie Murphy in the late-1950s.
Working with advisers, they collected grazing records,
milk yields, live weight gains and yields of hay and silage
from single fields throughout the country. Soil fertility
levels and the botanical composition of swards were also
measured. The results showed that, in stocking rate terms,
outputs of grass ranged from a respectable 1.4 acres per
livestock unit to a miserable 8.8 acres per livestock unit
(0.28 to 1.82 livestock units per hectare). This information
helped to set the framework for a grassland improvement
research programme.

An earlier large scale grazing trial by Joe Prendergast
and John Brady at Johnstown Castle compared commercial
and UK-bred strains of ryegrass and white clover.

The results demonstrated the enormous potential for
increased production from grass. Later work by Donal
Moloney and Willie Murphy gave new insights into the
level of animal performance that could be achieved from
newly established, well-managed grass/clover swards.
They showed that intensively managed grassland, with
high levels of fertiliser nitrogen, could give a beef live
weight gain of over 1,100 kg per hectare over the grazing
season, with the clover sward that got no nitrogen
achieving three-quarters of this level. These figures were
unheard of at farm level at that time. Similar trials were
carried out on the evaluation of grass/clover swards for
milk production.

Until then, farmers sowing white clover had to buy
inoculum, which enabled the clover to fix its own nitrogen.
However, a major investigation by Cyril Masterson at
Johnstown Castle on the symbiotic rhizobia bacteria that
fix atmospheric nitrogen revealed that clover plants had
the ability to select the most suitable strains of bacteria
from the soil. This groundbreaking discovery relieved
farmers of the problem of getting inoculum and the rather
troublesome business of inoculating white clover seed.

An illustration of the big variation of soil types in just one townsland.

Transforming Grassland

In the 1960s, a large number of trials were carried out at Johnstown Castle and at sites throughout the country on measuring the response to fertiliser use on permanent pasture. These showed that a combination of nitrogen and phosphorus could increase grass and silage yields by up to 50 per cent. The trials also played a major role in helping scientists and advisers to interpret soil test results and to provide fertiliser recommendations for individual farms. The dominance of inferior grasses, such as common bent grass, Yorkshire fog and red fescue, was also a huge problem in permanent pastures at that time, leading to very poor productivity. Scientists conducted an intensive research programme on methods to increase the proportion of ryegrass and clover in pastures.

An example of this was work by Tim Gleeson on non-ploughing methods to introduce ryegrasses into old permanent swards. Later, Noel Culleton, who is now head of Johnstown Castle, developed important blueprints for massively improving productivity of old swards. He found that good grazing management and effective fertilisation lifted the productivity of a sward, which had an initial ryegrass content of only 5 per cent, to 95 per cent of that of a fully reseeded sward. This work, which was replicated at a large number of research centres, made a huge contribution to transforming the quality and output of grassland.

The transformation was supported by recommendations developed from research at Johnstown Castle on the optimum levels of lime and fertilisers based on the interpretation of the results of soil testing and on the requirements of the range of farming systems. Scientists worked closely with advisers who disseminated the information to farmers.

A major component of the research on soil fertilisation was devoted to a better understanding of the chemistry of our soils and their powers to release phosphorus and potash. The industry looked to Johnstown Castle for guidance on all aspects of soil fertility and many of the fertiliser compounds produced for different systems of grassland and silage making were based on research conducted at Johnstown.

As new and improved varieties of grass and clover began to be developed, a huge amount of information was built up from research on the most suitable varieties and mixes for Irish farming conditions and for particular types of farming. Work by Johnstown Castle researchers, Tom Gately and Michael Ryan, on the suitability of early and late-flowering perennial ryegrasses is an example of some of the earlier work. They found that the late-flowering varieties were better for beef cattle as they had better growth rates for a longer period in summer whereas the early-flowering varieties were better for dairy cows as they had better growth rates when the cows were in full milk production and their more upright growth habit resulted in more clover growth in mid-summer.

Other research on the impact of grazing conditions, by Tony Brereton and Owen Carton, led to beneficial changes in grazing management. They measured the effects of grazing interval and severity of grazing on grass growth rates and tillering of the grass plants at different times of the year. They found very little difference in grass growth rate per day when paddocks were rested for between two and four weeks. However, longer or shorter rest periods resulted in either an accumulation of unusable grass or a grass scarcity. Further studies by Tony Brereton led to the development of the 'Johnstown Castle Grass Growth Model'. This is still used by Met Éireann in producing weekly forecasts of grass supply, which are published in the farming press.

Arable Crops Research

While the key focus of soil fertility research at Johnstown Castle was on grassland, major trials were also carried out on the nutrient requirements of tillage crops. During the 1970s and 1980s, Tom Gately investigated rates and timing of fertilisers for optimum yield and quality in the full range of cereal crops while Michael Herlihy conducted similar work on the fertilisation of sugar beet. Vital information was produced on tailoring fertiliser levels to the place of the crop in the rotation leading to big improvements in the quality of malting barley and sugar beet. Another outcome from the research was the formulation of different fertiliser compounds to match the requirements of particular crops, leading to a greater level of precision in tillage farming.

New equipment introduced in 1965 increased the speed of analysing soil samples for trace elements five-fold.

Dr Tom Walsh with staff of the soils division in Johnstown Castle in 1965.

Nitrogen the Key Primer

Until Nitrigin Éireann Teoranta (NET), the state-owned fertiliser company, went into operation at Arklow in the early 1960s, all sources of nitrogen were imported. These consisted of sulphate of ammonia, sodium nitrate from Chile and some forms of guano from the South Sea Islands. At first, NET produced only sulphate of ammonia but research at Johnstown Castle showed that calcium ammonium nitrate was superior to sulphate of ammonia for both grass and tillage. It acted quicker and did not acidify the soil, which was a serious problem with sulphate of ammonia. NET quickly moved to the production of calcium ammonium nitrate.

A that stage, urea was a much cheaper source of nitrogen but was regarded as inefficient and unreliable for the grasslands of Europe. Extensive research at Johnstown Castle showed that urea was equivalent to ammonium nitrate when used on grass up to around early-May.

Results from summer use were unpredictable because of the potential loss of nitrogen to the atmosphere. As most of the nitrogen on grassland is applied for spring and early-summer grazing and for first-cut silage, the Johnstown Castle research led to large-scale savings in expenditure on nitrogen fertiliser. The research also showed that the use of urea on spring-sown cereals was risky and its use in compound fertilisers in combine drilling often led to crop failure.

Johnstown Castle also designed systems for early and late grazing that increased productivity further. The research showed it was possible to bring forward the date of grazing by up to six weeks in spring and to greatly extend the autumn grazing season by good management and strategic use of nitrogen. Prescriptions were issued for different parts of the country to take account of soil and climate factors.

Adding sulphur increased second-cut silage crop yields by up to 50 per cent. As a result, sulphur was added to fertilisers and farmers were able to increase the productivity of grazing and silage over almost half of the country.

Money from Muck

The effective use of slurry was a major part of the Johnstown Castle programme for decades. Research was conducted by Marie Sherwood, Paddy Kiely, Hubert Tunney, and Owen Carton on the fertiliser value of slurry, spreading dates and spreading methods. A consistent finding was that the best responses were got from slurry applied in the spring. Methods of reducing nutrient losses were also the subject of detailed research. They included splash plate orientation, soil injection, trailing shoe applicators, band spreaders and acidification of the slurries. Soil injection was best but was unsuitable for most farms on account of the high stone content of the soils.

Aidan Conway, during a visit to Massey University in New Zealand, saw a coulter for grass seed drilling and felt a modification of this could solve the slurry injection problems in Ireland. The New Zealanders developed a prototype machine with specially designed coulters and this was shipped to Johnstown Castle for trial. Pioneering work by Paddy Kiely in adapting the machine led to the development of the 'band spreading' system. It resulted in much lower loss of nitrogen to the atmosphere and a big reduction in smell, compared to the splash plate system.

Solutions to Side Effects

As farming intensified, there were the inevitable side effects. One of these was an increase in the level of grass tetany, which was due to low levels of magnesium in the blood and led to the collapse and sudden death of high-yielding dairy cows. Research at Johnstown Castle by Aidan Conway, Michael Walshe and Paddy Smyth, a veterinarian in the Department of Agriculture, as far back as the late-1950s showed that cows grazing spring grass with high levels of nitrogen and potash were more prone to grass tetany. This threatened to undermine farmer confidence in the benefits of increased fertilisers. But the scientists found that dusting grass with calcined magnesite supplied small daily amounts of magnesium to the animal. This solved the problem and the practice of dusting pastures continues to this day.

Many years later, the solution to the problem of sulphur deficiency in the soil made a huge contribution to grass production, particularly in mid-summer. The problem arose as a result of the reduction of the sulphur content in fertilisers due to the big drop in the usage of sulphate of ammonia and superphosphate. Atmospheric release of sulphur from industrial sources was also being reduced. Trials by Matt Murphy and Jim Brogan found that sulphur deficiency was a major problem on a wide range of soils, leading to big reductions in grass production and silage yields.

Monitoring Grazing Behaviour

The effects of free range and rotational grazing on animal behaviour was examined by Michael O'Sullivan in the early-1980s. The cattle were fitted with sensors to monitor their movements and behaviour – walking, grazing, resting and rumination. The recordings were transmitted by radios mounted on the backs of the animals to a receiving station in the laboratory.

There were marked differences in behaviour between the free range and rotationally grazed animals, especially at the high stocking rates. The rotationally grazed animals ate for a short time until the grass supply was used up and then lay down waiting to be moved to the next paddock. The free range animals spent a much longer time wandering around looking for the next mouthful. The live weight gain of the rotationally grazed animals was higher. The difference in performance was equivalent to the energy expended by the free range animals in looking for extra grass.

Grass on Peat

Considerable research was carried out in the early years on growing grass on blanket peat and on cut over bog. The blanket peat research station at Glenamoy in north west Mayo was taken over by AFT from the Department of Agriculture in 1959. Minfhéir Teo had earlier tried to produce grass meal at the centre but with little success. As peat was deficient in almost everything, it was the ideal medium for research. The centre was managed by P J O'Hare, who later became head of tillage research at Oak Park. Good quality grass/clover swards were successfully established using a surface seeding technique and grazing trials were carried out. However, liver fluke was a major problem in both cattle and sheep and the centre was closed after about 10 years.

Paddy Lalor, (second from right), Parliamentary Secretary to the Minister for Posts and Telegraphs, on a visit to the peatland research centre in Lullymore, Co Kildare in 1969, with David Robinson (left) chief of the AFT horticulture and forestry division and scientists and executives from AFT and Bord na Móna.

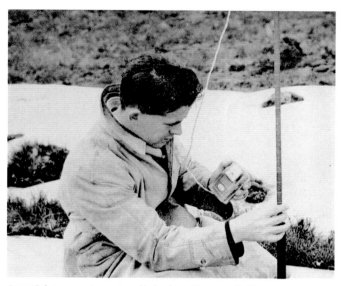

Liam Galvin measuring water table levels at Glenamoy, Co Mayo.

Jim Brogan, one of the early pioneers in grassland and soil fertility research.

Research on cut over bog was centred at Lullymore, Co Kildare, on land where Bord na Móna had produced milled peat. Research on cereals and potatoes on cut over bog had been carried out by the Department of Agriculture for four years prior to the establishment of AFT, which concentrated on growing grass.

The land was much drier than the blanket peat and the trials showed that good grassland was easily established. The research discovered particular problems with trace elements including what became known as the molybdenum/copper/sulphur complex and solutions were provided by Gary Fleming from Johnstown Castle and David Poole from Grange. The centre, which was managed by Andy Cole, developed livestock systems that were widely adopted. As a result of the research, Bord na Móna set up beef production units on land that became available from the milled peat operation.

The peatland centres were also used for other research, including vegetable growing and a range of industrial crops such as bamboo and fibre crops. There was also interesting research on wild fowl at Glenamoy where projects were undertaken in the 1960s on increasing the grouse population and on population trends and feeding habits of the mallard duck.

Evaluating the National Land Base

The National Soil Survey, established in 1959, was the first real attempt to survey, classify and map the soil resources of Ireland in a systematic manner. This was a major project and provided an essential framework for defining the productive capacity of the myriad of soil types and their suitability for different enterprises. It was also an important resource for overall land use planning.

The first generalised soil map of Ireland was published in 1969 by Pierce Ryan and Michael Gardiner. A second, and improved, edition and an explanatory bulletin was published by Michael Gardiner and Toddy Radford in 1980. Also, around that time, a peatland map of the country was published by Bob Hammond. Meanwhile, a systematic county soil survey was undertaken and around 44 per cent of the country was surveyed and mapped. Complete reports on 10 counties were published as well as reports on a number of regions and districts. The ten full counties with published soil surveys are Wexford, Carlow, Limerick, Clare, Westmeath, Meath, Laois, Kildare, Leitrim and Offaly. Surveys were also published for west Mayo, west Donegal and west Cork. When Teagasc was established in 1988, a decision was taken to discontinue the field programme. Twenty years later, there are now plans to revive this activity, which was given so much importance in the early decades of AFT.

The soil survey became an essential resource for advisers and planners and for studies on soil resources. It provided a framework for national strategic forest planning through the development of comparative data on forestry and grassland and was also used widely in the design of slurry management systems and in defining areas that were sensitive to groundwater pollution from nitrogen and other sources. The highest profile application is perhaps the legal challenge to the land valuation system in 1982 when the findings of the survey, through John Lee's work, played a significant part in the abandonment of

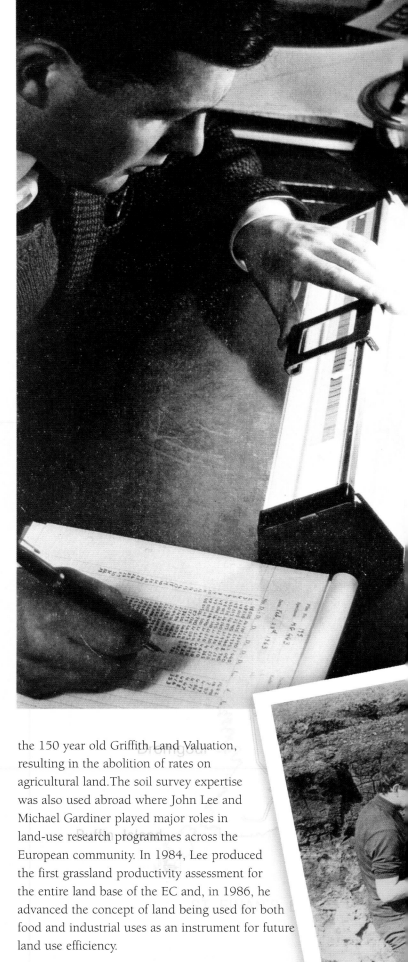

the 150 year old Griffith Land Valuation, resulting in the abolition of rates on agricultural land. The soil survey expertise was also used abroad where John Lee and Michael Gardiner played major roles in land-use research programmes across the European community. In 1984, Lee produced the first grassland productivity assessment for the entire land base of the EC and, in 1986, he advanced the concept of land being used for both food and industrial uses as an instrument for future land use efficiency.

Assessing drainage problems in Waterford during the 1960s.

Solving Drainage Problems

Information from the national soil survey was essential in identifying land drainage problems and in devising systems of drainage for different types of wetland. The scientists who led this work were Billy Burke, Liam Galvin, Tim Gleeson and John Mulqueen. A highlight of the drainage research was the development by John Mulqueen of the gravel mole drainage system for impermeable soils, which had significant impact on raising productivity.

Mulqueen, who worked at Glenamoy, Ballinamore, Creagh and UCG during his career with AFT and Teagasc, was the leading national expert on the mechanics and mathematics of water movement through different types of soils. As well as his innovations in agricultural drainage, he was also involved in developing drainage systems for some of the leading sports arenas in Ireland and the UK. They include Semple Stadium in Thurles, Fitzgerald Stadium in Killarney, Pearse Stadium in Galway and McHale Park in Castlebar. His expertise was also used to solve drainage problems at Ibrox, home of Glasgow Rangers, and at Ballybritt racecourse in Galway. Mulqueen, along with Tim Gleeson, also provided the essential science that led to the development of all-weather pitches.

Survey Scientists

The National Soil Survey was staffed by a large number of scientists, many of whom went on to senior research and management positions in AFT. Pierce Ryan, who subsequently became director of AFT and Teagasc, was head of the survey team from its inception in 1959. Michael Gardiner took over the reins in 1970 and led the team until 1981 when John Lee was appointed. Among the early scientists to be recruited were Michael Conry, Sean Diamond, John O'Callaghan and Tom Finch. Michael Ryan, Jim Kiely and Michael Walsh were also recruited in the early years. Other scientists included Bob Hammond, who specialised in peatland classification, and Michael Bulfin, who developed assessments of land for forestry. Joe Lynch was the survey team's cartographer and Ned Culleton, who later joined the national publications unit in AFT, was responsible for the laboratory in the early years.

Tracking the Trace Elements

Research on deficiencies and excesses of trace elements in the soil and understanding the complex interaction of elements and their effect on animal health and crop growth was crucial in the development of a modern agricultural industry. Much of this pioneering work was undertaken by the early AFT scientists and led from Johnstown Castle, with support from crop scientists and veterinary experts in the other research centres. Gary Fleming, who joined Johnstown Castle in 1950, spent 40 years on trace element research during which he acquired an international reputation.

Cobalt, which caused ill-thrift and 'pining' in sheep and cattle, was one of the first elements to receive attention. The deficient areas were identified and remedial strategies, in the form of dosing of animals or dusting of pasture, were devised. Research also showed that the problem was not just related to cobalt deficiency in the soil. In some soils, high levels of manganese resulted in cobalt being 'locked-up'. The end result was a major boost to sheep farmers in particular.

Selenium was next up, where in the 1950s advisers in Meath, Limerick and south Tipperary reported cattle and horses suffering hair loss and sloughing of the hooves. Drawing on US research, the scientists discovered that this was caused by an excess of selenium. However, national soil survey work and trials at Belclare involving the treatment of lambs with selenium showed that deficiencies also existed, particularly on limestone soils. It turned out that selenium deficiency was a much bigger problem than toxicity and injecting sheep with selenium vitamin E formulations became a common practice.

In other work, scientists found that high molybdenum levels induced copper deficiency, leading to serious animal performance problems. The research found that applying large dressings of lime to high molybdenum soils exacerbated the copper problem. The solution was to supplement the animal rather than the pasture with copper. This led to routine copper injections particularly to young growing cattle. Another element to receive attention was iodine, which was found to be deficient especially on soils with low organic matter. This led to the supplementation of iodine through salt licks or incorporation in the feed. This and other work on the effect of trace elements individually and collectively in soil-plant-animal interrelationships helped set the framework for the science-based industry we have today.

In the 1980s, work was undertaken on the role of trace elements/heavy metals in the environment. In particular, the heavy metal content of sewage sludges and its possible deleterious effects on soils on which sewage sludge was spread was examined. Attention was drawn to the possible danger of excess heavy metal intake by animals if sludges were applied to pastures.

In the 1990s, the compilation of a National Soil Database was begun as part of the National Development Plan. This work, involving Teagasc, the Environmental Protection Agency and other research institutes, led to the publication in 2007 of a Soil Geochemical Atlas of Ireland. It provided a sound, well-structured baseline of soil geochemical properties relevant to sustainable land use and soil management and to environmental, agronomic and health related issues.

The Development of Soil Testing

The soil testing laboratories at Johnstown Castle, which were a major part of the research and advisory effort on soil fertility during the 1950s and 1960s, date back to 1948. From around 1943, some limited soil testing was carried out at Ballyhaise agricultural college in Cavan using rudimentary methods. Shortly after his appointment as Minister for Agriculture in February 1948, James Dillon visited Ballyhaise college. He later described the soil testing kit as follows:

"I found an old man and a boy testing soil samples by a remarkable method. They had rigged up a bicycle wheel, with a medicine bottle tied to it, in which the sample was mixed with water. The boy turned the bicycle and thus the soil was tested".

The "old" man was Luke Mannion who, later in 1948, transferred to the new soil testing laboratory in Johnstown Castle, together with the famous bicycle wheel, by then obsolete. The government white paper of 1946 had given a commitment to establish a soil testing and advisory service and old stone farm buildings at Johnstown had been rapidly converted into laboratories. The scene was set for a massive soil testing drive. In 1949, 3,000 samples were tested. This increased to 33,000 in 1950 and reached 56,000 in 1951.

The Minister for Agriculture, Jim Gibbons (centre) opening the new soil testing laboratories (top) at Johnstown Castle in 1972 with, from left: Pat Ryan, assistant director of AFT, Dr Tadhg Ó'Tuama, chairman, Dr Tom Walsh and Frank Cantwell, architect.

Handling such an explosion in demand for testing required a large number of staff. These were mostly young and with no pre-training in handling chemicals or in laboratory work. That soil testing ran so efficiently and without any major mishaps is a tribute to many people but most especially to Tony McDonagh who supervised the day-to-day running of the laboratories.

The methodology adopted at Johnstown was based mainly on procedures developed in New England universities in the 1930s. A 'universal' soil extracting solution, called Morgan's, of ammonium acetate was used to extract the 'available' plant nutrients from the soil samples coming in from agricultural advisers countrywide. The solution was developed for acid soils and so was less suitable for soils high in lime.

The soil test values were divided into three categories, low, medium and high, with most soils falling into the low category. At first, recommendations for addition of lime and fertiliser were, of necessity, based on a limited number of trials relating increases in crop yields to the amounts of lime and fertiliser added. However, a big expansion in research work on the correlation of laboratory tests with field responses enabled more refined recommendations to be issued.

The number of soil samples tested at Johnstown Castle exceeded 100,000 in 1960. It remained at around that level throughout the 1960s as the national focus on lifting soil fertility continued. Charging for soil testing was introduced in the 1980s, leading to a big drop in demand and, by the early-1990s, the number of samples had dropped to just over 30,000. The introduction of the Rural Environment Protection Scheme (REPS) in 1994 and the more recent requirement for nutrient management plans on a growing number of farms have led to an increase in demand for soil analysis. In 2007, the number of samples tested at Johnstown Castle was 70,000, the highest in more than 25 years.

Meeting Environmental Challenges

Johnstown Castle research was re-focused as protection and enhancement of the environment became key components of European and national policies from the late-1980s onwards. The main objective of the centre, which was headed by John Lee from 1988, was to generate factual data that would enable preparation of codes of good practice for farming in order to ensure that agriculture would not cause pollution of soil, water and air.

A key achievement was the development of new protocols for the use of phosphorus in farming. We had now come full circle. From a situation of exceedingly low levels in the late-1950s, many farmers were now using too much phosphorus. The leakage of phosphorus to water bodies was leading to deterioration in water quality. This was not just in Ireland but a worldwide problem. Research led by Hubert Tunney produced new recommendations that led to a 30 per cent reduction in phosphorus usage by farmers, resulting in substantial savings in fertiliser costs and increased protection of the environment. The research programme on animal slurries was intensified with

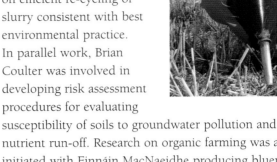

Owen Carton developing new management systems on efficient re-cycling of slurry consistent with best environmental practice. In parallel work, Brian Coulter was involved in developing risk assessment procedures for evaluating susceptibility of soils to groundwater pollution and nutrient run-off. Research on organic farming was also initiated with Finnáin MacNaeidhe producing blueprints for organic beef and pigs, followed by similar blueprints by Noel Culleton on organic milk production.

Confronting New Challenges

Noel Culleton, current head of soils and environmental research at Johnstown Castle, is adamant that research is as crucial now as it was when the early scientists built the foundations for today's modern industry. The environmental pressures, which have dominated the centre's agenda during the past decade, will become an even greater challenge for scientists in developing the technologies for efficient and profitable food production. Culleton sees Johnstown Castle playing a pivotal role in developing the scientific expertise to address the emerging environmental legislation on water quality and to meet the twin challenges of climate change and gaseous emissions.

Research on soils was one of the casualties during the financial cutbacks in the late-1980s and early-1990s. However, the scientific expertise at Johnstown Castle has been strengthened in recent years with the recruitment of experts in pedology, hydrology, soil science and soil chemistry. Research programmes have been established on ecology and biodiversity with the aim of developing production systems that are compatible with efficient farming and protection of water quality. Plans are also underway to complete the national soil survey. Because the environmental agenda dominates all aspects of farming worldwide, collaboration with other research centres in Teagasc and with research institutes in Ireland and internationally is essential in order to develop critical scientific mass. This is set to become an ever-increasing feature.

Statistics a Key Ingredient

The high scientific reputation acquired by AFT scientists was due in no small way to the professional support they received from the statistics department, which was an integral part of the research infrastructure from the very beginning. A group of qualified statisticians played a pivotal role in advising scientists on the design of experiments and surveys - no one would dream of undertaking an experiment or survey without consulting the statisticians on the number of animals or the number of people necessary to ensure an accurate result – and in analysing data.

Frank O'Carroll, the first professional statistician, was recruited in 1960 and has the distinction of installing the first real computer (an Elliott 803) in Ireland for analysis of experiments. Mal O'Keeffe, a technician who acquired professional qualifications through the Institute of Statisticians, joined the team soon afterwards and, in 1962, Dermot Harrington, a graduate in statistics from UCC, was recruited. The group rapidly developed a big national and international reputation.

During that period, AFT was regarded as being far ahead of other Irish institutions, public and private, in data analysis. For instance, Guinness used to rent time and programmes on the Elliott computer as did the Economic and Social Research Institute (ESRI).

Indeed, Roy Geary, the first director of the ESRI and considered Ireland's top statistician, paid public tribute to Frank O'Carroll for setting up a computerised input-output model of the Irish economy for the fledgling ESRI. A huge package of statistical programmes was developed and these were used not just by AFT scientists but also by some of the leading research institutes in the UK. Brian Coulter, a multi-talented soil chemist at Johnstown Castle, played an important role in the development of many of these programmes.

Following O'Carroll's move to the UK in 1963, to a senior position with Shell/BP, mathematician Denis Conniffe joined the team. Conniffe went on to become head of the AFT economics and rural welfare research centre and later became deputy-director of the ESRI. Aidan Moran was also a member of the early team and published many seminal papers during his AFT career. He later went on to become registrar of UCC. John Connolly was another statistician who achieved high scientific achievement. He joined the statistics unit in the late-1960s and, following 20 years with AFT, became a professor of statistics in UCD.

As well as providing professional support to scientists on experimental design and on data analysis, the statisticians did considerable original statistical research on their own and also participated in joint research projects with scientists involved in all areas of the AFT research portfolio.

The statistical strength developed in the early years was a key ingredient in building world-class research expertise. Like Mal O'Keeffe, many of those recruited as technicians obtained professional qualifications up to post-graduate level, enhancing their value to the research programme. Tony Hegarty, the last full-time professional statistician, retired from Teagasc in 2004.

The necessity for a central statistics unit waned over the years as the newly recruited scientists had better training in statistics. However, in recent years, especially with the rapid development of the bio-sciences, the need for a dedicated corps of highly-trained statisticians and bio-informaticians has again become evident.

Mel Deevy and Teresa Healy members of the staff of the statistics unit in 1985.

Farmers visiting Moorepark in 1962

CHAPTER 4
FROM GRASS TO MILK - THE MOOREPARK STORY

Joe Murray

The dairy industry that we know today hardly existed when AFT set about establishing a dairy research centre at Moorepark, outside Fermoy, in 1959. The country's 800,000 creamery cows had an average yield of a miserable 350 gallons. The average size of herd was seven cows. Around Fermoy, the heartland of dairying, 25 cows were regarded as a big herd. Dairy farms in Munster and in other milk producing regions were described as having the grass of 10 cows or 20 cows or 25 cows, hardly ever more because bigger herds could not be milked by hand.

An early analysis by the young Moorepark scientists showed that the farm of 25 cows might have extended to 100 acres. They estimated that the average dairy farmer was using 3.3 acres to maintain each cow. The conclusion was that on a farm with a herd of cows yielding less than 400 gallons the output per acre was little more than 100 gallons.

The quality of the milk was very poor and the market was demanding big improvements. Less than a quarter of farms had an adequate supply of water and fewer still had water on tap. So, most farms lacked the basic ingredient for cooling milk and washing equipment, not to mention a clean water supply for the farm home.

The majority of herds were milked by hand in tie-up byres. Expansion of herds was impossible without efficient machine milking. Most farms lacked electricity so there was no power for standard milking machines. Small, oil-powered machines were almost all unsatisfactory, a fact that became clear to farmers, who gave them up and reverted to hand milking. Winter feed for cows was predominantly hay. A survey by Roger McCarrick, who went on to pioneer research on silage at Grange research centre, showed that in the late 1950s just one farmer in 400 made silage. That was the extremely challenging scenario that faced Michael Walshe, the first scientist to be appointed to Moorepark in March 1959 and the man charged with leading the

establishment of the national centre for dairy research. With the group of young scientists who would join him over the following months and years, his mission was to provide the scientific leadership in establishing a modern dairy industry, offering an attractive way of life to the men and women who owned and milked the cows. He was starting from a green field in every sense. The Moorepark estate comprised 350 acres of totally neglected land and there was little or no research infrastructure in dairying in Ireland.

Urgent Research Challenges

Walshe recalls that before AFT was established there was virtually no animal research in Ireland. *"The amazing thing is that even though nearly all of our exports were agricultural - butter, store cattle and bacon - there was almost no research and no investment in research. So looking at New Zealand and other places later in life, I reckon we lost about 20 years of potential progress."*

Veteran journalist, former editor of the Irish Farmers Journal and later a chairman of AFT, Paddy O'Keeffe, agrees. Like Michael Walshe, he had identified low productivity as the root cause of Ireland's economic troubles, not just in agriculture. Paddy, who later established a large dairy farm of his own a few miles the other side of Fermoy, recalls that even though most Irish cows were calving in spring and producing milk off grass for supply to creameries, the science and economics of spring calving herds had not been researched.

Irish grasslands have a vast potential for increased livestock production

"Before AFT, research was minuscule. There was a small amount being done at the Albert College, which was part of University College Dublin and at Johnstown Castle, which belonged to the Department of Agriculture and was handed over to AFT in 1960. But grass-based dairy farming had never been examined in any state institution. Nearly all of the agricultural colleges were engaged in year-round milk production. The Albert College as the centre of training for agricultural graduates would never dream of having a spring calving herd," said O'Keefe.

Before coming to Moorepark, Michael Walshe was working as a research scientist with the Department of Agriculture at Johnstown Castle where he was investigating methods to prevent grass tetany and before that in the Glenamoy peatland research centre in north-west Mayo. Walshe had established a reputation as a top class scientist and a man who could get things done. His drive, energy and vision and his determination to get results made him an inspired choice as the leader of the Moorepark team. He was soon joined by Dan Browne and the work on laying out the farm, providing housing and establishing a dairy herd got underway. In parallel, Jim O'Grady, who had joined as a pig research specialist, was involved in establishing a pig unit.

From the beginning, Moorepark's mission was to find out how to expand creamery milk output under Irish conditions. Irish milk prices were very low by European standards, so the higher cost methods of production in the United Kingdom, Holland and Denmark had little relevance to Ireland. Irish creamery milk was produced almost exclusively on grass. It had to be.

How Many Cows?

One day in 1959 when the director, Dr Tom Walsh, was visiting Moorepark he asked Michael Walshe how many cows he thought they would need. Michael said he thought they would need at least 1,000. "The 'Doc' was highly amused but didn't dismiss the idea. Every few minutes during the visit he would break out laughing at the idea of a thousand cows." Twelve years later when Michael Walshe left Moorepark to join the World Bank in Washington, there were 1,100 cows on experiments at Moorepark. By then, the research centre had bought a second farm at Ballyderown, a few miles down the river from Fermoy, and Curtin's Farm across the main Fermoy/Mitchelstown road was also purchased. A number of research demonstration farms were also in operation.

The Birth of Moorepark

The Moorepark Estate had been used during the Second World War for military training. By the late-1950s, it was being administered by the Irish Land Commission and there was intense lobbying from local farmers to get a slice of the farm in order to bring their holdings up to an economic size. Fianna Fail was in government at the time and Paddy O'Keeffe remembers that one of the Fianna Fail TDs in the local Cork East constituency, Martin Corry, pushed hard for subdivision of the estate by the Land Commission. But his Fianna Fail colleague, John Moher, favoured the estate going to the new research centre and was supported by the Fine Gael TD, Dick Barry, who lived in Fermoy.

There was also strong support from Jerome Buttimer, a prominent Cork dairy farmer, who had been appointed to the first council of AFT the previous year and later served as President of the Irish Co-operative Organisation Society, the national representative body for the co-operative movement. As Paddy O'Keeffe puts it: "common sense and vision prevailed and Erskine Childers, the Minister for Lands at the time with responsibility for the Land Commission, gave 350 acres of the estate to AFT." The rest of the estate was given to Mitchelstown Co-op.

In an article in the Cork Examiner in 1980, celebrating the 21st anniversary of the establishment of Moorepark research centre in 1959, John Moher said his 'reward' for strongly supporting the handing over of the farm to AFT "was the loss of 800 votes in the 1961 general election".

"Smallholders in the vicinity of Moorepark would not be disabused of the notion that if the dairy research institute had been placed elsewhere the estate would have been parceled out to them by the Land Commission. In truth, the intention in such circumstances was to settle the place with migrant smallholders from Mayo," he wrote. In spite of the loss of 800 votes, John Moher held his Dáil seat in 1961 but lost it in the next general election in 1965.

Back at Moorepark, Michael Walshe had plenty of problems getting started. Sheep had been grazed on the estate on a per head rental basis and stockmanship was clearly not the best. The first task was to clean up about 150 sheep skeletons and carcasses. They also sold over 300 old and neglected trees at auction.

John Walsh discussing the Moorepark research programme with members of the AFT council.

The Minister for Agriculture, Charles Haughey, laying the foundation stone of the new Moorepark laboratories in 1965. Left: a model of the laboratories.

Very soon, Moorepark attained a stocking rate of 1.06 acres per cow. Clover was the main source of nitrogen with fertiliser nitrogen confined to the cutting area. Paddock grazing brought essential control into the management of both the grass and the cows. Work by Dan Browne on the relationship between nitrogen levels, timing of application, stocking rate and yield per cow and per acre was eagerly seized on by a large group of progressive dairy farmers.

Pat Gleeson, who joined in 1962, set about finding out how much meal should be fed to creamery cows in the winter. The simple answer was very little at prevailing milk prices. Irish conditions were different to any others in Europe and the Moorepark scientists realised that Irish answers would have to be provided to Irish problems.

The Basic Questions

The first heifers were bought in the marts and fairs. They were the ordinary heifers that were coming into the dairy herds of the country. In their first lactation in Moorepark, they gave an average of 400 gallons. The challenge was to find out how better management of grass could lift yields and by how much. The first experiments were very basic. Should cows be grazed in fields or in rotation, in paddocks? It was soon established that grazing cows in paddocks lifted output per cow by 10 per cent. More significantly, paddocks allowed stocking rates to increase. A stocking rate of one cow to 1.2 acres was shown to be readily attainable with low fertiliser use, a far cry from a cow to 3.3 acres that was the norm on most farms.

The Moorepark open day in 2006.

Management Blueprints

Led by Dan Browne, a calendar of events was developed at Moorepark: Farmers should turn out cows to grass at a certain time; close for silage at a certain time; close a certain proportion of the farm for first and second cut silage and breed their cows within a certain period. The prescriptions were initially met with cynicism from many farmers but a significant minority followed the Moorepark mantra. The early adopters of the Moorepark blueprints on grassland management and 'calendar' dairy farming saw yields and incomes grow. This boosted the confidence of researchers and advisers who actively promoted the new style of dairy farming, leading to more and more farmers dramatically changing their management practices. Of course, not all soils were equal and the guidelines had to be amended for different areas but the basic principles had been established. As Pat Gleeson pointed out, advisers were skilled at adapting the knowledge to their own areas.

The quality and management of the next generation of dairy cows also got priority from an early stage. Up to the early-1960s, replacement heifers were typically not put in calf until they were 27 months old, leading to the vast majority of heifers producing their first calf and first gallon of milk on around their third birthday. Work by Pat Gleeson showed that, with improved management, a heifer could be fit for breeding at 15 months of age, bringing her into milk production a full year earlier. A precise management and feeding programme was developed with achievable targets for growth rate during each stage of the animal's first two years. Within a short time, calving down heifers at two years of age became standard practice on an increasing number of farms, leading to big increases in productivity.

Ensuring that the animal is born alive and survives the early days and weeks after birth was a constant feature of the work at Moorepark. As herds got bigger, calf losses became a serious issue with deaths of 14 per cent recorded. A major investigation at Moorepark, involving Harry Green of the UCD Veterinary College and Moorepark veterinary expert, John Mee, identified the main causes of deaths. They developed management strategies and procedures that led to a reduction of two-thirds in mortality.

While the vast majority of dairy farmers calved their cows in spring, a significant number were also involved in winter milk production for the consumer markets of Dublin and other cities and towns. Also, as the range of products began to expand, co-ops were looking for manufacturing milk to be produced all year round. Research over many years by Moorepark led to the development of best feeding and management practices for winter milk production and also gave clear guidelines to farmers and industry on the cost differences between summer and winter milk production. In the early-1960s: there was 13 times more milk produced at the summer peak than at the winter trough. This peak/trough ratio was ultimately halved.

Moorepark also played a leading role in the development of recording systems to enable farmers to evaluate the performance of their herds and to compare profitability with that of other farmers. A prime example was the work done by Seamus Crosse and John Walsh on developing the dairy management information system (DAIRYMIS), a computerised system for recording and measuring the performance of dairy farms. It enabled farmers to track costs, output and profit and compare them against key targets set by research and with actual performance of other farmers of similar size and location. It brought a much-needed business approach to dairy farming and was a primer in the development of discussion groups.

Michael Gardiner from the soil survey team at Johnstown Castle addresses visitors at the 1963 Moorepark open day.

Getting The Message Across

From the beginning, Moorepark placed huge emphasis on getting its message out to as many farmers as possible. Michael Walshe had spent a year in the famous Ruakura dairy research centre in New Zealand where thousands of farmers attended open days in search of practical information.

"I copied the open day idea from Ruakura," Michael Walshe remembers. The first major Moorepark open day, in 1963, is legendary and was attended by 10,000 dairy farmers. Pat Gleeson, who was involved in organising many open days over the following 25 years, says: "What that open day showed me was that thousands of farmers were poised, ready to move ahead and were hungry for information. Their urgency was almost frightening, but it convinced me of the importance of Moorepark. The open days led to an incredibly good interaction between Moorepark staff and farmers and that goes on to this day."

Special open days, updating sessions and in-service days were run for advisers employed by county committees of agriculture and later ACOT as well as for dairy co-op advisers and for professionals working in the companies providing inputs to farmers. Emphasis was also put on open days and special visits by groups of farmers to the research demonstration, or 'satellite', farms. Moorepark scientists were also regular participants at farmer meetings run by county advisers and in articles and programmes in the farming media, especially the Farmers Journal and RTE.

Prescriptions for Different Soils

The land at Moorepark had one failing. It was too good to set a headline for farmers working the 50 per cent of Irish land that was classed as marginal. A hill farm owned by Waterford Co-op at Coolnakilla, near Fermoy was developed for dairying. Extensive work by Pat Gleeson and Jim Kiely, who had moved to Moorepark from the national farm survey team at Johnstown Castle, showed that reclaimed hill land could carry up to 80 per cent as many cows as dry mineral lowland.

The problem of dairy farming on difficult, hard to drain, lowland was also the subject of questions by farmers and advisers. Technician, Mick Reidy, remembers the questions: "Farmers visiting Moorepark were asking how many cows they could carry on their heavier, wetter land. We didn't know the answer. So Dan Browne and Gerry Barrett of Mullinahone Co-op decided to set up a dairy unit on a farm owned by the co-op in Tipperary. The farm was typical of 35 per cent of the land that was devoted to dairying in Ireland."

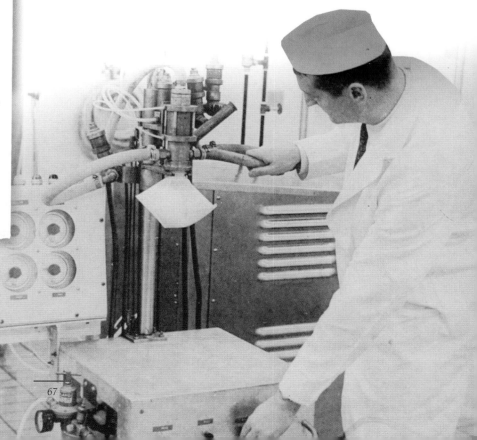

They found that the Mullinahone farm, which was managed by Mick Reidy in the early years, could carry about one-fifth fewer animals than a farm like Moorepark. Later, Moorepark also took over a wetland farm owned by Golden Vale Co-op at Kilmaley in Clare, currently managed by James O'Loughlin. Under the direction of Jim Kiely, this became a vital centre for demonstrating milk production on difficult soils. As well as developing tailor-made management practices, they also worked with Dermot Forristal in the agricultural engineering unit at Oak Park in devising adaptations for machines, which became standard practice and helped to transform farming on wetter soils.

The Satellite Farms

Mullinahone and Kilmaley were just two of a number of research demonstration farms established by Moorepark that played a crucial role in the dissemination of research results to farmers. These 'satellites' enabled the components of research to be applied in a whole farm situation on a scale with which farmers could identify. Other research demonstration farms, which were operated by Moorepark, included a farm at Ballyragget owned by Avonmore Co-op, farms at Kilmeaden and Castlelyons owned by Waterford Co-op, a farm at Solohead owned by Tipperary Co-op and an economic test farm at Herbertstown, Co Limerick.

This method of communicating research was unique to Ireland and gave huge credibility to the research programme. The popularity of these farms among farmers was due in no small way to the stockmanship and down to earth communications skills of the people who managed them. They include people like Mick Reidy and Tom Cullinane in Mullinahone and Kilmaley, Jack O'Mahony in Kilmeaden, Ted Horan and Oliver Carty in Ballyragget, Tim Doody in Herbertstown, Declan O'Grady in Solohead and Sean Hegarty in Curtin's.

In more recent years, Moorepark scientists operate a regional research programme at the Teagasc college at Ballyhaise, Co Cavan where blueprints for dairying on the more difficult soil types are developed and refined.

Better Milk Needed

Milk quality in the early-1960s was appalling. A survey in 1963 showed that only seven per cent of milk passed a three-hour Methylene Blue Test, regarded as the minimum quality standard for manufacturing milk. Milk was delivered daily to over 600 intake points. There was almost no refrigeration at farm level and cooling, if it could be carried out at all, depended on a good supply of clean cold water, a rarity on the farms of the early-1960s. An intensive campaign to set up rural group water schemes was an essential element in improving milk quality.

Demonstrating the use of a new milking machine.

The strategy included research at Moorepark, advice at farm and creamery level, penalties for poor quality and higher prices for quality milk. In 1965, the Department of Agriculture introduced a bonus of a penny a gallon for milk passing the three-hour methylene blue test. Kerryman, Michael Fleming, a young dairy scientist who started his career at the AFT laboratory at Ballinamore, Co. Leitrim, was one of those centrally involved in finding solutions and disseminating them through advisers and co-ops to farmers.

An important milestone on the road to quality was the introduction by Waterford Co-op in 1964 of refrigerated bulk tanks. Lough Egish Co-op in Co. Monaghan introduced a system in which their tanker lorries sucked milk by vacuum from farmers' tanks and cans. Following the first refrigerated tanks, Michael Fleming saw the pace of progress quicken. *"Refrigeration of either plastic or a single-skin steel tank came along. But refrigeration was limited by the amount of electrical power available on the farm. We set up a workshop in Moorepark for testing coolers. We introduced specifications. Any tank or cooler that came on the market had to meet Moorepark standards."*

Fleming has fond memories of the great bond of trust between the people in Moorepark, advisers, farmers and the staff in the co-ops. *"Together we got the job done. On a lot of farms, milk output increased tenfold over the next 20 years with a tenfold decrease of bacteria in the milk."*

Milkers and Milking Machines

In the early-1960s, most cows were still milked by hand. About half of the farmers who had installed milking machines had stopped using them. The most common reasons were that mastitis spread in the herd and milk quality deteriorated. With hand milking, the average rate per milker was only twelve cows per hour. So unless milking could be speeded up and streamlined, the Irish dairy industry was going nowhere. A small number of milking parlours were installed and bulk tanks were rare. The bulk tank in Moorepark attracted a constant stream of visitors on Sundays.

A team of researchers, assembled at Moorepark in the early 1960s, made an enormous contribution to milking technology in Ireland and internationally and this high level of expertise was maintained during the following decades, with huge benefits to the dairy industry. Led by Michael Cowhig, an agricultural scientist, it included veterinarian John Nyhan and Tow Dwane, an agricultural engineer. They conducted a survey that showed major problems with milking machines. The capacity of pumps was very low, vacuums were very poor and there was a lot of mastitis. Big strides were made in improving the technology and reducing mastitis levels over the first few years. But, in 1968, the three scientists were tragically killed when, on a flight to London, an Aer Lingus plane, the St. Phelim, crashed near the Tuskar Rock off the south east coast of Ireland.

Offices at Moorepark Dairy Production Research Centre.

Following the tragedy, John Walsh, who was a central player at Moorepark over many decades, took over responsibility for research on milking technology. The pioneering work continued and, in the early-1970s, Jerry O'Shea took over as head of the team. While farmer confidence in milking machines had increased, most machines still had faults. According to O'Shea, because the technology was only developing, many of the machines were hybrids and contained components from different manufacturers. So, rather than look at complete machines, the scientists examined the components. *"That made our testing a lot less complicated and less expensive. It also gave manufacturers the opportunity to replace poor components with parts from other manufacturers. Even some of the big companies did that on a temporary basis, until they improved their own components."*

O'Shea recalled that the Moorepark test results were not welcomed by all manufacturers and many battles were fought. But good science and technology prevailed and Moorepark standards became the norm for all components of milking machines. The scientists also played a key role in the design of milking parlours so that cows could be milked more quickly and they contributed to new technological innovations such as automatic cluster removal. Jerry O'Shea had a formidable team, with Eddie O'Callaghan as an agricultural engineer, Billy Meaney as a microbiologist, John Palmer who specialised in the cleaning of equipment and with constant animal health support from veterinarian Kevin O'Farrell.

Michael Cowhig   *Tom Dwane*   *John Nyhan*

The Tuskar Air Tragedy

Sunday March 24th 1968 is a date that will never be forgotten in the history of Moorepark. On that day, Aer Lingus Flight 712 crashed near the Tuskar Rock, off the south east coast of Ireland with the loss of 61 lives. Among the casualties were three young Moorepark scientists, Michael Cowhig, Tom Dwane and John Nyhan. They had been on their way to a machine milking conference in Reading and were flying to London.

News of the tragedy was delivered in a phone call from Aer Lingus to Moorepark that afternoon and Michael Walshe and Pat Gleeson, with the local priest, Fr Michael Cogan, had the awful task of breaking the news to Kathleen Cowhig and Mary Nyhan, wives of two of the victims. Both were living in Fermoy and had very young children. Tom Dwane was living in Limerick and Pat Gleeson asked a local priest, Fr David Rea from St Patrick's parish, to convey the tragic news to his family. Pat visited the family himself the following morning. Only 14 of the 61 victims were recovered. Michael Cowhig was one of them. Tom Dwane's and John Nyhan's bodies were never found.

The tragedy rocked Moorepark to the core. The centre was not yet 10 years old and was imbued with infectious enthusiasm, energy and comradeship. The three young scientists had already built national and international reputations in research on milking machines, mastitis and milk quality. Forty years later, Michael Walshe still regards them "as the most effective milking group in the world." He feels they would be comforted to know that the group that followed them was equally talented and continued to blaze a trail in research and leadership on this vital aspect of dairy farming.

Conor McGann discussing milk testing with industry representatives from left: Peadar O'Callaghan, Waterford Co-op.; Tom Whelton, Mitchelstown Creameries; John O'Connor, Department of Agriculture; Brendan Chambers, An Bord Bainne; Dr Tom O'Dwyer, AFT; Dave O'Connor, Fry-Cadbury, and Brian Daly, Lough Eglish Co-Op.

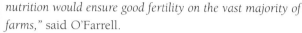

nutrition would ensure good fertility on the vast majority of farms," said O'Farrell.

The next priority was to improve heat detection. They discovered that the short duration of heat required farmers to observe cows five times a day if they expected to be 90 per cent successful in detecting cows that were ready for breeding. One New Zealand idea that was used in Moorepark was tail painting. It was a cheap and reliable way of detecting cows that were ready to be inseminated. It was promoted and fairly widely used but, according to O'Farrell, not widely enough. The difficulty in getting high genetic merit cows to go back in calf became a big issue in the 1990s. This is now being tackled through a change of focus in the new Economic Breeding Index (EBI), which includes fertility as a key component. Moorepark scientists have made a big contribution to this development.

Banishing Bugs

Hygiene, an essential on dairy farms, was an almost impossible goal at a time when piped water was a rarity on farms and when the available water supply was of such poor quality. John Palmer developed an innovative system of cleaning bucket-type machines, using a small quantity of boiling water and citric acid. He later developed a detergent that would clean pipeline machines using cold rather than hot water. It was enough to use a hot wash once a week or even once in two weeks. That cold cleaning system is still being used today. He also made an important contribution to the development of international standards for cleaning pipeline plants and he developed standards for dairy detergents that are still applied today.

Focus on Healthy Stock

The animal fertility, health and welfare programme at Moorepark was headed for many years by veterinary surgeon, Kevin O'Farrell. A calf per cow per year was the target set by the early scientists but performance at farm level fell well below that. *"There were a lot of people out there selling trace elements and minerals of all descriptions, which were supposed to be the elixir for all problems. But our research had shown that simple management and*

The Pioneer Farmers

*The remarkable success of the scientists during the early years after the
establishment of Moorepark was no greater than that of the farmers who
adopted the new technologies and expanded their dairy enterprises
throughout the early-1960s. The bravery of those farmers was spectacular.
They were breaking with a centuries-old tradition. They were borrowing
money to produce milk without any promise of better prices. They were
taking real and personal risks in search of a future that they decided had
to be better than the past.*

*Perhaps, like the scientists, they could have avoided the very real dangers
of change. If they failed they would pay dearly. They could have been
cautious. But conservatism and caution had held generations of farmers
in unacceptable poverty. Moorepark was offering a new deal. Compared
to the past the future might just be better. It was unlikely to be worse.*

*One of the early movers, Cork dairy farmer and former IFA and ICOS
president, Donal Cashman says: "The whole idea of tight grazing and
tight stocking was formulated in Moorepark. As farmers, we adopted
better ways of managing grass that were directly influenced by those bright
young researchers, all of them at the beginning of their careers and
brimming with enthusiasm." Cashman, whose first introduction to
Moorepark was when the Cork Chief Agricultural Officer, Tom Wall
brought Michael Walshe into his field in the early-1960s, singled out the
early work on machine milking technology by Michael Cowhig and his
team. "It was ahead of even New Zealand."*

*"As well as being a world leader in grassland research, Moorepark has in
more recent times led the way in investigating cow fertility, which has
emerged as a serious problem internationally," said Cashman.*

Kevin O'Farrell also remembers the huge impact the
state programmes to eradicate TB and brucellosis had on
the developing dairy industry, particularly in the 1970s.
He cites one particular piece of research carried out at
Moorepark by Brendan Cunningham and Leonard Dolan
of the UCD veterinary college, in collaboration with John
Walsh at Moorepark, that had a major impact on brucellosis
at farm level. They established how to break the cycle of
infection and minimise the spread of the disease. This led
to the development of a scheme called the Pre-Intensive
Brucellosis Eradication Scheme, which was adopted by the
Department of Agriculture. It involved the vet identifying
animals that were positive and isolating them, rather than
eliminating the whole herd which was the norm until then.
The scheme was a success and the disease in now down to
very low levels.

Another example of pioneering work in the animal
health area was work by Nola Leonard on the impact of
leptospirosis on dairy herds. In a major project with UCD
and Stormont, she found that the highly infectious disease
was widespread, resulting in abortions, the birth of weak
calves and sudden drops in milk yield. More than 95 per
cent of dairy farmers now vaccinate against the disease.

Research by Sean Arkins made a big contribution to
identifying and controlling lameness problems, which
became serious as the size of dairy herds grew. He found
that up to 30 per cent of cows were going lame, leading to
severe reductions in milk yield and fertility, not to mention
the animal welfare problems resulting from extreme pain.
Prevention strategies, including routine chiropody, foot
bathing, improving farm roadways and removing sources
of infection, were introduced and have succeeded in
dramatically reducing losses and associated welfare issues.

John O'Keeffe testing a bulk milk tank at Moorepark.

Excitement of Joining the EEC

It is hard to convey the sense of excitement among dairy farmers in anticipation of EEC membership, says Pat McFeely, who joined the team at Moorepark in 1970, from the University of Reading. Membership delivered everything that it promised, particularly to milk producers. There was a severe blip in cattle prices in 1974, which also affected confidence among dairy farmers. Recovery was quick and Pat McFeely described the period between 1975 and 1978 as the 'golden age of Irish dairying'.

He recalled that at the start of the 1970s, average yields were still only around 500 gallons. But, fuelled by Moorepark technology and with advisers spreading the gospel, huge leaps forward were made following EEC entry. The difference between the first and second half of the 1970s was quite amazing. Farmers had gone to a cow to the acre and some had pushed on to 0.7 acres a cow. By the late-1970s, cows were yielding between 800 and 1000 gallons, a very good performance for Irish cows at that time. *"For those of us working in Moorepark, it was a period of phenomenal job satisfaction,"* said Mc Feely.

Moorepark had a completely open door policy and McFeely remembers busloads of farmers visiting every week, usually with their advisers. Scientists talked and debated for hours with farmers and advisers about stocking rates, numbers of paddocks, intervals between grazings and nitrogen levels. But they never lost sight of the necessity to keep costs low. *"It was easy to boost yields with meals. All you needed to do was keep signing the cheques. There were farmers in the UK in the mid-70s producing 2,000 gallons but they were making less money than our good grassland farmers with 700 gallon cows."*

The Quota Shock

National milk output trebled between the early 1960s and 1984, when the imposition of the EU milk quota brought expansion to a shuddering stop. Before examining the impact of the quota shock it is worth recalling a milk production target set by Michael Walshe in 1973, months after Ireland joined the EEC. Walshe, who was then working with the World Bank in Washington, addressed the Irish Grassland Association. Based on the technology that was then available, he postulated that it was possible to have a dairy herd of five million cows in Ireland, almost five times the number we now have in 2008. This would have resulted in a trebling of agricultural output and, at a projected yield of even 700 gallons, would have given annual production of 3.5 billion gallons, more than three times what we had when quotas were introduced in 1984.

The imposition of quota had a particularly serious effect on farmers who were expanding actively, rearing heifers, and repaying development loans. It required a fundamental and immediate refocus of the dairy research programme on key technologies such as extended grazing, grass budgeting and

calving date that could cut costs and maximise profit from a given quota. As Pat Dillon, current head of Moorepark puts it; *"In times of expansion a lot of costs could be diluted by the increased output. But the industry was now in a new and harder environment."*

Pat Dillon cites the increase of North American Holstein genetics as an important new factor. It had really big implications for seasonal calving. The establishment of the Irish Cattle Breeding Federation in 2000 and the new Economic Breeding Index (EBI) in 2001 were stepping stones in addressing that issue. *"We are on the road now with our own Irish breeding programme. We know the kind of genetics we want and our decisions will be guided by our index,"* said Dillon.

Moorepark is now looking towards a quota-free situation where farmers can expand output but it must be done at low cost. Development of blueprints for a new type of dairy farming is dominating the energies of the current crop of Moorepark scientists. Aspects such as new technology to speed up genetic selection for improved grass strains are receiving priority. Dillon reckons the cow of the future will be a combination New Zealand Black and White with New Zealand Jerseys and Scandinavian genes in the mix. But at the base of it all will be a Holstein-Friesian, selected for fertility, milk production and calf survival.

Also, instead of traditional methods like progeny testing, new technologies will enable genes to be identified when the calf is born enabling scientists to speed up improvements using genetic markers.

Harnessing New Opportunities

Pat Dillon is very confident about the future for Irish dairy farming. While there are 40,000 fewer dairy farmers in Ireland now than there were in 1984 when quotas were introduced, our base of over 20,000 active dairy farmers in 2008 is much higher than in countries such as Holland and Denmark. This is due largely to our low cost structure, which enabled many farmers to survive on a relatively small quota.

Dillon believes a big number of dairy farmers are just waiting to be allowed to expand. The Moorepark emphasis on managing the grass and the animal together has placed Irish farmers in a strong position. *"It is to the credit of the dairy industry that they supported Moorepark through the dairy levy and it is vital that we continue to work together for the future."* As one of the new generation of scientists in Moorepark, Padraig French believes it is a great time to be a young scientist in dairy research. In contrast with a few years ago, farmers are looking forward. The lift in milk prices since 2007 and the likely abolition of quotas have dramatically changed attitudes. The challenge facing the Moorepark scientists and their advisory colleagues is to develop and disseminate innovative technologies in grass production and utilisation, nutrition, breeding, animal health, labour use and environmental protection that will underpin a new era in milk production and will enable Ireland to exploit opportunities for expansion.

Milk output trebled between the early 1960s and 1984.

CHAPTER 5

LEADING PROGRESS IN BEEF PRODUCTION

Paddy Smith

When AFT began its work at Grange, Irish cattle production was in a sorry state. A Department of Agriculture survey in the 1950s had revealed that stocking rates on Irish farms varied from a pitiful livestock unit to eight acres to a very exceptional livestock unit to an acre and a half. In today's metric measurements, that equates to a range of 0.3-1.8 Lu/ha, with the majority of farms tending towards the lower end of the scale. Winter feed consisted of poor quality hay and there was never enough of it. Soil fertility was very low and practically no silage was made.

Leabharlanna Poiblí Chathair Bhaile Átha Cliath
Dublin City Public Libraries

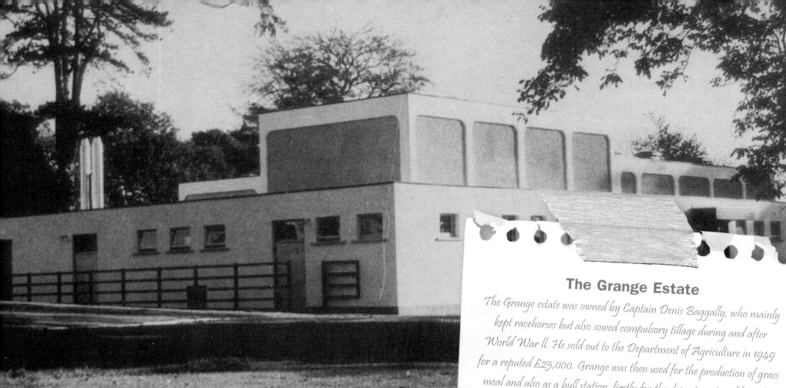

The main exports were live bullocks weighing around 8 cwt (400 kgs) at two years of age, with up to 800,000 head going to England annually for further fattening. There was a steady trade of blue-grey heifers from the West of Ireland to Scotland. The only meat factories in the country were pig factories and they were killing some cows to service the hamburger trade in the United States. The only other cattle being slaughtered by local butchers were heifers for the home trade.

The new research centre was faced with a mountain to climb if it was to be of any real benefit to Irish agriculture. Until then, most studies throughout the world on grazing management had been carried out with dairy cows, some with sheep but very few with cattle. So, the first task the Grange researchers set themselves was to develop firm recommendations for farmers that would enable them to lift production of beef from grass.

The first research scientist to start in Grange was Aidan Conway, a Wexford man who had been engaged in research work on grass tetany for the Department of Agriculture in Johnstown Castle. He arrived on January 16th 1959 and, with the staff already transferred from the Department, he set up grazing trials of two-year-old bullocks that would normally be exported, just to show how much could actually be produced from Irish farms. Even on the good land of Meath, the best-known cattle producing area of the country, an 80-acre farm carried a maximum of 50 bullocks.

An aerial view of the research facilities at Grange.

The meat research laboratory at Dunsinea, an integral part of research on meat yield and quality.

Developing Grazing Blueprints

Results from work on grazing management of dairy cows by the renowned New Zealand research scientist, Dr McMeekan, had shown that controlled methods of grazing substantially increased output. McMeekan had developed the 'paddock' grazing system and Conway set out to establish its potential benefits for beef production. He compared the effect of a ten-paddock rotational system against the conventional set stocking system, using low, medium and high stocking rates. He found that the rotational system gave slightly lower animal performance than set stocking on the low stocking rate, slightly higher on the medium stocking but performance from rotational grazing on the high stocking rate was a massive 50 per cent higher.

He also conducted a major trial over three years on the effect of stocking rate on animal performance and carcass weight. He compared three different stocking rates – 1.0, 1.75 and 2.5 animals to the acre. He recalls *a number of head-shakers in the Department who predicted that even the cattle stocked at one to the acre would die from starvation.* The results set the framework for more profitable production over the following decades. One of the key findings was that the performance of cattle on all three stocking rates was the same in the early weeks of the grazing season but the performance of the highest stocked group dropped significantly as the season progressed.

That led to another major study on the impact of manipulating stocking during the grazing season. This study, which ran over four years, showed that grazing two animals per acre until late-July followed by

one animal per acre for the rest of the season gave an additional 55 per cent live weight gain per acre than from running one animal per acre for the entire grazing season. This also had significant practical farm management implications. Part of the farm could be highly stocked for about two-thirds of the grazing season and the remainder could be cut twice for silage. Alternatively, all of the farm could be grazed intensively early in the season and, as cattle reached slaughter weight and were sold, the pastures could then be closed for silage.

Aidan Conway and Dermot Collins, who also joined Grange in the early years, continued to work on developing beef grazing blueprints. Later work included the issue of meal feeding on grass, with precise research-based recommendations on the economics of meal at different stocking rates. Dermot Collins produced vital information on responses to fertiliser nitrogen for both silage and grazing. He also showed that on the previously well-fertilised Grange soil, phosphorus could be omitted for a number of years on grazed pastures without affecting animal performance. This was to become a major issue more than 20 years later.

Animal health was an important research issue from the very beginning. Research work on the effects of internal parasites was carried out by Nigel Downey together with Alberta Kearney and Mike Hope Cawdery, who examined the efficacy of various anthelmintics, oral and injectible products and vaccines as well as contributing to an understanding of the life cycles of parasites, including liver fluke. Grange was also the centre for research on trace elements and, over many years, veterinary practitioners, Phil Rogers and David Poole, produced independent and practical information on the prevention and control of trace element deficiencies in all bovine animals.

Converting Farmers to Silage

Research into the conservation of grass meant, in the early days, searching for ways to make better hay. The first trial conducted by Roger McCarrick, who had been working on grassland conservation research in Johnstown Castle, was to compare three methods of hay conservation: tripod hay, cocked hay and dried grass. However, none could be relied upon to provide high quality winter feed at an economic cost. This led to the first of the silage experiments at Grange, which were conducted by McCarrick in 1959.

A 1957 survey indicated that hay made up 99.75 per cent of winter fodder in Ireland. Hay was the winter feed of choice and there was a very strong current of opinion among farmers that it was a better feed than silage. McCarrick set about changing attitudes. He received valuable backing from AFT director, Dr Tom Walsh and from Paddy O'Keeffe in the Farmers Journal, who was a member of the Royal Dublin Society and succeeded in getting financial support for an information campaign aimed at Macra na Feirme and the recently formed National Farmers Association (later the IFA). McCarrick had been to Finland, Denmark, England and Scotland to assess silage-making systems and he brought this thinking back to Ireland.

What followed was a huge body of research on the basics of silage making, on perfecting the formula for top quality and on ensuring that farmers could successfully avail of new developments in mechanisation and new methods such as the round bale. The first purpose-built shed, with housing for 120 cattle, was built at Grange in 1959. There were three silage pits with cattle accommodation each side of them, allowing nine comparisons of silage. The first single-chop forage harvester came to Ireland in 1958 and by the following year Grange had two: a Taarup and a JF, which could each handle one acre an hour.

The emphasis was on the practical application of research. During a particularly bad summer in the early-1960s when farmers could not make hay, Grange was asked to come up with ideas to resolve the crisis and Roger McCarrick made what became known as 'bun' silage. There were no concrete bases on farms so a gravel base was provided and grass was built with gently sloping sides to allow tractors to travel and compact all surfaces. An open day at Grange was built around this concept.

One of the two single-chop forage harvesters in Grange in 1959.

Measuring the Impact

By 1969, when McCarrick was leaving AFT for a new career in the beef processing industry and the number of silage-making farmers in the country was counted again, the figure had risen from that lowly 0.25 per cent to 13 per cent. Tillage farmers, who already had machinery, were the first to opt for silage, followed by dairy farmers, then drystock producers.

In 1983, the first big round bales of silage appeared on the scene, and Pádraig O'Kiely, who had now joined the team, recalled that these first bales were put into bags, which were then tied at the neck. Various forms of polythene wrapping followed, with a substantial amount of trial work at Grange, in co-operation with Dermot Forristal in Oak Park, going into the best methods of wrapping and how to prevent mould in the bales. In fact, the very last trial on mould in bales was completed by O'Kiely in 2008 as this book was going to press.

The strongest of views were always generated by the additives issue. Major trials were carried out involving AIVs (sulphuric and hydrochloric acids mixed), molasses, formic acid and bactericides. Roger McCarrick's early results found that additives were not necessary unless silage was made in adverse weather conditions. These were confirmed by extensive research carried out by Vincent Flynn in the 1970s and 1980s. The best way to make silage was to wilt the grass first and, if additives did become necessary, the best ones were molasses and formic acid. Sulphuric acid eventually became the additive of choice as it was much cheaper than formic acid.

Communicating Results

The New Zealand open day model, first used in Moorepark, was rapidly adopted by Grange to disseminate the results of research. The open days were run over four days – from Tuesday to Friday – with one day designated for farmers and the others for different target groups. From the beginning, AFT director, Dr Tom Walsh, insisted that research results be channelled to farmers through advisers. Field days and seminars were held for advisers and the results of every research project were disseminated through technical bulletins. The Irish Grassland Association, membership of which included scientists and leading farmers, was used extensively as was the Farmers Journal and other media outlets.

An Innocent Abroad

Cattle were bought-in for the feeding trials in Grange and the requirement for weanling bullocks meant that Roger McCarrick had to travel to fairs in Tipperary and Limerick (this was before the proliferation of livestock marts). It was here he came up against the tanglers – buyers who did not take kindly to an outsider coming to their fairs and driving up prices. The tanglers and their men would engage in conversation with the farmers who had stock to sell, thus keeping out anyone else who wished to buy. The farmers selling stock did not wish to upset the tanglers, who were there every week buying cattle, albeit in a buyer's market. To make a long story short, McCarrick returned to Co Meath emptyhanded. Grange resolved this situation by coming to an arrangement with a local tangler who bought on their behalf.

The big house at Grange, converted into offices for research staff.

Building Reputations

By 1963/64, Grange scientists had begun to make a real difference to the way cattle were being produced in Ireland and they were being invited abroad to present the results of their work. In Britain, in particular, researchers and farmers were interested in the Irish results of feeding and carcass composition work because there was very little of that type of research going on there. Groups of English farmers were also coming to Grange and other AFT research centres. Aidan Conway read a plenary paper at an International Grassland Conference in Brazil in 1965 on utilisation of grassland by beef cattle. "Ireland was coming to be known as a place where good research work was going on," said Conway.

Another man who began to receive international attention in the 1960s was Paddy Cunningham, who had joined AFT's animal breeding and genetics department in 1962 after completing his PhD on cattle breeding and genetics at Cornell University, New York State. In addition to his work in AFT, he taught animal genetics in Trinity College Dublin and was later appointed to a personal chair as Professor of Animal Genetics. He is currently chief scientific adviser to the Irish government.

Farm buildings expert Andy Kavanagh, demonstrating sloped-floor cattle housing.

Trends in Housing

From about 1964, an important part of Grange research involved devising cheap winter housing for cattle in a situation where farmers could not get bank finance for expensive sheds. The New Zealand idea of outwintering on pads was adapted by Roger McCarrick for Irish conditions. Then outdoor roofless cubicles were developed, with solid sides so that the cattle could not turn around. The concept never caught on generally due to the excess slurry/dirty water that had to be dealt with.

In recent years, the focus has switched back to outwintering pads and Grange research has shown significant gains in performance from wintering animals on pads constructed from a bed of woodchips as compared to animals fed in conventional slatted houses. The research has also shown earth bank tanks or reed beds/constructed wetlands to be effective methods of storing or treating the slurry generated by animals fed on the outwintering pads.

Specialist winter fatteners began to proliferate around the mid-1960s, housing cattle in straw sheds and feeding them silage, as a result of Grange research. Slatted housing was a major development through the 1970s. The first slats in Grange were in a 60-70 ft long shed designed and built by buildings engineer, Vincent Dodd. Slatted housing changed the face of overwintering, doing away with the intensity of the labour needed in spreading straw, collecting dung and scraping yards.

Changing Attitudes to Breeding

When Grange was established, beef breeding was tightly controlled by the Department of Agriculture. All bulls were licensed but the inspection process was based on visual characteristics only. According to Paddy Cunningham, the inspections were geared very much to the interests of live cattle exports to Britain and were at odds with any hope of real progress in genetics. Cunningham began to look at ways of improving recorded information and its proper analysis. In those early years it was frustrating for him because he was running against the tide of official policy and challenging the monopoly of wisdom held by the department. A nice irony in this context lies in the fact that when he left AFT in 1988, Cunningham was hired by a consultancy company appointed by the Department of Agriculture to advise it on how to divest itself of all responsibilities in animal breeding.

Beef breeding was based on visual characteristics only.

He wrote the report that the department used to eventually set up the Irish Cattle Breeding Federation (ICBF), which began to implement much of the technical solutions that he had been working on in the early part of his career.

Around 1970, the development of beef breeding shifted to the continental breeds and a large series of systematic trials were carried out at Grange by Gerry Keane, Michael Drennan, Richie Fallon and Gerry More O'Ferrall, evaluating continentals for cross-breeding in the dairy herd and as part of the suckler cow herd. This became a rich source of information for farmers and helped to guide the evolution in beef production from the dairy and suckler herds. Hereford and Angus were largely displaced by Charolais, Limousin, Simmental and Belgian Blue as production shifted away from live exports to beef exports.

Leading Production Trends

Through the decades, research at Grange has been to the forefront in leading production trends and in developing new systems in response to policy changes. For example, bull beef production was investigated by Joe Harte more than 30 years ago and showed the whole males grew faster, were more efficient at turning feed into liveweight gain and had significantly more lean meat and less fat. In the mid-1970s, a major research initiative was undertaken by a team led by Jim Roche on the effective use of growth promoters in boosting animal performance and meat quality. When growth promoters were banned by the EU in 1988, bull beef attracted a good deal of interest. It was possible to counteract the loss of performance from the banning of growth promoters by leaving the animals as bulls and, by the early-2000s, bull beef production had reached 12 per cent of total male beef production.

In the 1980s, Grange research had made it possible for beef farmers to achieve a carcass output of over 700 kg/ha, equivalent to the 1,000 gallons cow or the 10 tonnes/ha winter wheat crop. In the early-1990s, Gerry Keane was developing a more intensive system with a carcass output of 1,000 kg/ha. But the first major reform of the Common Agricultural Policy (CAP), implemented in 1992, led to a de-intensification of beef production in order for farmers to maximise their EU premium payments and the intensive production blueprints had little relevance.

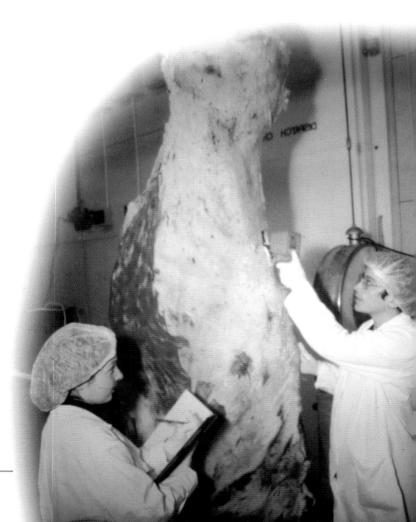

Suckler cow numbers more than doubled between 1984 and 2003.

Growth in the Suckler Herd

The development of the national suckler herd can be directly linked to the pioneering work carried out at Grange. In the early-1980s, Michael Drennan began assembling results from the vast amount of data that had been kept about animal performance and reproductive performance in the cattle at Grange. He showed that high levels of production could be achieved from a relatively low-cost extensive system of farming. The direct result of this research, coupled with EU subsidies, was a massive growth in the suckler herd. In 1968, the number of suckler cows was a mere 0.23 million, compared to 1.38 million dairy cows. Suckler cow numbers only reached 0.44 million by 1984, but following the introduction of the milk quota numbers began to expand rapidly. The size of the suckler herd had jumped to 1.17 million in 2003, equal to the number of dairy cows. Some 85 per cent of suckler cows are now bred to continental bulls and, between 1992 and 2005, the number of continental cross suckler cows doubled, from 36 per cent to 70 per cent of the herd.

Research on New Feeds

New types of feeds and feeding systems have been a constant feature of the Grange research programme. In the early-1970s, Vincent Flynn carried out some experiments with growing maize in the Dungarvan area and, 10 years later, Pádraig O'Kiely set about another attempt at this new feed crop, but it was not until the late-1980s that it became a serious option with the availability of better varieties. O'Kiely showed that maize could be a cheaper source of winter feed compared to grass silage if the yield was high enough. The new varieties and the use of plastic mulches in growing the crop, which was developed by researchers at Oak Park, have now made maize an important feed on a growing number of livestock farms.

Considerable research was also carried out on feeding fodder beet and on wholecrop cereals, which are a component of winter feeding on a significant number of farms today. An example of more recent work is the role of red clover as a source of silage where research by Pádraig O'Kiely has shown a yield potential of 16 tonnes of dry matter per hectare.

Despite the gradual change from hay to silage and the improvement in the feeding quality of the roughage, farmers learned from Grange research that energy and protein supplements were also required. The main concentrate supplement in the 1970s was barley and the importance of crushing the seed coat of grain to maximise its feeding value was promoted, as was the fact that good performance could be achieved from a simple concentrate feeding programme. Numerous studies over many years led to clear recommendations on the most cost-effective rations and feeding levels for all types of animals.

The impact of the feeding regime on carcass quality was central to these studies and, in more recent years, research has been carried out on producing beef to meet the needs of specific consumer markets. One of the aspects examined was the role of nutrition and diet on fat colour in beef, an important factor in some European consumer markets. Work by Aidan Moloney has shown that the timing of concentrate feeding can be used to manipulate fat deposition and colour. Moloney is also part of a team of scientists from Grange, Moorepark and Ashtown food research centre involved in a major project on the production of beef and milk with health-enhancing fatty acids. Grange research has shown that beef produced from grass has higher levels of conjugated linoleic acids (CLAs), which the medical profession accepts can protect against cancer, obesity and heart disease. Scientists have investigated methods to further increase these beneficial fatty acids. They have found that one way of increasing the level of CLAs is through the inclusion of plant oil in the diet of beef cattle prior to slaughter.

Leading-edge Reproduction Research

Scientists have been involved in leading-edge research in reproduction in dairy and beef cows, with a number of significant international breakthroughs during the past three decades. The research was initiated at Belclare in 1973 and continued at Athenry in more recent years. Under the direction of Joe Sreenan, the first programme focused on developing oestrous cycle control and the induction of twinning to increase the calf crop. Sreenan's work led to the development of protocols for oestrous cycle control that are now widely used. He also developed many of the embryo procedures, both *in vivo* and *in vitro,* that are in current practice. For example, the first description of successful non-surgical embryo transfer in cows emanated from this programme with subsequent studies demonstrating that it was possible to get twinning rates of 50 per cent following embryo transfer.

Sreenan was later joined by Michael Diskin and Dermot Morris and, towards the end of the 1970s, the research team were involved in ground breaking discoveries on the causes of reproductive failure in cows. They produced the first evidence that early embryo death was the main cause of reproductive problems and not fertilisation failure as was commonly believed. They found that 80 per cent of embryos were lost within the first two weeks after fertilisation.

This information on the pattern of cattle embryo growth, development and viability is internationally accepted as the definitive piece of research in this area.

The international standing of the research resulted in the scientists being awarded a number of EU-funded contracts, involving teams of multidisciplinary scientists from the UK, France, Germany and Italy. These initiatives led to the development of a number of key feeding and management procedures that are capable of increasing cow conception rate by up to 30 per cent. As a consequence of the sequencing of the human and bovine genomes, the programme is, in more recent times, using the latest gene chip and proteomic technologies to characterise the molecular mechanisms involved in embryo loss, with the aim of developing diagnostic tests to identify animals at greatest risk.

Since its inception, the programme has involved close linkages with universities in Ireland and the UK and with research centres right across Europe as well as AI stations and commercial companies at home and abroad. A measure of the scientific standing of the work is that the programme has received back-to-back EU grants over the past 25 years. Joe Sreenan and Michael Diskin have co-authored two books on bovine reproduction and have hosted a number of major international scientific seminars.

Rearing Better Calves

Research into calves was undertaken from the very start at Grange, first by Joe Harte and then later by Richie Fallon, with veterinary research being carried out by Nigel Downey. Grange protocols on feeding milk replacers became standard practice at farm level and, combined with research on concentrate feeding, disease prevention and grazing management, helped to underpin a dramatic improvement in the standard of calf rearing. Work was also carried out on preserving whole milk and on whole milk additives and this became very valuable especially for dairy farmers who found themselves with surplus whole milk in years when milk quota levels were exceeded.

The calf research programme also included a big focus on housing, a crucial factor in health and performance. Elaborate experiments were conducted over many years on ventilation, air movement, stocking capacity and many other factors affecting the welfare of calves during their vulnerable period indoors. These experiments led to the development of protocols that are now standard practice at farm level and have dramatically improved health, welfare and mortality levels.

Looking to the Future

The beef sector is facing very challenging times as a result of changes to EU policy on support payments and a possible World Trade Organisation (WTO) agreement. The expected dismantling of the EU milk quota after 2013 is likely to lead to an increase in milk production in Ireland and this in turn will lead to a greater proportion of national beef output coming from the dairy herd. For specialist suckler beef producers, increased emphasis will have to be placed on producing a premium product for high value consumer markets in order to deliver acceptable incomes.

Under the leadership of Edward O'Riordan, the Grange research centre will have a pivotal role in developing production systems that are grounded in efficient utilisation of grass and are fine-tuned to the different types of beef farming, including those practiced by the growing number of part-time farmers. The excellent research carried out at Grange during the past decades on the individual components of production provides the crucial ingredients for improved methods of production.

One of the most exciting developments at Grange is the imminent establishment there of a world-class animal bioscience centre that will take advantage of the far-reaching potential of genome sequencing. Using the most advanced molecular tools, this will enable the fast-tracking of genetic improvement in the Irish cattle herd that will lead to improvements in performance, efficiency and meat quality.

"Once we identify the genes controlling particular traits such as growth rate, milking ability, health or fertility, we can screen all animals for variations in these genes," said Sinéad Waters of Grange's bioscience department, pointing out that this latest science would allow them to vastly speed up genetic improvements by being able to accelerate, if not by-pass, the time-consuming and costly routines of traditional breeding programmes.

Grass as a Power Source

Grange is now involved in investigating the potential of grass for a range of non-agricultural uses. Pádraig O'Kiely is currently working with scientists in Belfast and Cork on a project that is examining grasses as a possible source of methane gas for power generation. O'Kiely is also looking at the potential of a range of grasses for other uses such as fibre for insulation or for reinforcing concrete. And, since grass produces lactic acid for silage, could it also produce acetic acid or ethanol? These are some of the questions that will be exercising the minds of scientists over the coming years.

John Litton addressing the assembled crowd at the official opening of the new facility at the National Sheep Research Centre, Creagh, Ballinrobe. The centre was formally opened in July 1965 by Paddy Lalor, Parliamentary Secretary to the Minister for Agriculture and Fisheries, and blessed by the Archbishop of Tuam, Dr J Walsh.

The first Finnish Landrace ewe and her triplets arrived in Grange in 1966.

CHAPTER 6

DEVELOPING A MODERN SHEEP INDUSTRY

Paddy Smith

In the late-1950s, the national sheep flock was just 1.8 million ewes. The sector was characterised by low stocking rates, typically two ewes per acre, or five ewes per hectare, with poor grassland management. Sheep farming was mainly a scavenging exercise with in-lamb ewes roaming the farm during the winter hoping to get a mouthful here and there. In the spring there was no grass available and there were all sorts of health issues. Lambing rates per ewe were low and poor spring grass meant that most ewes were not capable of rearing more than one lamb.

The national sheep research centre at Creagh was formerly a TB sanatorium.

Even then, lamb growth rates were very low. With the exception of farms with tillage, where new pastures were available, most lambs were sold as stores and were not fit for slaughter until their first birthday the following spring. The main lowland sheep systems were based on the Galway breed in the west and Galway, Cheviot, Border Leicester, Suffolk and their crosses in the east. For hill sheep, the Cheviot dominated in the east, mainly in Wicklow, and the Blackface along the western seaboard and on the hills of Waterford and south Tipperary.

Creagh, outside Ballinrobe, was the first dedicated national centre for sheep research to be established by AFT. Previously a sanatorium, Mayo County Council offered to sell the facility to AFT in September 1958. In February 1959, the AFT Council sanctioned the purchase of the buildings and 316 acres at Creagh for £7,000. Tom Nolan, one of the first staff to be recruited to Creagh, remembers the hospital being converted to offices and laboratories and a staff canteen being established in the nurses' home. Later, an additional 500 acres in two other farms in the Ballinrobe area - at Cloonagashil and Annefield - were leased and were used as satellite farms for sheep breeding research, which was to become a major part of the sheep research programme.

Pending the development of Creagh, the early research on sheep was carried out at the national beef research centre at Grange. The first research on lowland systems was carried out by Aidan Conway at Grange and involved simple systems for fat lamb production. It showed that 17 ewes per hectare, or seven ewes to the acre, could be carried on reseeded pastures, a big jump from the two ewes to the acre that was the norm on most farms. This was followed by a comparison by Tom Nolan of 10, 15 and 20 ewes/ha over a five-year period at Creagh. It confirmed that 15 Galway ewes/ha was near optimum for permanent pasture and that neither disease nor stomach worm problems increased with stocking rate. More than 30 years later, a final study by Tom Nolan at Athenry showed that it was possible to carry up to 17 Belclare-cross ewes per hectare of permanent pasture while achieving a weaning rate of 1.7 lambs per ewe.

The classic Kilmaine study gave a snapshot of sheep production soon after AFT was established. The study, which was carried out in 1962/63 by Pat Daly, a veterinarian working in Creagh, and published in 1966, surveyed 300 farms in the parish of Kilmaine, near Ballinrobe. It found that stocking rate was a mere six ewe equivalents per hectare in a cattle/sheep mix where around 60 per cent of the livestock units were sheep and the rest cattle; by that time, researchers had proof from the work at Grange and Creagh that a stocking rate three times higher was attainable.

The Mixed Grazing Formula

The farming systems in Kilmaine were very typical of those in the majority of parishes. It was unusual to have sheep only on farms. Most farms had sheep and cattle and the AFT scientists set about examining how a well-defined system of mixed grazing could improve overall performance of sheep and cattle. This led to the establishment by Aidan Conway of mixed grazing trials at the newly acquired AFT research demonstration farm at Ballintubber in Roscommon. The results showed a big increase in overall performance and profitability, mainly due to a big lift in the performance of sheep. Out of this developed a major research programme, conducted by Tom Nolan, Denis Conniffe and John Connolly, which perfected the mixed grazing formula and which was adopted widely by farmers over the following decades.

Mixed grazing of sheep and cattle and its adoption at farm level is a prime example of a concerted approach by researchers, advisers, veterinary practitioners and farmers. The science behind the system resulted from research work at Creagh by Tom Nolan and John Connolly, mainly from a large experiment involving a total of 13 variations: three all-sheep, three all-cattle and seven mixes of cattle and sheep with different stocking rates and ratios. Researchers worked with advisers, local veterinary practitioners and the veterinary laboratory to monitor disease and parasite levels as well as all other economic aspects on farms where the new systems were being pioneered.

Slowly, the concept began to spread locally and within a few years bus loads of farmers were being ferried from all of the main drystock counties to open days on Tom Mannion's, and other farms, in the south Roscommon area to see the new system in operation. Adviser Frank Young and P J Dwyer of the Department's Veterinary Laboratory in Athlone were leading figures in promoting the system, working very closely with AFT. The system originally established blueprints for calf-to-beef and sheep and later for suckler beef and sheep.

Developing the Belclare Breed

Genetic research in the 1960s compared a range of breeds as terminal sires – Suffolk, Oxford, Hampshire Down and Texel – with seven rams from each breed being tested. Research centred on a flock of some 1,000 pedigree and commercial Galway sheep, which were built up at Creagh to enable the establishment of a genetics programme on Galway sheep. These sheep were bought-in as hoggets from all over the country and the research team, led by Vivian Timon, showed that it was possible to obtain a 1.5 per cent genetic gain per annum. This work, which went on for some 20 years, was one of the biggest experiments in the sheep sector.

Ireland could not capitalise to the same extent as Britain on crossbreeding because farming patterns here were not suited to this approach. In 1966, the researchers decided to import the Finnish Landrace, which had poor conformation but boasted a litter size of at least 2.5, in an attempt to develop a more productive breed without having to rely on within-breed selection. Then, at a time when the approach to genetic improvement was to look at families, Timon returned from a visit to England with the concept, advocated by a leading geneticist there, that the genes from individual animals as well as families should be used in programmes of genetic improvement.

This led to the setting up of the so-called High Fertility Flock, made up of individual exceptional sheep from all over the country. Average litter size of the foundation ewes after purchase was 2.1 and the daughters had an average of 1.75. This high fertility flock was kept at the tillage research centre at Oak Park from 1964 to 1970, because of a shortage of accommodation in the west, but was then moved to Creagh and was subsequently used in the formation of the Belclare breed.

The Finnish Landrace was crossed on the Galway ewe to produce the Finn cross Galway. Then a Welsh breed, the Lleyn (pronounced 'Clean'), was crossed on top of that. The resultant progeny was the Belclare Improver. Later, Seamus Hanrahan introduced another variation, using three-quarter Texel rams on the Belclare Improver in order to add more leanness. The progeny was three-eighths Texel and that is essentially what the Belclare breed is today.

"The key point here is that we selected Finn sheep for high ovulation rate," recalls Hanrahan. *"This was successful and increased ovulation rate by about 70 per cent. The objective was to increase it enough that we could produce a three-quarters Texel/one-quarter Finn with a prolificacy equal to that of the Belclare Improver. Then we could get Texel genes into the new breed and capture the benefits in carcass composition."*

The present Belclare was therefore produced by crossing Belclare Improver stock with the Texel/Finn rams. The Belclare has a litter average of 2.2 and, in further research, when crossbred daughters of Belclare rams were compared with crossbreds by seven other breeds, the Belclare cross ewes reared between 15 and 20 more lambs per 100 ewes than any of the other crosses.

In spite of its inspiring history and performance, the Belclare has failed to dominate the composition of lowland ewe flocks.

A Chance Encounter

A traffic hold-up in Athlone on a Sunday in 1963 meant that Vivian Timon diverted to Shannonbridge on his journey from Roscommon to Dunsinea. And fate brought him in contact with a farmer who helped to change sheep breeding history in Ireland. The farmer was driving a flock of 40 Galway ewes over the bridge and told Timon in conversation that one of them had eleven lambs in 12 months. Curiosity got the better of the AFT man who accepted an invitation to the farmer's home where he was shown local newspaper coverage of the ewe with four lambs in March 1962, another three in September 1962 and a further four in March 1963.

Timon later checked out the story with the local adviser and then tried to buy this prolific ewe from the farmer for research purposes, without success. On the basis that there must be other individual ewes with similar levels of multiple births, prepaid postcards were printed and issued to advisers in all the sheep areas of the country seeking ewes which had four or more lambs or three successive sets of triplets or lambed more than once in the year. As a result of the hundreds of replies, work began on assembling these prolific animals, with either Timon or a technician or two students, who happened to be future scientists, Joe Sreenan and Seamus Hanrahan, visiting the farmers. Because relatively few of the farmers would sell – AFT would only pay good commercial rates – they collected only about 50 ewes in the first year. A total of 149 ewes were acquired between 1963 and 1965.

Hanrahan has theorised that since the Belclare Breed Society was established in 1985 producers have been more concerned with keeping up ewe numbers, in order to claim premiums, than with productivity. In addition, they were more inclined to buy-in replacements rather than breed them, or they bought rams with the choice dictated by the marketing of the lambs in the next year rather than on any longer-term consideration of genetic potential of the flock.

Micheal Lawlor withdraws a sample of food in the course of digestion through the rumen cannula of a fistulated sheep.

An Enterprising Postman

A determined Co Roscommon postman should get some of the credit for the development of the Belclare sheep breed. He delivered a letter to farmer, Johnny Mee of Four Roads, and the only address on the envelope was 'Roscommon Sheep Society, Roscommon'. This was in 1974 and the Roscommon Sheep Association had been defunct since the 1920s but Johnny Mee was a well-known sheep breeder, which is why the postman came knocking on his door.

Seamus Hanrahan, who was trying to persuade farmers to take on Finn-Galway rams in order to raise litter size, was speaking at a meeting of farmers in south Roscommon and Johnny Mee showed him the letter. It was from John Peters, a Welsh farmer in Anglesey who had heard from the older people in his area that they used to travel occasionally to Roscommon to buy some Roscommon rams and use them on their own breed, the Lleyn, for a bit of size.

In Ireland, there was farmer resistance to the new Finn-Galway cross, mainly based on appearance, and Hanrahan decided, on the basis of the letter which had described the Lleyn breed in glowing terms, to take a trip to the Lleyn peninsula where he visited a number of breeders. He was searching for a crossing breed that would incorporate an acceptable appearance into the Finn-Galway, while at the same time not compromising litter size. The Lleyn appeared to fit the bill and 13 ewes, highly selected on litter size, were eventually imported in 1975/76 and used in the development of the Belclare Improver.

By 2006, two-thirds of the ewes in the lowland flock were sired by Suffolks, but only one in twenty by Belclares. However, a survey of ewe lambs kept for breeding in the 2007 flock revealed that just over 10 per cent were Belclare, evidence Hanrahan felt that, with the advent of decoupling production from premia, farmers were finally beginning to change their attitude to the Belclare.

Top: Aidan Conway taking farmers around the Grange lamb production trials in 1963.

Components of Efficient Production

Researching all the components of production and knitting them into systems that can be effectively adopted by farmers has been at the core of sheep research for the past 50 years. Aspects such as grazing management, disease and worm control, housing, winter feeding, breed evaluation and many others have been examined and refined.

A significant research programme on sheep parasitology was run by Alberta Kearney, who developed guidelines on the use of anthelmintics along with grazing management to control the impact of parasites on lamb growth in intensive systems. A key element from her work was that in all-sheep systems a maximum of three anthelmintic treatments should suffice for the lambs and ewes were not dosed, thus helping to minimise selection for drug resistance and eliminating unnecessary expenditure.

Alberta always emphasised the importance of combining worm dosing with good grassland management such as moving lambs to 'clean' grazing at weaning – either aftergrass or fields that were not grazed by sheep earlier in the season. Current research by Seamus Hanrahan, along with parasitologist Barbara Good, has been focused on identifying sheep that are resistant to parasites and on identifying the genes responsible to enable the use of molecular genetic tools to breed sheep that have a high resistance to roundworms. Resistance of roundworm parasites to drugs has been growing in significance as a potential problem on sheep farms and the researchers have been examining the best ways to manage the parasite problem and the genetic make-up of the resistant sheep.

After the establishment of a Common Agricultural Policy for sheep, it became easier to import the continental breeds into this country and scientists made a major contribution in evaluating these breeds as sires for fat lamb production. An early project, undertaken by Gerry More O'Ferrall, led to the identification of the Texel as an alternative to the Suffolk as a crossing sire. He made a major contribution to the establishment of the Texel Breed Society and the promotion of genetic improvement programmes in the pedigree flocks of the main terminal sire breeds – Suffolk, Texel and Charollais. In later years, Seamus Hanrahan carried out a comprehensive evaluation of the benefits of a large number of breeds as terminal sire breeds, including the Charollais, Dorset, Ille de France, Bleu du Maine, Rouge de l'Ouest, Beltex and Vendeen. The results of this work, which went on until 1999, showed that the Suffolk still beat them all, with Charollais coming next, followed by the Texel. However, the Suffolk would not win out if the ewes were already Suffolk crosses. A 2005 survey revealed that, in lowland flocks, 55 per cent of the rams were Suffolk, the next breed being Texel at 18 per cent, followed by Charollais at 14 per cent.

Silage as a winter feed for sheep was pushed from the early-1960s. At that time and into the 1970s, hay was the feed of choice, being self-fed from the so-called 'sheep cock' in the west, a large hay cock built up around a vertical pole in the ground. Tom Nolan showed that there was no need for sophisticated set-ups when feeding silage and that an average of 7.5 cm per ewe at the silage feeding face was sufficient using an uncovered slatted unit on a concrete base. The thinking before this was that 30 cm was necessary for each ewe, but studies of the behaviour of the ewes showed that at any given time only a quarter of a group of sheep would be actually feeding at the silage face.

Eugene Grennan, who began his career in grassland research at the peat land centre in Glenamoy in north-west Mayo, played a vital role in developing recommendations on fertiliser nitrogen levels and on the contribution of clover pastures to profitable production. He also established guidelines on the ideal sward height for maximum lamb growth rate. Liam Sheehan led research on the nutritional requirements of pregnant ewes and finishing lambs while Seamus Fitzgerald did a huge amount of work on feeding silages and root crops to hill lambs and lowland stores. The results of much of their work are now common practice on farms today.

The Electric Fence

The introduction of electric fencing for sheep dates back to work at Belclare in the 1970s when there was a certain amount of success in developing a system. Then, in 1980, Sean Flanagan was in Kentucky on a farm with 3,000 sheep and he saw a system of 5-strand electric fencing with hardwood stakes from New Zealand. In spite of the 5,000-volt kick from the wiring, no insulators were needed because the stakes were derived from the Eucalyptus tree species. A similar set-up was soon in operation in the Blindwell paddock system after enquiries revealed that the New Zealand company had an agent in Cork.

In other research, Murray Black was responsible for a significant body of work on sheep housing, including open-air slats and covered slats. Sheep physiology research by Sean Quirke included ewe lamb breeding and hormone usage to increase growth, although this latter work was rendered redundant by the EU's blanket ban on animal growth promoters in 1988.

Research Locations

Creagh, from which the bulk of pioneering research emanated in the early years, had limitations as a research station due to the relatively small amount of consistent quality land there. From 1972, it was decided to concentrate research at Belclare, Co Galway. A total of 800 acres were leased and Belclare became the Western Research Centre with responsibility not just for sheep research but also for research on animal reproduction and for disseminating the results of Moorepark research to the growing number of western farmers who had moved into milk production. Vivian Timon, who had taken over as head of research in the west in 1970, recalls that at Creagh they would have been lucky to get 200-300 farmers at open days; there were 4,000 farmers at the first open day at Belclare in 1973. Following the establishment of Teagasc, Belclare was closed and sheep and animal reproduction research was concentrated in Athenry where it continues today.

Research in Practice

The development of the research demonstration farms, or economic test farms, as they were variously called, enabled all the components of research to be put together in a system that enabled farmers to readily relate the information to the scale of their own flock enterprises at home. In addition to the farm at Ballintubber, which was used to demonstrate research results on mixed grazing of cattle and sheep, an all-sheep demonstration farm was established at Blindwell, outside Tuam. It was a self-contained 25 hectare farm carrying 360 ewes and achieving an output of over 20 lambs per hectare and run by one man, Peter O'Malley.

Sean Flanagan, who had overall responsibility for Blindwell, remembers the large numbers of sheep producers countrywide who came to the farm to see and discuss the principles of intensive flock management and many returned repeatedly on an annual basis. When Blindwell closed, a farm at Knockbeg in Carlow was used to demonstrate the best techniques in intensive sheep production, where a particular focus was placed on handling facilities and on extending the horizon in grassland management. These farms, which are the subject of a personal reflection by John Shirley elsewhere in this book, played a vital role in the dissemination of research result.

Hill Sheep Research

From the beginning, the research programme gave strong emphasis to hill sheep production where technologies and targets were very different to those for lowland sheep. Hill sheep research started in 1965 on Muckross Estate, outside Killarney, but, due to pressure locally in Muckross where it was felt that the sheep would interfere with the running of the famous herd of red deer, it was moved after three

The Mock Auction

A mock auction, staged at Athenry mart, was one of the features of the Telefís Feirme 1970 series of RTE television programmes on sheep production, presented by AFT man, Vivian Timon. The aim was to raise awareness of the opportunities that Common Market membership would bring sheep farmers. Lambs were selling at £25–£27 per head at the time. In the mock auction, lambs made £70 per head, a foretaste of what would happen when the French market opened up.

years to Maam, Co Galway. In more recent years, research on hill sheep has been located at Leenane, Co Mayo.

The key initial objective was to reduce the losses of ewes and lambs on the hills. Michael O'Toole worked on a system that entailed the selective feeding of the 12-15 per cent of the ewes who were thin and who would die if left on the hill. Bringing the whole flock down off the hill would not have been cost effective, but he showed that bringing down the thin sheep could increase overall productivity from a low 60 lambs per 100 ewes to 100 lambs per 100 ewes. Ewe mortality was cut from 10 per cent to 2 per cent. Later work by Michael O'Toole on better grazing management and winter feeding enabled hill sheep producers to reach a target of 1.2 lambs per ewe. On another front, production trials involving purebred Blackface and Blackfaces crossed with Belclares showed that financial output could be improved dramatically by crossbreeding, depending on the proportion of lowland available. The pure Blackface system was applicable where no lowland existed.

Around the turn of the millennium, interesting work on environmental issues was carried out by Michael Walsh at Leenane, which had a flock of 500 Scottish Blackface. In response to a view that sheep were overgrazing

commonages and hill farms, the Leenane experiments used the cutting edge satellite technology of GPS tracking collars to show clearly that this was not the full story because sheep were very selective about the type of vegetation they ate on the hillsides.

Numbers Rise and Fall

When Ireland joined the EEC, many of the technologies for profitable sheep had been developed by AFT. It was a time of great expectations for sheep farmers but it turned into a decade of frustration as they enviously watched other farming sectors receive massive boosts from entry into the EEC. The sheep men's ambitions were thwarted by the antics of a French government anxious to protect its own sheep farmers and denying free access to the lucrative French market to outsiders, including the Irish.

In 1980, the national breeding flock, at just over 1.5 million ewes, was even lower than in 1958. The arrival of the Common Agricultural Policy for sheep in 1980 heralded a new era for sheep producers, leading to unprecedented expansion of the national breeding flock. Driven by the 'ewe premium', which was an integral part of the new policy, profits increased substantially. Numbers peaked in 1992 when farmers claimed the 'ewe premium' on 5.3 million ewes, a three and a half fold increase on the 1980 flock size. Even some dairy farmers added a sheep enterprise. However, policy changes since 1992, poor prices and the continuing shift to part-time farming have all combined to take the gloss off sheep production during the past decade or more. As a result, the national ewe flock is now below 3.5 million.

Focus on Wool

Wool contributed a very significant proportion of a sheep farmer's income in the 1960s and was an important focus of the Creagh research programme in the early years. Sean Flanagan researched the characteristics and physical features of wool from different breeds for industrial use. There was a wool evaluation laboratory at Creagh, although by 1970 it was no longer in use. He also set out to do something about the lack of skilled shearers in Ireland, where practically all shearing was done manually.

Discovery of New Gene

A Belclare Improver ewe was found in 1983 with 18 ova, an exceptionally high ovulation rate. Ewe 700 (her tag number) was mated with a Texel, which was the most unprolific of the breeds available at Belclare, as a test of her own prolificacy. As a ewe lamb, her daughter produced seven ova, again an exceptional number. This was part of research on the biological control of litter size, specifically ovulation rate and embryo survival, under Seamus Hanrahan and Sean Quirke.

Family 700, as her descendants were described in scientific literature, were studied in subsequent years and the research eventually led to the discovery of a new gene controlling ovulation in sheep. The work involved collaboration with the agricultural research institutes of France and New Zealand. This gene is also involved in the control of ovarian function in other animals and in humans. "The potential impact of all this, ultimately, is that it greatly extends our understanding of how the ovary functions in humans as well as animals," said Hanrahan.

One of the Creagh farm workers, Seamus Brannick, had an interest in the skill of shearing and, at Flanagan's instigation, he was sent to Scotland for training in 1965. Brannick, who trained a nucleus of machine shearers in the west, later went on to win the All-Ireland shearing title and at Maam he set a new Irish record for the most sheep shorn in a single day.

Remembering the Demonstration Farms

John Shirley*

When reporting on beef and sheep research emanating from AFT, the satellite demonstration farms always held a special attraction for me. Farmers too held in high regard units like Ballinalack near Mullingar, which was involved in cattle, Blindwell near Tuam, which was devoted to sheep and Ballintubber in Roscommon, which was used to demonstrate cattle and sheep in mixed grazing. In contrast to the large centres of multi-component research, the outside farms were run as self-contained farmlets, with which the farmer could identify. The managers of these units communicated effectively in farmer language and people such as Paddy Coakley in Ballinalack, Peter O'Malley in Blindwell and Aidan McLoughlin in Ballintubber were some of the unsung heroes of AFT.

Ballinalack was linked to the Grange research centre. Initially under Aidan Conway, it demonstrated topless cubicles as well as grassland management. At that time, little emphasis was placed on managing slurry on farms. If you constrained most of the slurry solids few questions were asked. In the early 1970s, Vincent Flynn took over as director of the farm, which was split into two 60-acre units, one in calf-to-steer beef and the other in weanling-to-steer beef. Both were extensions of Grange trials and research. Interestingly, the cattle were mostly Friesian steers from the dairy herd. Suckler cow numbers nationally then were less than half those of today.

Ballinalack's innings straddled the introduction of implant growth promoters and the cattle in the unit were used for implant comparisons. In spite of the availability of implants, the slaughter weights of the steers at Ballinalack ranged from 300 to 320 kg, poor by the standards of today. The mantra was that beef should be produced from grass and silage. There was a general assumption that meal feeding was not economical. Subsequent trials at Grange by Gerry Keane showed that concentrates had been underrated in the production of beef. With concentrates now hitting new price records maybe the Ballinalack silage results should be revisited.

Ballintubber came into the ownership of AFT in the mid-1960s via the Land Commission. At 60 acres, it was bigger than most of the neighbouring holdings in north Roscommon. Under the direction of Aidan Conway, it was used for fundamental research on mixed grazing of cattle and sheep. It was shown that mixed grazing of cattle and sheep was highly beneficial for the sheep and was neutral for the cattle. Ballintubber experiments also showed that rotational grazing and fertiliser transformed the botanical composition of the sward in a short few years. Both of these lessons are as relevant today as they were 40 years ago.

Blindwell was sold in the 1980s and there was farmer clamour for sheep research in the east of Ireland. This led to the opening of Knockbeg near Carlow. Under the direction of Sean Flanagan, Knockbeg during the 1990s and right up to 2005 carried out fundamental assessment of clover pastures, winter grazing, Belclare sheep and outdoor lambing. Again, the trials were conducted within a farm-like system under Willie Kelly.

Other satellite farms run by AFT and later Teagasc include the hill sheep farm at Maam in Galway and more recently in Leenane. In Maam, Michael O'Toole introduced the first measurement and recording into an enterprise that was almost without documentation. Of course, the ewe subsidy, introduced by Ray MacSharry in the 1992 CAP reform, led to hills being packed with ewes.

Over the years, when AFT and later Teagasc became strapped for funds, the test farms were vulnerable. Their activity was not seen as pure research. They also offered the prospect of a capital injection on disposal. However the passing of the Ballinlacks, the Blindwells, the Ballintubbers and Knockbegs was a loss to farmers. They are recalled with fondness.

The upgraded Galway ewe, infused with genes for prolificacy.

For lowland sheep farmers the names Blindwell and Knockbeg carry a resonance. Blindwell operated as a sheep farm from the early-1970s and incorporated the lessons on grassland management, fencing, housing, and breeding that had been researched by scientists like Sean Flanagan, Vivian Timon and Tom Nolan at Creagh. Farmers from all over the country flocked to the open days at Blindwell, where they saw topless slats, electrified sheep fencing, sheep fed on silage, all developments that had to be seen before being confident to try them out on one's own farm. The upgraded Galway sheep infused with prolific genes were also assessed there.

* John Shirley is former beef/sheep editor with the Irish Farmers Journal

Manuel Ribeiro discussing new grass
varieties with visitors to Oak Park in 1972.

CHAPTER 7
CUTTING EDGE TILLAGE
TECHNOLOGY AT OAK PARK

J o e   M u r r a y

An analysis of 50 years of tillage research by AFT and Teagasc is probably the classic example of how usable technology can transform an industry and bring real benefits to farmers and the economy. While Ireland is not by any means the most suitable place in the world for tillage farming, today's tillage farmers have regularly the top yields of wheat and barley in the world. This phenomenon is the result of high scientific endeavour, the fine-tuning of technologies to Ireland's unique climate and the combined efforts of scientists and advisers in disseminating the technologies to a group of highly professional tillage growers.

Oak Park House, now the Teagasc head office, dates back to 1830.

In 1960, the national acreage of cereals was over 1.1 million acres (450,000 ha) and the annual output was less than one million tonnes. Today, cereal growers produce over two million tonnes of grain a year on just 60% of the area planted in 1960. Fifty years ago, crops were all sown in spring, with oats as the most popular crop, followed by wheat and barley. Around one-third of acreage is now made up of winter cereals and spring-sown barley is the most important crop.

The first tillage scientists employed by AFT in 1959 were located in the Sugar Company premises in Thurles. Bernard Crombie, chief plant breeder with the Sugar Company, was appointed as head of the new AFT plant sciences and crop husbandry division and all new recruits were located with the new boss until a permanent home was found. In 1960, Oak Park, on the outskirts of Carlow, became the home and has remained since as the powerhouse for tillage research, first under the direction of Bernard Crombie and later under P J O'Hare, Tom Thomas and Jimmy Burke, who is now responsible for the national tillage research programme.

Acquiring a Stately Home

Oak Park House and 850 acres was bought by AFT from the Land Commission in 1960 as the headquarters for the new plant sciences and crop husbandry division. It would later become the national tillage research centre of AFT and Teagasc.

The property had been owned for 180 years by the Bruen family, a dynasty of substantial landowners who at one time owned over 20,000 acres in Carlow alone. The first Bruen came to Ireland as an officer in Cromwell's army in the mid-1600s. At the end of the Cromwellian campaign, he was given land near Boyle in Roscommon. A wealthy descendant of his, Henry Bruen, came from America in 1775 and bought Oak Park. He was the first of five Henry Bruens to own Oak Park, the last dying in 1954 without a male heir. In 1957, Brownshill Farms, an English syndicate that already owned a substantial amount of land in the area, bought Oak Park, which then consisted of the house and 1600 acres. Poor harvests and local agitation to have the land divided resulted in the syndicate selling out to the Land Commission in 1960.

The newly-established AFT bought the house and 850 acres of the estate from the Lnd Commission, Carlow golf club, which had been rented from the Bruen estate since 1922, was also purchased from the Land Commission and land was also made available to Carlow rugby club. The remaining 450 acres of the estate were allocated to farmers, some of whom adjoined the estate and others came from further afield.

Oak Park House, which is now the Teagasc head office, dates back to 1830. It was designed by William V. Morrison, a well-known designer of stately homes during that period. Most of the records of the building and reconstruction works during the 19th century are now preserved in the National Library. However, magnificent as it was, it offered strange accommodation for the young scientists, technicians and support staff joining AFT in 1960. As Tom Thomas, one of the first scientists into Oak Park remembers: "Our desks were located in grand rooms with high ornate ceilings and magnificent fireplaces. We even had a man who kept the fires going all day long for us, so it was very comfortable and grandiose. But it wasn't really built for research."

While Oak Park was an inspired choice, being in the heart of Ireland's tillage area, the purchase was almost an accident. Land outside Thurles was the original choice but this did not materialise before Oak Park became available.

Dr James Ryan, Minister for Finance, at the official opening of the AFT plant sciences and crop husbandry division in 1964.

Aerial view of Oak Park.

Transforming Grain Growing

The role played in transforming grain yields is perhaps the most striking contribution by Oak Park during the past 50 years. Following the establishment of the research centre, the early concentration was on improving soil fertility and developing the basic scientific knowledge on fertilisation, weed control and mechanisation in spring-sown cereals. It was the 1970s before the real technological revolution took place in cereal growing. Cereal disease work in the 1960s was largely confined to the control of eyespot and take-all through crop rotation. Very significant progress was made by the first Oak Park plant pathologist, Colm Cunningham, in establishing patterns of disease progress and the particular strains of disease in Ireland.

develop growing systems for winter cereals provided the platform for the development of production systems most appropriate for Ireland.

The implementation of the research programme received a boost following a visit by a group of growers and others to the University of Gembloux in Belgium where research under the direction of Professor Lalous showed the immense yield potential of winter cereals when grown on scientifically based practices. Although a simple concept, the use of tramlines, which facilitated accurate spraying and fertiliser application, raised considerable interest. Plant pathologist, Brendan Dunne recalls: *"The tramlines were pre-formed wheel tracks to permit repeated crop treatments such as spraying and top dressing with fertiliser. The yield targets were almost unbelievable to us.*

Harvesting winter cereals at Oak Park.

Tom Thomas, one of the first AFT crop scientists.

With the introduction of high yielding winter cereal varieties, new fungicides, herbicides and growth regulators in the 1970s, research was focussing on developing systematic approaches to growing winter cereals, which would greatly enhance grain yield and quality. In this regard, on-going work in Western Europe, Belgium and Northern Germany looked particularly interesting. Research led by Tom Thomas and colleagues at Oak Park as well as enterprising cereal growers who were anxious to

At that time in Ireland, you got your seed into the ground, you came back a few weeks later and sprayed for weeds and then you closed the gate and waited for the harvest. You might spray a bit of fungicide on spring barley."

The task for researchers in Oak Park was firstly to select varieties of winter wheat that were best suited to climate and soil conditions in Ireland and develop systems that would exploit the genetic potential of these varieties. Early findings

showed that while all components in the growing system were important the most critical were sowing in good soil conditions before the end of October, adequate nitrogen fertiliser, prevention of lodging through the use of growth regulators and, especially, comprehensive disease control. Eyespot and Septoria were the main target diseases as both were caused by the relatively wet Irish conditions. Colm Cunningham and Brendan Dunne identified the most appropriate fungicides, their optimum doses and the critical timing of spraying.

The Ten Tonne Club

The uptake of research findings on winter cereal growing by groups of farmers from Cork to Louth was quite amazing. Soon they were striving to get 10 tonnes/ha. Membership of the '10 tonne club' was much sought after and many set higher targets.

Jimmy Burke, who joined Oak Park in 1976, remembers the enormous interest among tillage farmers in the new technology at the Oak Park open day that year where large crowds assembled throughout the day around the various trials. At the time, it was not possible to buy the tramline attachments for the corn drills. *"The first electronic tramline attachments were developed at Oak Park for a commercial company and Oak Park staff also fitted the tramlines on new corn drills."*

Gay Corcoran and Liz Durak evaluating wheat quality.

Michael Conry, who joined the Oak Park research team from the national soil survey unit, was given the task of developing techniques for high yield winter barley growing. He recalls that in 1977 there were just 300 acres of winter barley in the entire country and farmers were crying out for information. His headline findings showed that sowing date was critical. *"For every week that sowing was delayed after mid-September, yields would be reduced by 0.1 tonne per acre. Sowing from November onwards would give a poor crop"*, said Conry.

Aerial spraying being demonstrated at Oak Park.

New type of sprayer being tested at Oak Park in 1961.

Michael Conry says the early research results offered great hopes for winter barley and winter wheat in Ireland. In the case of winter wheat, these hopes were all fulfilled but not so for winter barley. The problem was that that both crops were competing for the same good, heavier free-draining land and wheat, because of its higher yield potential, won out. Winter barley, while still an important crop on many specialist tillage farms, has rarely exceeded 20,000 hectares (50,000 acres) a year.

Getting the Recipe Right

Similar advances in technology also enabled big productivity gains in spring-sown crops. Research on sowing date and fertiliser nitrogen levels helped to ensure Ireland's internationally-renowned reputation for the production of high quality malting barley. A study in 2003 carried out by consultant Gerry Boyle, who is now the director of Teagasc, showed that Oak Park research on malting barley gave a 95 per cent return on investment, which is 19 times higher than the minimum rate advocated by the Department of Finance for public sector investment projects and compares very favourably with the best international figures.

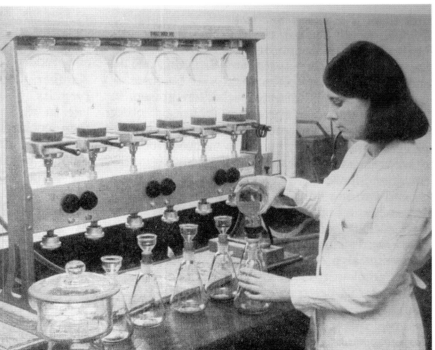

Up to the mid-1970s, the range of crop chemicals was very small. But as winter grain increased fungal diseases became more and more of a problem. New fungicides brought almost magical results but the ability of diseases to develop resistance became ominously impressive. Several generations of crop chemicals later, scientists and farmers are still struggling to keep ahead in the never ending race between new fungicides and the inevitable new disease resistances. The part played by Oak Park in fine-tuning successive generations of chemicals to Ireland's unique set of disease challenges made a big contribution towards Irish grain growers achieving the top yields in the world.

Advisers played a huge role in the yield revolution through the transfer of the new technologies to tillage farmers who had to become familiar with a whole new vocabulary in relation to crop growth stages and time-critical crop management decisions. The demand from farmers for expert guidance on the identification of diseases, weeds and pests and the precise rate and timing of the most effective chemicals and fertilisers dramatically increased. This led to a transformation in the intensity and methods of advice. Timing was the key to achieving top yields and advisers were available to farmers during the full daylight hours during the crucial crop growing periods. Indeed, tillage advisers were the first professional group to be equipped with mobile phones in the late-1980s, a time when coverage in many rural areas was far from perfect. The entire episode is a classic example of how an integrated research and advisory structure can deliver huge productivity gains.

Stephen Flynn using the LECO FP428 Nitrogen Determinator for protein analysis.

With the increasing availability of plant protection products, Michael Clancy and Joe Eades tested a range of chemicals for both efficacy and residues and made recommendations for Irish conditions. In some instances, these were at variance with what was being recommended by manufacturers. The work gave assurance to advisers, growers and consumers that an acceptable balance between efficacy and environmental sustainability could be achieved with proper use.

Jimmy Burke stressed the importance of developing Irish solutions to Irish problems. *"For instance, the control programme for the leaf disease, septoria, which can drastically reduce yields, is totally different in Ireland than in the UK. Also, in recent years, Oak Park scientists were to the forefront of a Europe-wide effort to come to terms with the failure of a group of chemicals, called strobilurins, which until then had given excellent control of septoria"*, said Burke.

Another example of the importance of home-grown research expertise was the discovery in 2001 by scientists Eugene O Sullivan and Brendan Dunne of 'ramularia', a new fungal disease in barley. It was the first time the disease was identified in Europe. Once identified, it was easily controlled with relatively cheap chemicals. A few years earlier, growers and scientists were confronted with a mysterious disease that devastated yields of one barley variety, Cooper. Research at Oak Park found that the variety was susceptible to light-induced spotting particularly when periods of cloud followed high temperature. Again, Oak Park research came up with solutions to overcome the phenomenon.

Finding all the Links

According to Tom Thomas, the disease challenges in Ireland are so high that one missing link in growing the crop can result in a severe breakdown with the inevitable effect on yield and income. He believes that Oak Park work on barley yellow dwarf virus (BYDV) was vital in the survival of winter barley growing. *"Our understanding of how to deal with aphids, which spread the disease, literally saved the crop."*

Tom Kennedy, who has worked on BYDV control for many years, recorded a yield drop of over one-third due to the disease and devised a strategic spraying programme to control aphids. However, he has also done extensive research on biological control of aphids and other harmful pests. While ladybirds have the reputation of controlling aphids, the research does not confirm this. A group known as the rove beetles have been found to be more effective predators. The research has shown that their larvae climb up the plants at night and feed on aphids. By daylight, they have disappeared back into the ground.

Up to recently, scientists were not aware of the job these creatures were doing because it was all happening in the dark. The increased attention to the role that useful insects can play has led to a better use of chemicals.

During the past decade, Tony Fortune and other mechanisation experts have examined the effect of minimum tillage, or 'min-till', on work rates, energy usage, machinery and labour costs, pest and weed control and yield. The results overall were positive and this system has been adopted by an increasing number of Irish growers. Problems unique to Ireland were identified and solutions to minimise their impact were developed. This work has also shown that 'min-till' has the potential to reduce damage by aphids and slugs and to lead to an increase in the number of beneficial slugs and earthworms but it can lead to more problems with weed control.

The Yield Ceiling

Considering the enormous advances in yield in recent decades, might we now be reaching the limit? Jimmy Burke is adamant there is still a long way to go and that we can continue the upward trend in yields for the foreseeable future. New technologies are enabling scientists to predict what new and future varieties can yield and the impact of genomics and mapping will play a very significant role.

"It is not uncommon for Oak Park trials to yield 14 tonnes/ha of winter wheat so this must be our next national target as new developments in plant physiology, genetics and disease resistance will help us reach these new goals", said Burke.

He regards genetic engineering and the whole genome revolution as the biggest development in world agriculture in the past 20 years. More than 100 million hectares of GM crops are grown worldwide and the area is increasing by double percentage figures every year since 1996. The acreage of GM maize has just begun to expand in Germany and Spain and this trend is likely to expand in the years ahead.

Technological Revolution in Sugar Beet

While sugar beet was an important crop since the 1930s it was under significant economic pressure in the early-1960s. On the formation of AFT, two major constraints were identified. These were low yield and a very high labour requirement, in the growing, harvesting and haulage of the crop. These constraints were the focus of a comprehensive research programme initiated by AFT in collaboration with the Sugar Company, which had an existing development programme in sugar beet breeding and mechanisation.

Around the time AFT was set up, sugar beet yields averaged just 10 tonnes/acre (25 tonnes/ha) and, while now difficult to imagine, the crop was thinned and weeds removed by hand and hoe. The crop was also harvested by hand and manually loaded for transport, taking about 350 man-hours to produce one acre. Advances in technology dramatically changed the scene and, by 1976, yield had increased by over 50 per cent and labour input reduced by over 80 per cent.

The entire crop was sown with monogerm seed and over 70 per cent sown to a final stand. Chemical weed control was carried out on the entire crop with almost 100 per cent mechanically harvested. In the mid-1980s, some growers were able to produce beet with just 4 per cent of the labour required 30 years earlier – a remarkable tribute to the dedication of all those involved in the sugar industry in Ireland.

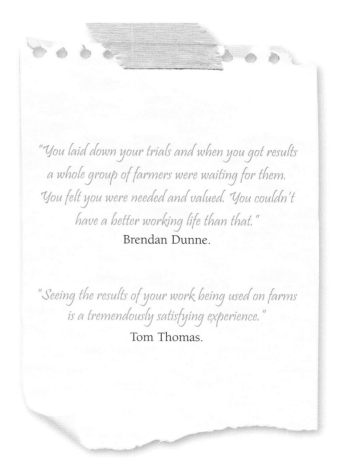

"You laid down your trials and when you got results a whole group of farmers were waiting for them. You felt you were needed and valued. You couldn't have a better working life than that."
Brendan Dunne.

"Seeing the results of your work being used on farms is a tremendously satisfying experience."
Tom Thomas.

Improved varieties in respect of root yield, sugar content and sugar extractability were produced in the sugar beet breeding unit in Thurles. The successful programme was initiated by Bernard Crombie and carried forward by Larry O'Connor and Pat Fitzgerald. Weed control research, started by Tom Thomas in 1960, coincided with the development of pre-emergence herbicides, followed by the introduction of selective post-emergence herbicides, leading to the development of techniques which could give season-long control of virtually all annual weeds. By the mid-1970s, all crops were sprayed pre-emergence.

Seed treatment to protect sugar beet seedlings from disease and pest damage was also crucial to the successful use of monogerm seed and sowing to a stand. Albert Feeney identified the main pests of sugar beet seedlings in Ireland and, in conjunction with the Sugar Company, was highly influential in developing effective control measures.

Tom Thomas remarked: *"As well as delivering a good income, sugar beet was also a very important part of the crop rotation. In fact, malting barley and sugar beet became the basis for the farming economy in a number of tillage areas, particularly Wexford, over a long period."*

Work done from the late-1970s helped to push yields further. An example of this was work by Jimmy Burke on the factors affecting sugar loss and quality deterioration during storage, which led to a more efficient system for scheduling the beet harvest as well as a storage system for sugar beet that shortened the beet harvesting season by over four weeks. In the early-2000s, the better growers were achieving yields of 70 tonnes per hectare (28 tonnes/acre), nearly three times the levels in 1960 with additional significant improvements in overall sugar yield, quality and extractability.

"Our better growers were matching the yields of their counterparts in England, Holland and Belgium. Unfortunately, the relatively small scale of the Irish sugar operation along with drastic alterations to the EU sugar beet regime saw the closure of the Irish sugar beet industry in 2007. It would be wrong to say that sugar beet ceased in Ireland because our farmers were not able to attain top yields", said Burke.

Expanding the Crop Base

Oak Park has also been to the forefront in devising production strategies for a range of new and industrial crops. In the 1960s, spring and winter varieties of oilseed rape were tested by Michael Neenan but yields of 2.5 tonnes/ha for the best varieties were not sufficient to make the crop viable at that time. As a result of improved winter varieties the crop did become viable and was sown by a number of specialist growers in the 1980s. More recent work has provided growers with a non-cereal break crop that has the potential to both produce oil for human consumption and for the emerging bio-fuels market although profitability still remains the main barrier to increased acreage.

Other crops tested by Michael Neenan and later by Jim Crowley included linseed, camelina, poppy, sunflower, soya bean and crambe. With the exception of camelina, these crops did not offer much promise in Ireland. Flax and hemp were also tested as fibre crops and reached the stage where a small commercial project was established in Bunclody by former AFT chairman, Rory Murphy. While a total technology package was developed by Michael Neenan, the worldwide collapse of the natural fibres market terminated the project. In the early years of the new millennium, there is now renewed interest in natural fibres so the wheel has turned full circle.

The introduction of maize as a fodder crop to Ireland in the late 1970s offered a high quality alternative winter feed to dairy and beef producers. However, maize is not suited to the relatively low spring soil temperatures that occur in Ireland and the early results were disappointing. The limiting factors at that time were suitable varieties for Irish conditions. In the mid-1990s, research into the use of plastic mulches and new varieties showed that high yielding, high quality crops can be produced consistently.

Leaders in Potato Breeding

If you are on holidays in any country in the Mediterranean region or in the Canary Islands you are quite likely to be served potatoes that were bred at Oak Park. Harry Kehoe, who joined AFT in 1960, led the potato breeding programme for more than 40 years and became one of Europe's most renowned potato breeders. He and his team bred more than 35 potato varieties, many of which were outstandingly successful at home and abroad and still earn significant royalties for Teagasc.

How Rooster Was Named

Like Cara and Clada, the names of many of the varieties, such as Burren, Slaney, Malin and Setanta, which were bred at Oak Park, have strong Irish associations. Others, such as Habibi, Kikko, Romeo, Galactica, Emma, Cristina, Savanna and Camelot, have more exotic names. There is a story behind the name of each variety but the background to the christening of Rooster is worth recalling.

The new variety or, to use the breeders term, the new cross, was being tried out on Owen Phelan's farm on the outskirts of Kilkenny. All it had at that stage was a seven digit number – no one had got round to thinking of a name. It was autumn 1987 and, more than 20 years later, Owen Phelan can still recall the sequence.

"After we had weighed the potatoes from the plots and after Harry Kehoe had kept back enough seed, we could always sell the rest of the crop. I gave a few of these red potatoes to a neighbour to try out. He was back within a couple of hours to tell me they were the best potatoes he ever ate and immediately bought a couple of bags."

"The following year we grew the cross again and the neighbour's commendation had spread because there was great demand for the red spuds, which still had no name. My father, Paddy Phelan, asked me what name we would put on them. Call them 5059, I said – the first four digits in the number that Harry had given them in the trial plots."

"A few minutes later, I saw him with the red marker printing ROOSTER on the paper bags. That's the name for them now' he told me, 'Rooster, always on top of the pile.' My father didn't live too long after that but he got to name the most popular potato on the market today."

The first varieties they produced were Cara and Clada. Clada was for the home market and Cara was originally for the UK. It became quite successful and took 10 per cent of acreage in England. It was also exported as seed to 15 countries in the Mediterranean region and it did very well there and in the Canary Islands. Around 15,000 tonnes of Cara seed is still sold every year and internationally it is the most successful potato variety to come out of Oak Park.

Harry Kehoe says that while Clada also did well, the fact that it was white skinned created a problem. "A lot of inferior potatoes can be passed off as good white varieties, because whites are hard to distinguish by variety. So when I was looking for a replacement for Clada, I decided to look for a red skinned potato and that is how Rooster came about", said Kehoe. Rooster now has 50 per cent of the Irish market and is taking an increasing proportion of the market in the north of England.

Plant pathologist, Leslie Dowley, who joined Oak Park soon after Harry Kehoe, provided technologies on disease prevention in potatoes. Potato blight was still a major problem in potato growing in the 1960s. Intensive investigations, initially by Carmel Frost and later by Leslie Dowley, led to the development of highly successful control strategies, which are now adopted on farms. The research also identified the development of blight fungus strains that are resistant to specific fungicides.

In more recent times, a state-of-the-art plant biotechnology facility has been established at Oak Park and scientists with expertise in key areas of biotechnology have been recruited. Greater emphasis is now placed on disease resistance in a continual drive to lower chemical inputs. New technology such as marker-aided selection and the sequencing of the potato genome, which Teagasc is now researching, will greatly aid the selection of new high-performing disease resistant varieties thereby enhancing the effectiveness of potato breeding.

More than 35 potato varieties have been bred at Oak Park.

Success in Grass Breeding

Oak Park also acquired an international reputation in clover and grass breeding. The scientist who led this activity for more than 40 years was Vincent Connolly. He produced a number of highly respected white clovers, acknowledged for their long growing season and their persistency. The Aran variety is widely grown across Europe as well as in Australia and New Zealand. Susi and Chieftain are popular in Ireland and the United Kingdom. Other Connolly-bred varieties include Emeraude and Pirouette.

He also bred many successful varieties of perennial ryegrass. Among these are Millenium, popular across Europe and in Australia and New Zealand. Green Gold is widely grown in Ireland and the UK while two newer varieties, Magician and Glenstal, are taking an increasing share of international markets. Other Oak Park varieties of ryegrass include Cashel and Shandon.

Testing the Machines

Testing of machines was one of the earliest services set up by AFT. At the first two meetings of the AFT Council, on August 19th and September 9th 1958, the issue of research on farm mechanisation and testing of machines was one of the dominant issues. A new era of farm mechanisation was getting underway with machines being imported from Holland, Denmark and Germany. They were designed for conditions very different to those in Ireland. Importers and agents knew little about the capability of the new machines and neither did the farmers who were buying them. Therefore, an independent specialist testing service was an urgent necessity.

The new service was established in 1959, with Brendan Cunney as its first recruit. He was joined soon afterwards by Pat Comerford, Tony Fortune and Bernard Rice.

In the early years, the unit was part of the rural economy division but was later transferred to the crops research division at Oak Park. The role of the unit was to set standards so that farmers would know that the machines on sale would actually work on their farms.

Bernard Rice remembers that grass machines imported from continental Europe ran into particular problems. *"There were a lot of difficulties with mowers and silage making equipment. Many of the forage wagons that came in were built for a light crop of fairly dry material on dry ground. When they were confronted with old Irish grassland with a thick, wet butt, they just weren't able to perform. The manufacturers had to adapt these machines, or else the imports came to an end."*

The manufacturers who followed AFT advice and adapted their machines to suit Irish conditions found a ready market in an Irish agriculture that was expanding rapidly. Many of the continental manufacturers came to use Ireland as a testing ground. The maxim was: "If it will work in Ireland, it will work anywhere". In fact, Ireland's reputation as a tough environment for machines gave valuable credibility to Irish farm machinery makers when, a generation later, they went out in search of world markets. The high standards imposed by the Oak Park engineers also provided a valuable assurance.

Wetland Machines

As mechanisation became more sophisticated through the decades, Oak Park continued to provide operational guidelines to manufacturers and farmers on the full range of machinery for tillage, grass, silage, hay and winter feeding. A lot of emphasis was placed on machinery for different types of farming. One example was work done by Dermot Forristal, who joined the team in the 1970's, on the development of machines that would travel on soft ground.

The result of the research, carried out on the AFT wetland research farms at Kilmaley in Clare and Ballinamore in Leitrim, was a set of machinery adaptations that now allow farmers and contractors to work on land where, a generation ago, machines could not venture.

Work by Dermot Forristal and others has also ensured that farmers are more conscious of machinery costs. Detailed Oak Park assessments of machinery costs on a wide range of farming systems are now being widely used by farmers in making machinery purchase decisions. Researchers and their advisory colleagues continue to play an important role in defining how the latest technology in farm mechanisation should be adopted by farmers as they strive to keep tight control of costs.

Crops for Fuel

Veteran researcher, Bernard Rice, probably holds the world record for the length of time that he spent investigating bio-fuels. Bernard and his colleagues at Oak Park were investigating bio-energy long before its real significance was appreciated. When the first oil crisis happened in the early-1970s, there was a lot of research internationally on alternative fuel sources. But oil was still incredibly cheap and when it got plentiful again, the alarm died down and much of the research worldwide was put to bed until the next crisis. There were no worries back then about environment, greenhouse gases or global warming. At Oak Park, Michael Neenan was in charge of the earliest trials on growing willow for biomass. His work on varieties, cultural practices and disease control led to the development of growing blueprints that are still relevant today.

The relatively small bio-fuels research programme that was maintained at Oak Park since the 1980s by Bernard Rice has resulted in valuable information now that oil prices are steadily rising, there are real concerns about climate change and there is economic and political pressure to devote some land to renewable energy.

Work at Oak Park on bio-diesel production from low cost materials, such as recycled cooking oil and animal fats, has led to the establishment in 2008 of a bio-diesel plant in New Ross.

Miscanthus research, started by Jimmy Burke and Tom Thomas in the early-1990s and still ongoing, is yielding invaluable long-term information. If crops for bio-energy can compete with crops for food in the future, Irish farmers have the technology to grow them.

Shaping the Future

As it enters the second half of its first century in research, Oak Park is well equipped to provide the scientific leadership to enable the Irish tillage sector to maintain its position at the forefront of grain growing and in harnessing new opportunities in plant breeding and in alternative sources of energy. The centre's new state-of-the-art plant biotechnology facility opens the door to the use of genetic fingerprinting in further increasing yields of cereals through more focused and cost-effective disease control and in breeding higher yielding, higher quality and more disease-resistant varieties of grasses, clovers and potatoes.

Facilities on their own are of little use without the scientific expertise to exploit them. In recent years, scientists with skills and international experience in plant biotechnology have joined the Oak Park research team. They include Dan Milbourne, Susanne Barth, Emma Guiney and Ewen Mullins, who are leading a 20-strong team of scientists and post-graduates. The facilities and expertise are also in place to provide clear scientific data that will enable informed debate on the benefits and risks of genetically modified crops and, if deemed appropriate, to formulate guidelines on the use of these crops in Ireland.

The development of second-generation bio-fuels is also a key part of the new research portfolio where newly recruited scientists John Finnan and John Carroll are collaborating with research groups in the universities in exploring a range of possibilities including the transformation of lingo-cellulose into bio-ethanol. Other new areas include the development of novel plants designed specifically for energy purposes as well as the production of other high-value bio-molecules, chemicals and pharmaceuticals. The focus on the new sciences combined with the long-established expertise in agronomy, physiology, breeding and pathology ensures that Oak Park is set to remain at the leading edge of research and development.

Delegates at the Congress of the European Society for Rural Sociology, organised by the AFT rural economy division and held in Maynooth in 1966. It was the first time that women were allowed to sleep in the rooms of the seminary.

CHAPTER 8

FIFTY YEARS OF ECONOMIC AND RURAL DEVELOPMENT RESEARCH

Brendan Kearney

When AFT established the rural economy division in 1959, the Irish economy was reaching the end of a decade of despondency and gloom. The agricultural sector was characterised by low growth, traditional methods of production and little by way of innovation. Farm incomes were in a very depressed state as shown in the first National Farm Survey conducted in 1955 and there was little by way of improvement in the remaining years of the 1950s. There was a dearth of knowledge on the economics of the sector, on the relative costs and returns and efficiency in the different enterprises, on the markets for and the marketing of the main farm products, on the organisation and structure of production and on how the sector was adjusting to developments in the wider economy and society.

In the previous year, the First Programme for Economic Expansion was published with its emphasis on achieving maximum economic progress by *"stimulating public interest and support, ensuring co-ordination of effort and limiting the scope for misunderstanding and inconsistency"*. In Europe, two groups of countries, the European Economic Community (EEC) and the European Free Trade Association (EFTA), had recently come together to further their economic, social, and political interests. The EEC was a much more comprehensive grouping embracing an initially limited common policy framework, of which the Common Agricultural Policy was the overwhelmingly dominant feature. That policy, either in anticipation of its potential impact or in regard to its eventual effects, was destined to have a paramount influence on the fortunes of Irish agriculture and the research carried out by the fledgling rural economy division.

This was the national and international context in which the early economists and sociologists framed their research programmes. Jim Byrne was appointed as first chief of the division in early 1959 and he was joined soon afterwards by economist, Ted Atwood, who later went on to become chief economist at the Department of Agriculture. The early programmes were focused on developing baseline information on key aspects of farm production and in investigating how Ireland could enhance its trading position in the context of changing supply and demand conditions in the major importing countries. The home market also received some attention, particularly in regard to consumer trends and distribution.

Early Teething Problems

At that time, economic research and analysis was in its infancy. The Economic and Social Research Institute (ESRI) was not even established until 1960, two years after AFT. So, there was always going to be some teething problems. As early as 1961, the division experienced difficulty in recruiting and retaining staff with the necessary qualifications and training for research in agricultural economics. The call for extra resources was only partially met and this and other issues led to a somewhat turbulent birth for the division culminating in the departure of the first chief of division in 1961.

There were no qualified agricultural economists available in the late-1950s and early-1960s as this option was not in the university curriculum in Ireland at that time. Therefore, the vast majority of the research staff recruited in the early years did not have a professional agricultural dimension to their third-level qualification. While this in no way reflected on the technical competence or research ability of the staff concerned, it was felt important that a blend of agricultural expertise should be incorporated into the research capability. This led to the recruitment of a number of agricultural graduates in the early-1960s, all of whom were sent to the United States for further training in agricultural economics and related disciplines, under the aegis of the Kellogg Foundation Support Programme for Ireland.

Advisers attending a seminar run by the AFT farm buildings department.

Tomás Breathnach was appointed chief of division in 1961 and, under his stewardship, the research programmes evolved quite rapidly mainly led by the industrious, versatile and prolific Ted Attwood. Ted had a voracious appetite for hard work, and in those early years, had a prodigious output of papers and publications. He was strongly supported by John Heavey, the first agriculturalist to be recruited to the research staff. John would be inextricably linked with the National Farm Survey for the next two decades or more.

National Farm Survey

Since its inception, the National Farm Survey has had the greatest impact on the economic research programme and has been given the biggest resource commitment. As well as providing comprehensive information on trends in farm incomes, costs and productivity, it became an invaluable resource to research staff working across all the farm enterprises in assessing production trends and in developing research programmes to address the needs of different types of farmers and enterprises.

It also became a vital source of information for the advisory service and for companies providing services to farmers and was used by governments and policy makers in framing agricultural policy. Almost 50 years later, the National Farm Survey is still a vital resource to the agriculture and food industry. John Heavey was followed as head of the survey by Dick Power and, in more recent times, by Liam Connolly who heads the survey team today.

Also central to the organisation and analysis of the survey from the early days was Barth Hickey, who later became the production economist on the beef enterprise. Another key member of the survey team from the outset was Maurice Roche, who remained a dedicated and indispensable member of the unit until recent times.

In addition to the survey, the establishment of which was a major undertaking, the early economic research portfolio ranged from enterprise and farm management studies to projects on the structure of farming and the factors of production. The need to provide the individual farmer with specific information to achieve high levels of economic and technical efficiency led later to the introduction of management information systems and a farm management manual.

Socio-Economic Sceptics

Of any body of research associated with the agricultural sector, the socio-economic dimension is usually the most controversial and so it has been proven in the case of the research history of the rural economy division. From the outset, some farm spokespersons were of the view that only projects which related to "putting money into farmers pockets" were worthy of inclusion in the research programme while projects having welfare or distributional dimensions or overtones, or those concerning the wider rural economy, were occasionally frowned upon or even viewed with hostility.

The first major study on rural development was the West Cork Resource Survey where the division's economists and sociologists combined with other scientists to undertake an appraisal of the area's demographic, economic and physical resources and to make recommendations to enhance the economic and social development of the area. Studies on the Congested Districts and other area research surveys also featured in the early years. Pakie Commins, who joined AFT in 1960 as the first rural sociologist, was one of the key people involved in these studies and went on to become a major figure nationally and internationally in rural development research.

Responding to the Trading Environment

Ireland's agricultural sector suffered frustrating times in the early-1960s with an unfavourable trading environment. Failure of the application to join the EEC was compounded by the involvement of the UK in the EFTA. The substantial protection being given to Britain's own farmers and Ireland's difficulty in gaining access to export markets had a serious impact on prices and farm incomes. Revised trade arrangements were negotiated between Britain and Ireland resulting in the Anglo-Irish Free Trade Agreement of December 1965 and this greatly improved trading relations. The increasing interest in export markets unleashed a plethora of studies by economists in the rural economy division on the market situation for the main farm products in Europe and the prospects for the main farm enterprises in Ireland. These studies provided important information on the potential for exports and on the relative efficiency of Irish agriculture.

Short-term forecasting was also incorporated in the research programme in the early-1960s and was later significantly expanded to a review and outlook analysis for the main farm enterprises and the agricultural economy. Among the key players involved in these studies in the 1960s and who helped to establish the identity of the centre were Aidan Power, Micheál Ross, Rosemary Fennel, Fergus O'Neill, Barbara O'Carroll and Síle O'Neill.

Economic Test Farms

The first in a series of economic test farms was established in Herbertstown, Co Limerick in 1960. The farm became a model for the application of new dairying technology emanating from Moorepark research centre. It was followed by the establishment of similar economic test farms in Ballinalack, Co Westmeath on beef production; in Drumboylan, Co Roscommon on dairy farming on drumlin soils; in Blindwell, Co Galway on sheep production, and in Castledermot, Co. Kildare on tillage farming. The farms, which were established to assist in assessing the economic value of new farming techniques and systems, became important locations for the demonstration of efficient farming practices and were visited by tens of thousands of farmers during the following 25 years. They involved strong collaboration between leading researchers in dairying, beef, sheep and tillage and economists and farm management specialists in the rural economy division. In 1971, their operation was taken over by the appropriate enterprise research centres.

Towards the late-1960s, comprehensive marketing research was undertaken, particularly in the dairy sector, with studies on the costs of milk assembly and the economics of milk utilisation and processing being undertaken by Tom O'Dwyer, one of the agriculturalists who joined in the early-1960s and had participated in post-graduate training in marketing in the United States. Tom later went on to an illustrious career in the European Commission and has served as Chairman of Teagasc since 1998. During the 1960s, economists also assembled a lot of valuable information on the domestic marketing of cattle and on trends in cattle supply. The Department of Agriculture was not pleased at the findings of one particular marketing study that forecast a surplus of cattle in the autumn of 1967. This was a politically sensitive topic in the context of the previously negotiated Anglo-Irish Free Trade Agreement. However, the exercise was repeated the following year without any fuss or negative reaction.

Billy Fingleton, who specialised in the economics of dairying for much of his 40 years in the rural economy centre.

Changing the Focus

Personnel changes in the late-1960s and early-1970s saw Denis Conniffe taking over from Tomás Breathnach as head of the centre while Ted Atwood had moved to the then Department of Agriculture and Fisheries. Andy Conway, another of the early recruits who had also gone to the United States for post-graduate training, had taken over

responsibility for the economics programme and Tom O'Dwyer was in charge of the marketing component. They were supported by experienced researchers like Fergus O'Neill, Pat Cox, Michael Keane, Cathal Cowan, Brendan Riordan, Frank Bradley and Michael Igoe. The centre was now called the economics and rural welfare centre, presumably to signal a greater focus on rural development issues.

The main focus of marketing studies until then was on the major commodities – butter, bacon, live cattle and beef – reflecting their dominance in our home and export markets. A considerable body of marketing information had also been amassed on key areas of the horticulture sector.

Following entry to the
EEC, the focus changed to consumer studies and
the need to increase the flow of market information
to consumers. Later, changes in the traditional channels
of trade and newer meat technologies were mirrored in
projects on vacuum packed beef and the development of
specifications for wholesale cuts to comply with butchery
practices in some of the major markets in Europe.
Meanwhile, the rural sociology programme had begun
to give growing attention to the small and low-income
farm problems.

EEC entry also brought the requirement for the economic
data in the National Farm Survey to be provided each year
to the EEC Farm Accounts Data Network, a requirement
that still applies today. The publication of the survey
had by then become a high point in the annual AFT and
agricultural calendar and the quality and reliability of the
information ensured there was no difficulty in complying
fully with the EEC requirement.

Disseminating the Information

From the beginning, there was heavy emphasis in
disseminating the results of research to the widest possible audience.
This was done through publication of scientific papers in international
research journals, including the Irish Journal of Agricultural
Economics and Rural Sociology, which had been launched in
1967 and became an important outlet for research staff.
The results of all research projects were also disseminated in
publications of various sizes to farmers, advisers and all sectors
of the agriculture and food industry as well as to policy makers.
Research staff were also in great demand as speakers at
conferences and on radio and television programmes and
were prolific writers in the national and agricultural media
on a vast range of topics on agriculture, food and rural affairs.

In 1974, the first annual Rural Economy Conference was launched
as a forum for disseminating the results of research and for discussion
with and feedback from key stakeholders. It focused on
change and adjustment in the rural economy, including an
examination of the new EU directives. Aspects such as
preservation of the environment also featured.
Over the following 15 years, these conferences were an annual
meeting point for leading executives in the industry, the
farming organisations, advisers and key policy makers and
were organised by the capable Ann Confrey.

They were not always to everybody's liking. We had the negative
reaction of a prominent member of the AFT Council to
a paper delivered at the 1976 conference by sociologists,
Patricia O'Hara and Carmel Kelleher, on adjustment
problems of low income farmers. The comment was: "sure what
would these girls know about farming." In 1977, the then
Deputy President of the IFA, Joe Rea, described a paper
by this author on the efficiency of milk production and the
constraints on expansion as "an exercise in stargazing."
The then chief economist of the IFA, Lorcan Blake, did not
entirely concur with the assessment.

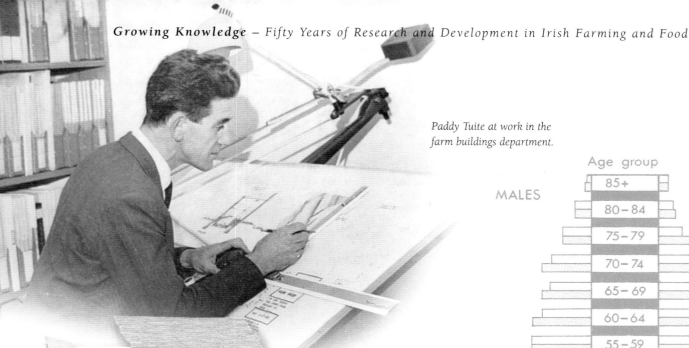

Paddy Tuite at work in the farm buildings department.

Farm Buildings and the Environment

Research on farm buildings was an integral component of the work of the rural economy centre form the beginning. During the 1960s and 1970s, a group of engineers and architects, led by Paddy Tuite, produced blueprints on alternate systems of livestock accommodation and on the control of farm sources of water pollution. Attention was also given to the development of efficient and inexpensive waste management systems and to the renovation, alteration, renewal and heating of farm dwellings. A major proportion of the department's time and resources were employed in specialist advisory work covering hundreds of cases, many of which involved visits to farms. The main players in that department were Vincent Dodd, Andy Kavanagh, Tony McGrane, Fearghal O'Farrell and later Owen Daly.

As far back as the 1970s, an experimental passive solar house was erected at Oak Park designed to utilise the natural advantages of an open site to conserve energy. Later, as concern on environmental protection increased, a handbook was produced on the impact of farm buildings on the environment. It outlined the possibilities that existed for the farming community to contribute to and enhance the rural environment and landscape. It presaged the huge emphasis which was increasingly being placed on farming and the environment, culminating in the introduction of the rural environment protection scheme (REPS), which today has some 60,000 farmer participants. Nevertheless, a leading agricultural journalist of the day scoffed at the publication and suggested that the resources employed in its preparation would be better employed elsewhere.

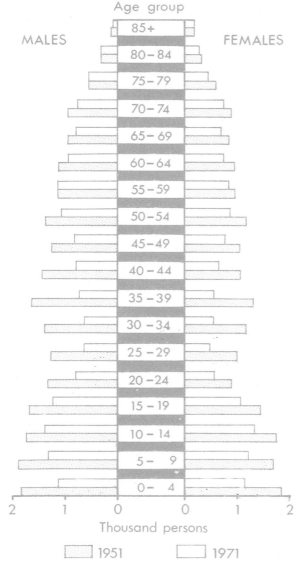

A 1970s paper by the Economics and Rural Welfare Research Centre showed the contraction in almost every age group in county Leitrim between 1951 and 1971.

The National Farm Survey team in 1980: Liam Connolly, director Pierce Ryan, Michael Harkin, John Heavey and Maurice Roche.

Shift in Research Funding

The following years marked the beginning of a shift from a completely public-funded research programme to a combination of public and private funding. In the mid-1970s, up to a third of staff resources were devoted to research funded by the industry. This showed the recognition by industry of the economic, marketing and sociological expertise in AFT. It was also a reflection of national budgetary constraints and the growing need for researchers to 'earn their own keep'. The centre was also involved in a number of important national and EEC initiatives. An example was the provision of analysis and other management services to the fledgling Irish Farm Accounts Co-operative (IFAC), which today is a major provider of accounting services to farmers nationwide.

The centre also became a partner, under the guidance of Mick Harkin, in the EEC Harmonised Consumer Survey, the purpose of which was to monitor trends in consumer spending, savings and living standards. A further illustration of the service provision of the centre was the establishment of Agriline, which was a system for disseminating and retrieving computer-based information using telephone lines for communications and television sets for displaying the information.

Following completion of Ireland's transition to full EEC membership in the late-1970s, the research programme placed emphasis on the analysis of output response to price changes and on measures to increase efficiency of production. The large increase in farm incomes from 1974 to 1978 had more to do with higher output prices than any increase in the volume or efficiency of production. Consequently, the research programme was adopted to focus more on the factors influencing farm performance and efficiency. A study by Jim Frawley on the issues influencing farmers' adoption of recommended farm practices and improved technology is an example of the work carried out during this period. There was also a stronger focus on rural and regional development while the land market was the subject of a number of studies relating to patterns of transfer and prices, with important studies by Paul Kelly and Jim Higgins. These included the establishment for the first time in Ireland of a land price series and an examination of the factors determining the price of land. The channels of communication from the consumer back to the producer were also given attention.

When this author took over as head of the centre in 1980, about two-thirds of research personnel were involved to a greater or lesser extent in projects funded by domestic or EEC sources, reflecting the squeeze in funding from the national exchequer. Research highlights in that period include comparative studies on Irish farming and that in other EEC countries, which provided vital benchmark information for the production research programme, for advisers, farmers and the industry as a whole. A particular example was a major study on the dairy sector with respect to price comparisons and technical performance by Michael Keane, Eamon Pitts, Billy Fingleton and Paul Kelly. In the study on price comparisons, the average gap in milk prices being attained in Ireland and that in six other member states corresponded to a difference of about 10 per cent of the target price for milk, with the cost of milk assembly being substantially higher in Ireland. The centre was also commissioned by the Cereals Authority of Ireland to provide a market information service, which was largely initiated by Liam Dunne and consisted of the provision of a series of regular bulletins.

Incomes and Funding Downturn

The early 1980s were characterised by a major downturn in farm incomes and this received much attention in the centre programme. For example, economists undertook a major study for the National Economic and Social Council (NESC) on farm incomes and on the policy adjustments that could effectively narrow the gap between farm and non-farm incomes. Productivity studies as well as rural development and part-time farming issues also gained prominence in the programme at this time. Gerry Boyle established procedures for measuring productivity and the technical efficiency of Irish agriculture as well as the returns on investment in agricultural research. This work established the foundation of much of Teagasc's work on competitiveness over the following years.

outlook studies continued to feature. The sensitivity of the farming organisations to income forecasts in particular is well illustrated when, in 1987, a significant income recovery was forecast, it incurred the wrath of a prominent farm leader who used colourful language to equate the timing of the exercise as similar to the arrival of a certain equine stinging insect when weather conditions take a turn for the better!

The economic and policy analysis capability of the centre was now well recognised and this resulted in its involvement in a number of major national and international reports and events. These included a significant contribution to an NESC project on a Strategy for Development 1986-1990 and a major input into a national seminar on agricultural policy, organised on behalf of Taoiseach, Garret Fitzgerald, in 1986. By then, the first stages of what were to become radical changes in agricultural policy had begun to take place. The imposition of the milk quota in 1984 fundamentally changed the focus of the research programme with the holding of a dedicated conference on the issue and the execution of a succession of projects that helped to develop a national strategy for maximising profit from milk in an era of static output. The bulk of this work was undertaken by Andy Conway, Gerry Boyle, Billy Fingleton and Lynn Killen.

The 1984 annual centre conference was devoted exclusively to marketing issues, especially changing consumer trends and attitudes, and market issues in the dairy and beef sectors. More intensive work was also conducted during this period on part-time farming, rural social services, alternative sources of farm income, rural development and environmental protection, reflecting the changing agenda. The incorporation of food issues into world trade talks also led to a number of studies on international trade and the comparative efficiency of Irish agriculture. Situation and

Half a Century of Change

Since the establishment of AFT in 1958, there have been dramatic changes in agriculture and its place in the national economy. The proportion of the labour force working in agriculture has fallen from 36 per cent to just over 5 per cent while the primary agricultural sector has declined from 25 per cent to a little over 2 per cent of national income over the 50-year period. The shrinkage in the contribution of agriculture to the national economy has been particularly pronounced over the past 15 years or so because of the rapid and unprecedented growth in employment and national output in the rest of the economy.

While the farm labour force has declined almost three-quarters, from 420,000 in 1958 to around 115,000 today, the volume of agricultural output has risen by 130 per cent. Labour productivity has, in consequence, risen eightfold over the period. Incidentally, the growth rate in output was about three times faster in the period before the introduction of the dairy quota in 1984 than in the two decades since.

There have also been big changes in the structure of farming. The change in the number of farm holdings has been much slower than in the labour force, falling by a little more than half, from an estimated 270,000 in 1958 to about 131,000 in 2007. Meanwhile, the role of part-time farming has grown in importance from about 10 per cent of all farms at the foundation of AFT to roughly 40 per cent today. In the wider rural economy, the most positive development has been the stabilisation of the rural population in those rural electoral districts where formerly continuing decline was the norm.

The Exodus of Staff

The late-1980s was a traumatic time for the centre. The merging of AFT and ACOT into Teagasc in 1988 and the accompanying drastic cut in financing from the national exchequer resulted in a large-scale exodus of staff from the centre. Some took up employment in other areas of the public sector while others availed of a voluntary early retirement scheme and moved to the private sector. In the first few years after the establishment of Teagasc, economic and rural development research received little support from the higher echelons of the governing authority and often its programme was treated with indifference and even disdain.

Despite these setbacks a number of important studies were undertaken. Pakie Commins, who had taken over from this author as the head of centre in 1989, and Jim Frawley published a major report on the changing structure of Irish farming. They classified farms according to their economic and demographic viability and presented scenarios for the following decade. Another major landmark study to which economists and rural development researchers made a substantial contribution was a report on developing the rural economy for the NESC, which laid the foundations for the first White Paper on Rural Development in 1998 and eventually the National Spatial Strategy in 2002. This put particular focus on adopting a territorial approach to rural development policy.

With more resources from the Structural Funds and other EU sources, the centre programme began to move up a gear and more studies were undertaken on competitiveness, particularly in the pig, dairy, sheep and tillage enterprises. A wide range of market studies on consumer behaviour, value-added foods and food industry competitiveness was also undertaken at the National Food Centre, which had taken over responsibility for marketing research soon after the establishment of Teagasc.

A New Beginning

The programme area that has most transformed the work of the centre over the past decade or so has been the FAPRI project. It arose from a visit of the Taoiseach, John Bruton, to the Food and Agricultural Policy Research Institute at the University of Missouri. He was highly impressed with the ability to analyse policy options using models of world commodity markets. Coincidentally, Bruton's economic adviser at the time was professor Gerry Boyle, the current director of Teagasc and he played an influential role in establishing the basis for the subsequent development of the FAPRI-Ireland partnership.

Following negotiations between Teagasc and the University of Missouri, the FAPRI-Ireland partnership was established in 1997. Three new economists, Kevin Hanrahan, Trevor Donnellan and Thia Hennessy were recruited and, with the guidance of Robert Young, a leading member of the FAPRI team in Missouri, the new economic and policy analysis service was bedded down. The overall leader of the project was Brendan Riordan, a long-serving member of the rural economy centre since the early days of AFT. Led by Teagasc, the partnership also involved the major universities.

The FAPRI project immediately began to bear fruit with a conference on the outlook for agriculture in December 1998. Since then, the unit has recruited additional economists and has carried out a large number of studies, including the impact of the Berlin (Agenda 2000) Agreement of 1999, the analysis of the Luxembourg CAP

Reform Agreement, the analysis of various WTO reform scenarios and the implications of various milk quota and other policy options. The unit has also produced a number of income and outlook studies. Since its inception, it has played an important role in assisting the government in crucial EU and world trade negotiations.

An Expanding Programme

The rural economy research centre, as it is now called, was led by Eamon Pitts during the late-1990s and early-2000s. It relocated from Dublin to Athenry in 2004 and, under the leadership of Cathal O'Donoghue, the current head of the centre, the research programme has been substantially expanded and new economic and analytical expertise has been added in several areas.

Among the recent innovations is the creation of a spatial analysis unit using advanced geographical information systems and remote sensing to map agricultural and environmental data. There is a renewed focus on rural sociology and the impact of environmental issues is now one of the research programme priorities. The centre is also working closely with the Teagasc advisory service in evaluating and improving methods of technology transfer.

The high-level modelling capacity has continued to expand. An example of a new feature is a simulation model of the Irish local economy, which has the capacity to assess how farmers and rural dwellers react to economic, environmental and rural development policy changes. The FAPRI model has incorporated new dimensions such as greenhouse gas emissions and has been pivotal in negotiations at government level on the effect of climate change policy on agriculture. The National Farm Survey remains the backbone of the analytical capacity of the centre and has been expanded to include income from activities other than farming. Environmental data has also been added to the survey.

Following a dip in the resources devoted to economic and rural development research throughout the late-1980s and 1990s, the rural economy research centre is again a key component of the research, advisory and training infrastructure. Throughout the past 50 years, it can justifiably take pride in having done the state some service, thanks to its dedicated staff, many of whom spent all or most of their working lives serving the interests and committed to the welfare of the rural economy.

Kieran Kilcawley ascertains odour
characteristics of cheese at Moorepark.

CHAPTER 9

BUILDING WORLD CLASS ABILITY IN FOOD RESEARCH

Brian Gilsenan

Compared to the high profile activities in agricultural research in the early years of AFT, food research had more humble beginnings. The emphasis on developing the science that would improve grassland management, crop production and animal management was regarded as the main national priority in the late-1950s and early-1960s. As a result, the early food scientists had to play second fiddle to their farm production colleagues.

Sean Egan examining shelf-life of tomatoes.

AUGUST-SEPTEMBER 1990   Price £2.50 (including tax)

FARM & FOOD
RESEARCH Teagasc

Factors Affecting Silage Effluent P
Observations on the Quality of La
Developments in Butter and Dairy
A New Foliar Disease of Oats 28

Kay Cormican, Kinsealy, preparing samples of a new food product developed at Moorepark for taste panel evaluation.

Notwithstanding that, the early scientists did important and valuable work. Reflecting the times, it was of a more basic nature than the high tech activities that characterise much of food research today. Fifty years ago, the major pre-occupation was the quality of milk and meat. Very poor quality milk and toughness and flavour of meat were causing headaches for the food industry and these dominated the work of food scientists in the 1960s and 1970s. As Liam Donnelly, current director of food research in Teagasc puts it: *"These problems may seem trivial today, but they were major barriers to the development of the food industry where butter, beef and bacon dominated exports."*

Food research advanced through the 1980s but was still overshadowed by farm production. It was not until the 1990s that a major shift in emphasis took place and since then substantial investment in staff and facilities has been undertaken in the two food research centres at Moorepark, Fermoy and Ashtown, Dublin. Further investment of €30 million, which is underway as this book goes to print, will further enhance capability in food research and development. Half of the research scientists in Teagasc are now working in the two food centres and food research accounts for around 20 per cent of total Teagasc expenditure on research, advisory and training services. Food scientists are also among the leading competitors for research funding from the EU and other sources.

The other big development in recent years is the collaboration between food researchers in Teagasc and universities in Ireland and internationally. For example, close linkages between Moorepark and University College Cork has put Irish scientists at the forefront internationally in research on food and health. Teagasc food scientists are now involved with many multinational companies. Three of the top four infant formula manufacturers and seven of the top 10 food companies in the world are numbered among their clients.

The Early Scientists

Michael Mulcahy and Michael Carroll were the first two food scientists to be appointed by AFT. Mulcahy was given the task of establishing a dairy processing research facility at Moorepark while Carroll's job was to establish a meat research section, first at the Department of Agriculture's laboratories in Thorndale on the northside of Dublin and later at nearby Dunsinea, which is now the home of the Ashtown food centre. Both started from a blank canvas.

Michael Mulcahy recalls that apart from the serious problems with milk quality and its consequent effect on the quality of butter and other dairy products, there was suspicion and some animosity from the dairy processing industry about the new 'scientific messiahs'. The Department of Agriculture was also less than forthcoming in its support, mainly because they felt that AFT director, Tom Walsh, who was moving at breathtaking speed in setting up research centres, was hell bent on taking over everything in the industry. Skill and diplomacy helped to break down these initial barriers and good working relationships were built up fairly quickly with industry and the department.

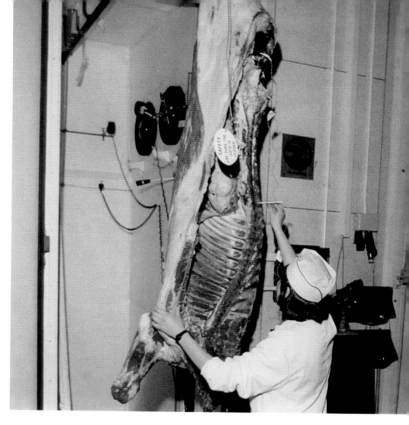

Michael Carroll, who came to AFT from Reading University and also had taught in the butchery school in Smithfield Meat College in London, began to identify the immediate skills to underpin a research programme that would tackle meat quality problems. The first two meat scientists appointed were Vincent McLoughlin and Robin Joseph. In Moorepark, Michael Mulcahy was joined by Conor McGann and Matt Murphy. These six scientists formed the nucleus of the AFT food research programme in the early years.

Improving Product Quality

As Moorepark scientists in the milk production area conducted an all-out campaign to improve hygiene, machine milking and disease prevention practices at farm level, their colleagues in dairy processing began to develop the technologies to underpin the manufacture and keeping quality of dairy products. Liam Downey, who joined the food science team a few years after Moorepark was established and later became director of ACOT and Teagasc, recalls that in the 1960s there was little or no knowledge about the quality, keeping quality or the storage ability of dairy products. Methods for measuring fat and protein levels in milk were very slow, involving scientists and technicians labouring over a laboratory bench for two or three days. One of the first notable breakthroughs in this area was work by Conor McGann with a company called Foss Electric in developing automated systems for measuring the constituents in milk. These systems became universally used throughout the dairy industry.

In the 1960s, most milk went into butter and much of the early work was concentrated on the factors affecting the keeping quality of butter, which was a major problem for the dairy industry. At that stage, butter was wrapped in parchment and when stored in supermarket cabinets the constant light penetrated the wrapping and caused oxidation and bad flavour. Moorepark scientists solved the problem by wrapping the butter in foil. An Bord Bainne, now the Irish Dairy Board, was then in the process of developing the famous Kerrygold brand and it is no coincidence that from day one all Kerrygold butter was wrapped in foil.

The scientists also discovered that the level of copper in milk was a major determinant of the keeping quality of butter. It was found that tinned copper surface milk coolers or milking components were major contributors and this problem was eliminated by the upgrading of equipment with stainless steel instead of tinned copper. Tim Cogan, Tony O'Sullivan and Joe Phelan had now joined the team and the group embarked on a major scientific programme on the keeping quality of a range of dairy products and on new technologies for processing milk.

An example of this was work done by Liam Downey and Tim Cogan with Waterford Co-op on manufacturing lactic butter, a product not used in Ireland but had a big market in Europe. Later on, Joe Phelan worked with dairy processors on the development of more spreadable butter, or dairy spreads as they became known. He recalls the idea being frowned on initially by many in the industry, as these were not pure 'dairy' products, but competitive pressures soon forced manufacturers to include the spreads in their product mixes.

New Processing Techniques

With skim milk powder becoming a big product area following entry into the EEC, Tony O'Sullivan, Joe Phelan and later Phil Kelly worked with industry in developing new technologies and on improving the keeping quality of milk powders. A big issue was the considerable loss of product into the atmosphere from spray driers and Moorepark gave valuable assistance to manufacturers in reducing these losses and in lowering effluent. A service continues to this day to help dairy plants comply with Environmental Protection Agency (EPA) licensing. The first oil crisis in the early-1970s focused attention on energy efficiency and work by Moorepark in refining the manufacturing process helped manufacturers to halve the amount of oil needed to produce a tonne of skim milk powder.

New techniques were also developed to produce new products from whey, a by-product from cheese manufacturing. The objective was to utilise every part of the whey and one of the outcomes was the production of food quality alcohol, which was eagerly taken up by industry. Seasonality of milk production, where farmers produced 13 times more milk in summer than in winter, was creating quality and shelf-life problems with some products. Scientists helped in introducing modifications in processing that enabled the industry to confront this problem. The peak/trough ratio was eventually reduced to half of its previous level.

According to Joe Phelan, innovations in the 1970s led to a growing confidence in the dairy industry in the value of Moorepark. *"They could see measurable benefits through more efficient and new processing techniques. This, combined with the work of production researchers, led to the establishment of the dairy levy fund, a contribution by farmers that helped greatly in funding the Moorepark research programme"*, said Phelan.

Big Advances In Cheese

Tim Cogan, who spent a lifetime in cheese research, initially confronted inconsistent quality and flavour. The starters being used to ferment milk for cheese were largely mysterious cocktails of unknown bacteria. Cogan standardised starters, so that the processors would know what they were using and how they worked. A lot of work was done also on factors that influenced the flavour of cheese. The very successful Dubliner cheese, made by Carbery and marketed by the Irish Dairy Board, emerged from this research.

Another innovative venture was the introduction of microbial rennets for cheese making, instead of the traditional rennet which came from calves' stomachs. Cogan and his team also helped industry to adapt cheddar making technologies to produce other cheese varieties, such as Emmental, Leerdammer and Regato. In more recent times, the Moorepark cheese team, led by Tom Beresford, has advanced technologies further. A recent ground breaking achievement was the sequencing of the complete genetic composition of a bacterium, called *Lactobacillus helveticus*, which has strong flavour enhancing properties in cheese. This discovery also has exciting potential in the development of functional foods with health enhancing properties, such as the ability to reduce blood pressure.

Finding The Perfect Steak

The early meat scientists concentrated on quality problems in pig meat and beef. Vincent McLoughlin's first project was investigating a problem in pork called 'pale soft exudative' meat. He found that the problem was largely due to animal stress before slaughter and advised on how it could be prevented. A related issue in cattle, called 'dark dry firm' beef, which resulted in meat that could not be sold, was investigated by Vivian Tarrant, who later went on to become head of what is now the Ashtown Food Centre. *"In 1974, former Moorepark scientist, Dan Browne, who had then moved to the meat industry and was manager of the IMP plant at Midleton, showed me a row of carcasses that couldn't be sold,"* said Tarrant. Following a comprehensive investigation, Tarrant found that the problem was caused by exhaustion due to mixing of animals from different sources in the pre-slaughter period, not by weather or nerves as had been previously thought. *"By 1980, I was able to write the bible on dark cutting beef,"* he recalled.

A lot of early work was carried out by Ted Hood on vacuum packaging and pre-packing of beef. While this technology was not taken up by the industry until some time later, many of the problems, such as discolouration of meat, were ironed out by Hood and in later research by Michael O'Keeffe and Paul Allen. Meanwhile, John Dempster provided important scientific guidance to pig processors on counteracting spoilage during curing with brine and this led to a specialised curing service being provided by AFT for the bacon industry. A multi-needle brine injection system, which was widely used by the industry, was established by Brian Riordan.

Work by Robin Joseph on beef tenderness in the early years centred on hanging methods and led to the practice of hanging carcasses by the hip rather than by the Achilles tendon. Since the 1980s, Declan Troy, who is now head of Ashtown food centre, has studied tenderness and eating quality of beef in detail. He came up with the 12/12 rule – the temperature should not fall below 12 degrees in the first 12 hours of chilling. *"This ensures microbial safety and, if the carcass is left hanging for seven days, there is a 95 per cent certainty of getting tender beef,"* said Troy. He has also examined the role of enzymes in tenderising beef but they gave very variable results. Researchers are still looking for the magic probe that would give an instant tenderness reading.

One of the latest experiments on beef quality involves taking out the choice cuts and wrapping them tightly in plastic film. In this way, the cuts keep their shape in the chill and do not shrink and toughen. Called Pvac, it has been shown at research level to give high quality, tender beef much more consistently than any other system. There are also potential energy savings because the same energy is used to chill bones, fat and cheaper cuts as for high value cuts. Declan Troy feels that this new innovation could be the way forward. *"It gives consistent high quality meat and removes the cost of chilling bones."* Another area of ongoing research on meat quality is the examination of the part played by genetics in distinguishing the tough from the tender. This could lead to a more rapid test for tenderness and to better selection of animals with superior genes.

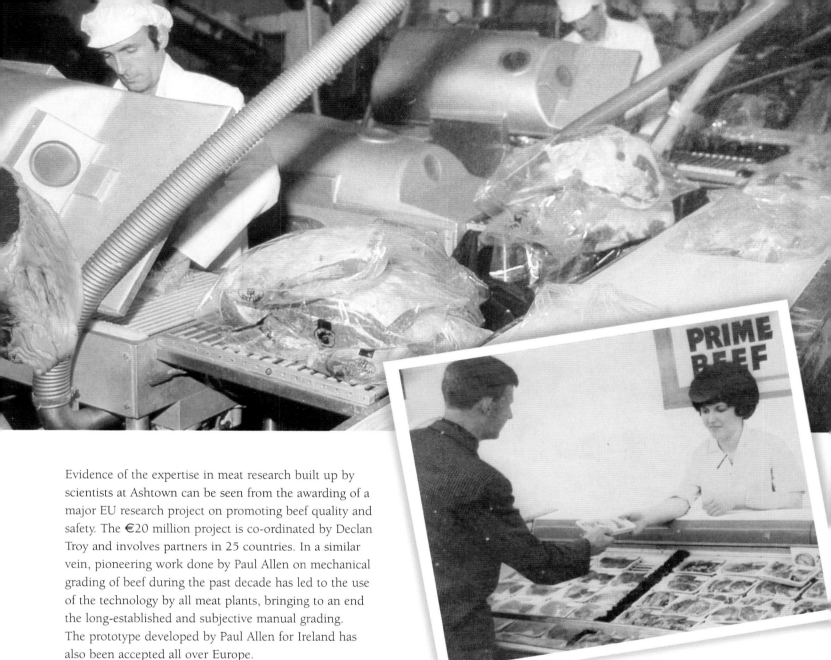

Evidence of the expertise in meat research built up by scientists at Ashtown can be seen from the awarding of a major EU research project on promoting beef quality and safety. The €20 million project is co-ordinated by Declan Troy and involves partners in 25 countries. In a similar vein, pioneering work done by Paul Allen on mechanical grading of beef during the past decade has led to the use of the technology by all meat plants, bringing to an end the long-established and subjective manual grading. The prototype developed by Paul Allen for Ireland has also been accepted all over Europe.

Excellence In Food Safety

In contrast to the early days, research on food safety now forms a very substantial part of the programme in Moorepark and Ashtown food centres, reflecting the increased threat of and greater public concern about food scares. During the past 15 years, expertise on food safety has increased more than 30-fold, particularly at Ashtown, which is among the leading food safety research centres in Europe. In 1991, there were just two microbiologists at Ashtown. Today, there are almost 40 working on food safety projects and a further 20 working in the food residues area. Evidence of the scientific excellence of the work in food safety can be seen from the fact that in 2008 scientists at Ashtown were working on 29 different projects, with funding by the Department of Agriculture Fisheries and Food, the Food Safety Promotion Board and the EU.

Understanding the pathogens that cause food poisoning or gastroenteritis or worse and developing methods to control them is at the core of food safety research. Among the biggest threats are salmonella, campylobacter and *E.coli*, all of which are present in the stomachs of animals and can be spread at any point along the food chain. Work in the 1990s on the lethal pathogen, *E. coli* 0157:H7 earned Jim Sheridan, former head of food safety at Ashtown, an international reputation. This pathogen can result in kidney failure and death, with the elderly and the very young most susceptible. Today's group of food safety experts, under the leadership of Geraldine Duffy, are building on Jim Sheridan's early work and are extending the frontiers of science in developing methods to combat this and other food-borne threats to human health.

Among the many achievements is the development of a full risk assessment for *E. coli* 0157:H7 in beef, which has been adopted by the Food Safety Authority of Ireland and the World Health Organisation. Similar risk assessments are being prepared for salmonella in pork and for other pathogens in other foods. These are high-science activities, involving microbiologists and mathematical modellers and linkages with scientists in Irish universities as well as research institutes in Europe and the US Department of Agriculture. Meanwhile, food safety systems, based on hazard analysis and critical control point (HACCP), and geared to the needs of Irish plants have been developed for the beef, pig meat and sheep industries. Scientists have also worked with many food companies in developing 'safe' systems for the manufacture of food products.

Another side of the food safety research agenda at Ashtown is the development of anti-microbial peptides, or small proteins, which are produced by animals or plants and have the ability to combat harmful bacteria. The challenge is to identify these products, extract them and either feed them to the animal or add them to the food during processing. Scientists are working on a number of different products that are showing potential against *E. coli*. At Moorepark, there is also a substantial body of food safety research, with emphasis on pathogens in milk and dairy products, such as listeria in cheese. In food safety the only certainty is that new challenges will always emerge. As Geraldine Duffy puts it: *"There is always going to be a new bug. Micro-organisms are very good at adapting to survive. The challenge is to keep ahead."*

Another aspect of food safety is tracking residues in food. The National Food Residue Database, run by Michael O'Keeffe, tracks all residues in food, including heavy metals, mycotoxins, pesticides and drugs. It contains one million tests covering all the major food types. Michael O'Keeffe has worked with partners in UCD and the Department of Agriculture, Fisheries and Food in assessing exposure and risks from residues. After years working in the area, he is confident there is no threat to human health from residues in food. A unique feature of the service is the availability of a fully open database on a website.

At the launch of the Moorepark food biotechnology programme in 1984: Jerry McAuliffe, AIB, programme sponsors; the Taoiseach, Dr Garret Fitzgerald; Niall Crowley, chairman AIB; Tim Cogan and Liam Donnelly, Moorepark.

Dr David O'Beirne working on a dessert at Ashtown.

Food And Health

Much of the food research programme is now geared towards finding new foods and new ingredients that can confer health benefits. Barry Connolly, who joined the Moorepark food research team in 1975, was one of the first scientists to get involved in this area. In the 1980s, dairy products were getting a bad name, particularly the relationship between milk fat and heart disease. In conjunction with Trinity College and St James Hospital in Dublin, Connolly carried out a large integrated study in which the total dietary intake of a group of people was measured. They found that feeding very high levels of dairy products to a sample of people made no difference to their level of cholesterol or lipoproteins. In spite of this information and other international studies, he found that it took a very long time to convert health experts to the view that dairy foods were not bad for your health.

Around this time, a new biotechnology programme was established at Moorepark. Colin Hill, now professor in UCC, was the first molecular geneticist appointed and he worked on the improvement of flavour cultures in cheese. This led to research on food and health and later to the development of cultures with health benefits, which is such an important part of the programme today. Moorepark is now one of the leading international centres in the development of novel technologies for the development of functional foods, or 'foods for health'.

Paul Ross, who now leads the food biotechnology programme at Moorepark, worked in the 1990s on probiotic cultures, in association with scientists in UCC. He was studying bacteriocins – small proteins produced by some bacteria which can kill a range of pathogenic bacteria, including the hospital bug MRSA and clostridium. At first, the focus was on food safety, but more and more it moved to human health. Particular areas for attention include bacteria that might improve gut health and food elements that might have a positive influence on cardiovascular disease, obesity, and infant nutrition. In the latter case, Ross feels that the food that infants eat can have a big effect in later life. It is possible to influence the gut flora and immune system at an early age with beneficial effects later on.

Benefits of Collaboration

The work on food and health is a classic example of collaboration between scientists across a wide range of institutions. The team includes clinicians, professors of medicine and scientists in universities as well as Moorepark. Where once they may all have competed for funds, now they have very big collaborative programmes. An example of the depth of collaboration is the Alimentary Pharmabiotic Centre, a joint venture involving UCC and Moorepark, which is coming to the end of its first five-year programme. It has brought together a large multi-disciplinary group of scientists who have made a big impact in the whole area of gut health and how food affects it.

Paul Ross believes this leading-edge technology offers huge scope for Irish food companies to expand the portfolio of functional foods products. There are already a number of successful innovations. An example is a probiotic cheese developed by Catherine Stanton, another of the leading Moorepark scientists, and colleagues in UCC. This is now manufactured in Ireland, licensed by the Irish Dairy Board and on sale in Britain under the Pilgrim's Choice brand. Another innovation, also involving Catherine Stanton, relates to conjugated linoleic acids (CLAs), a group of fatty acids with anti-carcinogenic and other health benefits. Irish and international research has shown that milk and beef produced from animals fed a grass-based diet have particularly high levels of these fatty acids. Scientists at Moorepark and Grange have worked on methods to increase CLA levels by adding oils to the animal's diet. A breakthrough was also made on microbial production of CLA as an alternative to getting it from milk and beef. This discovery has now been patented.

The most sophisticated equipment is used by scientists as they strive to expand the technologies in functional food development. Phil Kelly highlighted two recent additions to the armoury at Moorepark that enhance research capability.

The biofunctional food engineering facility provides technologists with the most up to date process to separate, stabilise, and deliver bioactive ingredients in food products with commercial potential. It enables a fast-tracking of the transfer of ideas from the laboratory to the pilot plant. The second facility, the national food imaging centre, which was funded by the Department of Agriculture, Fisheries and Food under the Food Institutional Research Measure, enables a wide range of food materials to be closely studied, ranging from individual biomolecules to complex food products. In simple terms, according to Phil Kelly, it allows scientists and food manufacturers to get an insight into how components of food work if new ingredients are incorporated.

Other important developments taking place as this book goes to print include the establishment of a National Functional Foods Research Centre. This is an initiative involving four major dairy companies - Carbery, Dairygold, Glanbia and Kerry - and Enterprise Ireland. It is a large five-year programme in functional foods and links scientists in Moorepark, UCC and UCD with food company technologists, ensuring that research is closely tied to the requirements of the market place. Another project at Moorepark, called ELDERMET, funded by the Health Research Board, is studying gut flora in the elderly.

Diversifying The Product Mix

There is also a strong focus on functional foods in the Ashtown research programme where scientists are looking at the bioactives that are naturally in meat. Another major project is searching for valuable components in algae, seaweed and fish in order to identify novel marine food ingredients and products. Called the Marine Functional Food Research Initiative, it is managed at Ashtown by Declan Troy and involves collaboration with the Marine Institute and five Irish universities, with funding of over €5 million from the Department of Agriculture, Fisheries and Food. Ronan Gormley, who cut his research teeth working on the quality of tomatoes, mushrooms and other horticultural foods in the 1960s and 1970s, is also involved in this latest work. In more recent years, Gormley and his colleagues did innovative work on the development of new functional foods based on fish and horticulture. Examples include a project on a fish amino acid, called taurine, which can restore elasticity to the arteries of young smokers, a salmon lasagne and a gluten-free ready meal.

Under the leadership of Gerry Downey, who is now head of the prepared foods department at Ashtown, comprehensive work of direct benefit to food manufacturers is taking place on a wide range of processing techniques. Of course, the Ashtown centre has a long history of scientific and technological support to emerging food companies and to established companies involved in expanding their product range. Hand-holding by scientists and technologists and access to the food processing pilot plant at Ashtown have been vital in launching new companies and products on the market.

Vivian Tarrant cited the merging, in 1988, of AFT scientists who were then based at Ashtown and Kinsealy with food technologists from the Institute of Industrial Research and Standards as a major landmark. It created critical mass in food research but the scientists suffered a funding famine during the following five years where little long-term research was undertaken. One important achievement during that lean period was the introduction of food quality management systems to the Irish food industry. As a result, food companies were able to operate to international standards and were accredited by an independent agency. When the funding situation improved with the introduction of EU structural funds in the mid-1990s, Ashtown had the intellectual capacity to win major research projects against top international competition.

Things have come a long way since the days of trying to keep milk from going rancid within hours of taking it from the cow and tackling basic problems in beef and bacon. Fifty years ago, scientists were concentrating on reducing the number of bacteria in milk by several hundred thousand. Now, their counterparts are separating "good" bacteria from "bad" ones and putting the good ones into our food. The early research provided the foundation on which the recent studies are built.

World Class Facilities

Scientists now have access to the most sophisticated equipment as they extend the barriers in food research. Facilities have been transformed during the past two decades and some of the leading scientists in the world recruited. Among the milestones are the biotechnology centre and the joint Teagasc/industry pilot plant at Moorepark. At Ashtown, a food processing pilot plant has been established and the meat development unit was extended. A new food industry training unit was also developed. New facilities have also been provided in the universities with which Teagasc food scientists are in close collaboration. A prime example is the Alimentary Pharmabiotic Centre in UCC.

The €30 million investment in food research, which is underway in 2008 under the Teagasc 'vision' research programme, will maintain scientists at the forefront of international research. This involves the extension of the Moorepark biotechnology centre and the development of a new facility at Moorepark that will examine the health benefits of food ingredients using pigs as models. A new state-of-the-art facility at Ashtown will investigate nutraceuticals in all types of raw food products.

Supporting New Products

Food scientists have contributed to the development of a wide range of products, demonstrating the role that publicly-funded research can play in food innovation. The achievements in recent years include a range of value-added cheeses, baby foods, beverages, functional foods and cream liqueurs, as well as ingredients for a variety of snack foods and prepared ready meals. Technology developed at Moorepark led to a new infant formula, which is manufactures by the multinational, Wyeth, at its plant at Askeaton, Co Limerick and now sold worldwide. It is based on alphalac, a constituent protein of whey. Alphalac is also a major component of mother's milk so this innovation represents a further stage in the 'humanisation' of infant formula. It also demonstrates the role that innovative public research can play in embedding a foreign multinational food company into the Irish innovation system.

Moorepark scientists played a central role in the development of new value-added cheese varieties. A blue-veined cheddar developed for the Carbery Group at Ballineen, Co Cork is just one of a number of novel cheeses either already commercialised or in the process. New technologies also led to big advances in the manufacture of mozzarella cheese and technological support was given to small food companies in producing new farmhouse cheeses and a range of other products, including Irish coffee and cream liqueur. Innovations in food ingredients include the development of a yeast extract flavour ingredient for the Carbery Group and the improvement of customer processes for production of cheese-based flavour ingredients. These ingredients have wide application in snack foods and prepared ready meals and are spear-heading the entry of Irish dairy companies into flavour ingredient markets.

New technology has also played a key role in the production of a range of natural food colours by the successful Waterford based company, Cybercolor. The company has built up a major market in North America for its products. Another innovative company, National Food Ingredients in Limerick, availed of Moorepark technology to produce a flavour concentrate for use in a range of value-added confectionery products. In the beverages area, a division of the multinational giant, Diageo, has used the Moorepark pilot plant to produce flavour concentrates from malt and roast barley. This concentrate is being exported to more than 50 countries for use in a range of beverages.

Thousands of operatives, technologists and executives in the food industry have benefited from training provided by the Ashtown and Moorepark centres over the years. The vast bulk of the training is provided by specialists at Ashtown where a new training unit was added in recent years. The presence of research scientists and training specialists on the same campus has added greatly to the depth and relevance of the training. The training covers the full spectrum of food production with aspects such as food safety, innovation and consumer foods dominating in recent years.

Training of regulatory staff in government departments in Ireland and in European countries has also featured. An example of overseas involvement in recent years was a course provided for officials in the Cypriot Ministry of Health. Food trainers have also collaborated with Teagasc rural development advisers in providing intensive courses for farmers and rural dwellers interested in setting up a small-scale food enterprise.

Unique Pilot Plant

The establishment of Moorepark Technology Limited (MTL), the joint Teagasc/industry pilot plant, was a major technology milestone. The brainchild of Liam Donnelly, current director of food research, it is a unique example of food companies coming together and developing a topnotch research and development facility on the same campus as a major food research institute. Established in 1993, MTL has the big Irish food companies and dairy co-operatives among its shareholders. Managed by Sean Tuohy, a former scientist in Moorepark, it provides pilot scale facilities that companies could not afford to build themselves. It enables companies to conduct their own trials and pilot scale manufacturing on a completely confidential basis while having access to the scientists and technologies at Moorepark food research centre. In addition to well-established companies interested in bringing an idea for a new product or process to pilot commercial scale, it is also used by start-up companies, many of which continue to manufacture the new product at Moorepark for relatively long periods until they have established their own manufacturing premises. Since its establishment, MTL has contributed well over 100 product and process innovations to food companies. The technology for many of these developments originated in the public research programme at Moorepark. The pilot plant is also serving the national strategy for inward investment and food multinationals are prominent among the customer base.

Alice Nongonierma preparing cheese extracts to determine levels of key peptidase activities known to be contribute to cheese flavour.

CHAPTER 10

SUPPORTING THE EXPANSION OF FARM FORESTRY

N u a l a   N í   F h l a i t h b h e a r t a i g h

Forestry has been an important feature of the research portfolio in AFT and Teagasc for most of the past 50 years. Michael Bulfin, whose career in research spanned more than 40 years, was one of the early recruits to the national soil survey, which was established at Johnstown Castle in 1959, and played a central role during the 1960s and 1970s in assessing the suitability of different land types for forestry. Toddy Radford, another long-serving member of the forestry research team, also started his career as a technician with the national soil survey.

Dr Michael Woods Minister for the Marine and Natural Resources and a former Kinsealy scientist, at the launch of the research initiative on forest productivity at Kinsealy in 1998, with scientists Michael Bulfin and Pádraig MacGiolla Ri.

Highlighting the Potential

During the 1980s, Michael Bulfin led a major EU-funded research project that involved the classification of the site and soil characteristics on 1,200 forestry plots throughout the country. The project, *Determining the Role of Private Forestry on Highly Productive Forest Sites,* provided vital technical, economic and social information on the potential of forestry. AFT research also helped in highlighting the productivity and environmental barriers to planting trees on some of the oligotrophic peat soils. This ultimately led to the development of guidelines on planting and management of trees on these soils.

In the early-1990s, Bulfin led a team that produced an indicative forest strategy for Co Clare, which was conducted on behalf of the Forest Service of the Department of Agriculture and Food and quantified the potential of forestry across a range of soils. This led to the biggest single project on forestry conducted by AFT and Teagasc during the past 50 years. Supported by the Forest Service and the Environmental Protection Agency, it involved a multi-disciplinary team of eight scientists and technologists who, between 1998 and 2006, produced soil and forest productivity maps for every county in the country using remote sensing and aerial photogrammetry. The national dataset of soils and forest productivity rankings were a central component of the Indicative Forest Strategy published by the Forest Service in 2007.

Current research, led by Niall Farrelly, is building on the earlier work and is developing site-specific information on planning, management and ecological practices for profitable and sustainable timber production. Another example of current work is the use of remote sensing and aerial photography to quantify the wood resources from farmer-owned forests. Funded by COFORD, the national council for forestry research and development, researchers are quantifying the wood resources from clusters of farmer-owned forests so that economies of scale are achieved in management, thinning, harvesting and marketing.

Through the development of comparative data for forestry and grassland, the soil survey provided a framework for national strategic forest planning. A classic example was an in-depth examination of the potential for forestry in Leitrim, which was carried out as part of the Leitrim Resource Survey in the 1970s. Led by Michael Bulfin, it concentrated on the relationship of soil type to forest productivity and highlighted for the first time the high potential of wet mineral soils for growing Sitka spruce. It included a forest productivity map of the county, based on the soil survey map. This was the first such map in Ireland or the UK and a precursor of the concept of indicative forest strategies.

The publication of the survey was followed by a multi-disciplinary study, involving agriculturalists, foresters, economists and sociologists, on the scope for forestry in Leitrim, which is dominated by wet mineral soils that are marginal for agriculture. The study concluded that afforestation provided a good land use option for Leitrim. The timing of the report coincided with the most buoyant period in farming, following our entry into the EEC. While there was some opposition to the report at local level, it marked the beginning of a national debate on the role of forestry in economic and rural development and led to a series of studies by AFT and subsequently Teagasc that have helped to shape forestry development particularly during the past two decades.

Advisory specialist Mary Ryan discussing shaping of broadleaves with forestry growers.

Assessing the Economics

In addition to identifying the most suitable soils for trees and providing scientific guidance on planting and management, crucial economic data was also assembled and this provided policy makers with the ammunition to support the case for national and EU funding for forestry, which ultimately led to the position today where some 15,000 farmers and land owners own a forest. Up to the 1980s, the state accounted for almost all forest planting. (This function was handed over to a new state agency, Coillte, in 1988.) It was not until the introduction of the western package afforestation scheme in 1982 and, more especially, the afforestation programme following the first major reform of the Common Agricultural Policy in 1992 that private planting began to take place.

During the 1970s and 1980s, a series of studies by AFT highlighted the economic incentives that were necessary to underpin the development of private forest planting. As part of the Leitrim Resource Survey, published in 1978, Barth Hickey, an economist in the economics and rural welfare centre, and Michael Bulfin recommended the introduction of an annual income for farmers to compensate for the loss of income while the forest was being established.

While the western package included planting grants and other incentives, there was no provision for an annual income payment. A number of reports on the impact of the western package showed that private forestry would never be adopted unless an annual income was paid. The EU-funded report, led by Michael Bulfin and referred to earlier, included a major section on the economics of farm forestry and again emphasised the need for an annual income until plantations became productive. It also recommended improved planting grants, a specialised forestry advisory service, demonstration farms and highlighted the role of co-operatives in expanding farmer-owned forestry. All of these recommendations are included in the current forestry programme, including the payment of an annual tax-free premium. Farmer-owned forests now account for almost 40 per cent of the national forest estate of 700,000 hectares. During the past decade, over 90 per cent of all new forests have been planted by farmers and private landowners. Several studies by Jim Frawley during the 1990s on the socio-economic potential of and barriers to the development of farm forestry and work in recent years by economists in the Teagasc FAPRI unit have continued to inform policy makers and the forestry sector on the adaptation of policy to meet changing circumstances.

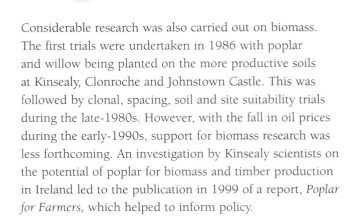

Diversifying the Species

The need to diversify the species range and to include a greater proportion of broadleaves in our forest estate became apparent in the 1990s and scientists provided the information and technology to help make this happen. Trees on the Farm, a book published in 1992 by Michael Bulfin, helped raise awareness of the potential for species diversification and mixtures in Irish forestry. A research programme at Kinsealy on the management and shaping of broadleaves resulted in the development of protocols that were adopted into national policy and are now part of the management guidelines for broadleaves. Research on the development of protocols for the management of broadleaf plantations is still ongoing, a current example of which is work by Ian Short and Toddy Radford on the thinning of broadleaves on farmer-owned plantations.

Scientists have also made an important contribution to improving seed sources for two native broadleaves, birch and alder, which have considerable potential in species diversification. A birch improvement programme was initiated in 1998 and this was expanded to include alder in 2006. Seed orchards have now been established for the two species. The broadleaf improvement programme at Kinsealy also includes work by Gerry Douglas on the investigation of micro-propagation and vegetative propagation

techniques with the aim of conserving the gene pool of veteran trees. This research is also addressing issues such as brown bud ash, an alien species that may threaten the native stock of ash. The broadleaf improvement programme will continue to be an important part of the research programme, with improved planting material for other tree species being developed.

Considerable research was also carried out on biomass. The first trials were undertaken in 1986 with poplar and willow being planted on the more productive soils at Kinsealy, Clonroche and Johnstown Castle. This was followed by clonal, spacing, soil and site suitability trials during the late-1980s. However, with the fall in oil prices during the early-1990s, support for biomass research was less forthcoming. An investigation by Kinsealy scientists on the potential of poplar for biomass and timber production in Ireland led to the publication in 1999 of a report, *Poplar for Farmers,* which helped to inform policy.

Looking Forward

The amalgamation in 2004 of research, advisory and training staff in Teagasc into a single management unit, combined with the very close linkages with COFORD and the Forest Service section of the Department of Agriculture, Fisheries and Food, ensures that Teagasc research and development is firmly focused on the needs of the sector. The incorporation of forestry into the FAPRI economic and policy analysis model will also advise and steer the farm forestry sector into the future. Research in the future will concentrate on the best practices for private forest owners in the areas of forest management, thinning, harvesting, marketing and infra-structural development as well as perfecting management practices for broadleaves. Aspects such as carbon sequestration, tourism, recreation and non-wood forest products will also be prioritised. Alternative farm forestry systems such as agro-forestry and riparian buffers will also be investigated.

The Minister for Agriculture, Mark Clinton and Taoiseach Liam Cosgrave on a visit to Kinsealy in 1975, with scientists Michael Maher and Paddy Gallagher.

CHAPTER 11

HOME GROWN TECHNOLOGY FOR HORTICULTURE

Lorcan O'Toole

When the first horticultural research scientists were appointed by AFT in 1959, the sophisticated production, distribution and marketing channels that exist today were but a pipedream. There was little supermarket development, no centralised distribution or cool chains. Horticulture was still a protected sector with high import tariffs and preferential licensing during our natural production season. Production had changed little over the preceding 20 years and a limited range of fruit and vegetable crops were produced on a small-scale market garden basis. The Dublin wholesale market was predominant, setting prices on a national basis and acting as a clearinghouse for home grown and imported produce to country wholesalers, van men, greengrocers and small family grocery stores.

Within a year of its establishment, AFT had acquired a research facility for soft fruit at Clonroche in Wexford and a centre for top fruit research at Ballygagin, near Dungarvan. A farm of 100 acres at Kinsealy was purchased for £12,000 as the headquarters for the division and the centre for research on vegetables and glasshouse crops. By the time the Kinsealy centre was officially opened by the Taoiseach Seán Lemass in 1962, a comprehensive research programme was underway across all areas of horticulture.

From the beginning, the scientists realised that much of the available foreign research data, even that from Europe, was not directly applicable to Irish growing conditions. A comprehensive programme of home grown basic research was required to establish crop protocols. This led to a concentration on component research in the early years leading to the development of recommended production systems later. Priority was given to finding Irish solutions to Irish problems. In this regard, early attention was given to research on problems of fungal diseases such as botrytis or grey mould in strawberries, which were exacerbated by our cool, damp climate. Finding the right weed control techniques for Ireland's long growing season was also top of the agenda. The development of peat as a propagation and growing medium was another priority, due to the home and export potential of peat-based composts. An overarching theme across all horticulture crops was research on the impact of treatments on the quality, flavour and nutritional aspects of the product. The programme was led by an outstanding group of scientists, supported by a dedicated corps of technicians and farm staff, the majority of whom gave a lifetime of service to research. David Robinson, who led the team from the early-1960s until the late-1980s, became an international figure in horticultural research and presided over a programme that laid the foundation of the modern commercial sector of today

Technologies for Vegetables

The modernisation of vegetable production started with the development of extensive food processing by Erin Foods, a subsidiary of the Irish Sugar Company, and by Bachelors.

The companies had a requirement for a range of crops to be grown on a field scale and programmed to deliver an even supply of suitable produce for processing. The challenge to the research scientists was to develop production protocols for a wide range of crops that would meet the processing specifications and would deliver an acceptable income to growers. This involved a massive research programme on varieties, growing methods, nutrition and mechanisation, the development of weed, disease and pest control strategies, best harvesting techniques and the examination of post-harvest physiology. It involved a multi-disciplinary team of scientists that was led by Cyril Cassidy, who specialised in weed control, and included Paddy Gallagher on nutrition, Ted Ryan on plant pathology and Dixie Dunne on entomology while Owen Goodman, Maria Prendeville and Barry Murphy concentrated on variety selection and crop husbandry.

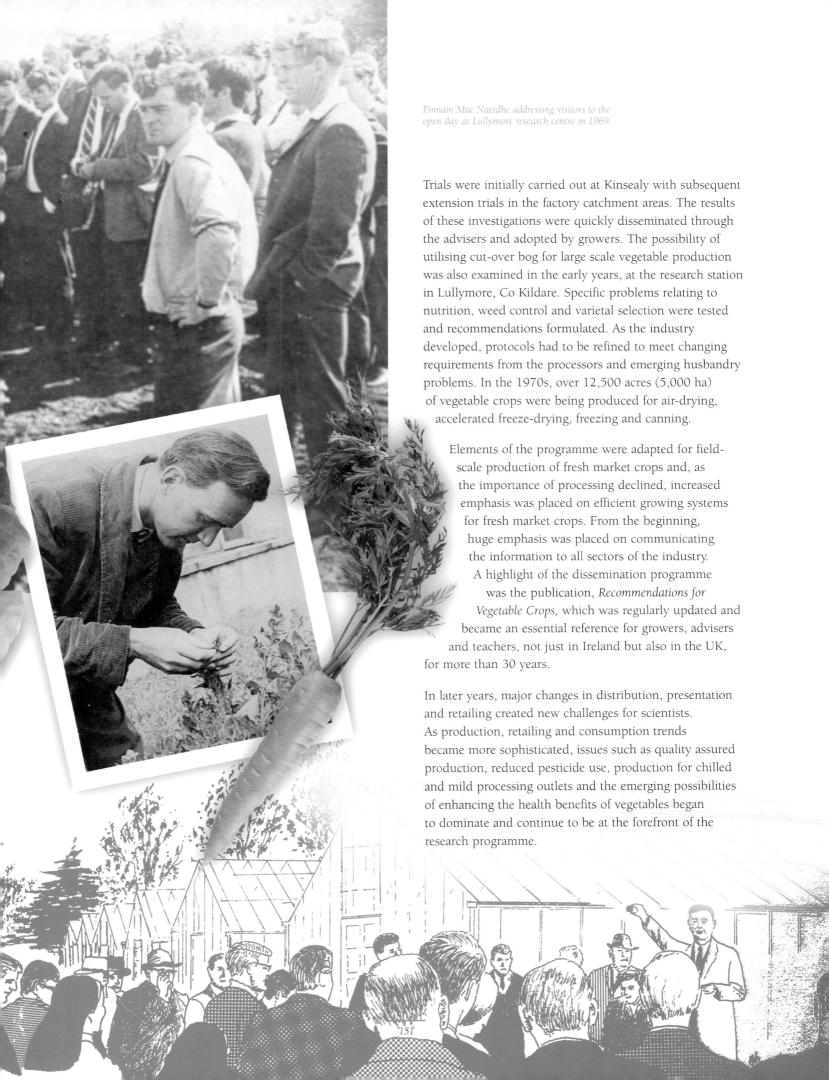

Trials were initially carried out at Kinsealy with subsequent extension trials in the factory catchment areas. The results of these investigations were quickly disseminated through the advisers and adopted by growers. The possibility of utilising cut-over bog for large scale vegetable production was also examined in the early years, at the research station in Lullymore, Co Kildare. Specific problems relating to nutrition, weed control and varietal selection were tested and recommendations formulated. As the industry developed, protocols had to be refined to meet changing requirements from the processors and emerging husbandry problems. In the 1970s, over 12,500 acres (5,000 ha) of vegetable crops were being produced for air-drying, accelerated freeze-drying, freezing and canning.

Elements of the programme were adapted for field-scale production of fresh market crops and, as the importance of processing declined, increased emphasis was placed on efficient growing systems for fresh market crops. From the beginning, huge emphasis was placed on communicating the information to all sectors of the industry. A highlight of the dissemination programme was the publication, *Recommendations for Vegetable Crops,* which was regularly updated and became an essential reference for growers, advisers and teachers, not just in Ireland but also in the UK, for more than 30 years.

In later years, major changes in distribution, presentation and retailing created new challenges for scientists. As production, retailing and consumption trends became more sophisticated, issues such as quality assured production, reduced pesticide use, production for chilled and mild processing outlets and the emerging possibilities of enhancing the health benefits of vegetables began to dominate and continue to be at the forefront of the research programme.

Doubling Tomato Yields

In 1960, output of tomato production in Ireland was characterised by low yields, indifferent quality, short cropping season and overproduction in the mid-summer period. In anticipation of increased competition from the Netherlands and the Channel Islands under free trade conditions, a national glasshouse grants scheme was introduced to update production and grading facilities for growers. In parallel, a team of highly skilled and enthusiastic scientists at Kinsealy developed blueprints that were quickly adopted by growers. Within seven years, yields had more than doubled and quality improved dramatically.

Joe Mahon outlines the results of research on tomatoes.

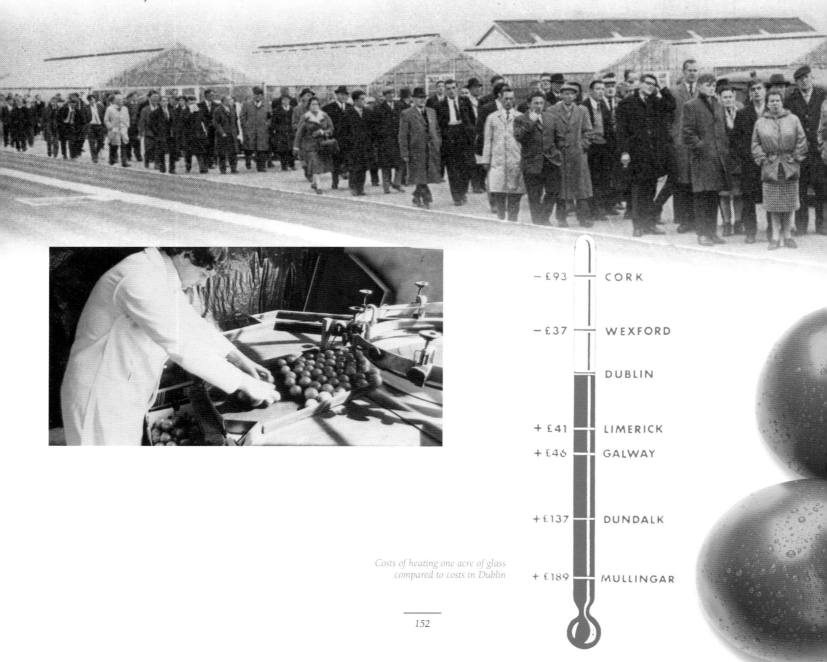

– £93	CORK
– £37	WEXFORD
	DUBLIN
+ £41	LIMERICK
+ £46	GALWAY
+ £137	DUNDALK
+ £189	MULLINGAR

Costs of heating one acre of glass compared to costs in Dublin

The research team, involving Michael Woods, Michael Maher, John Seager and Luke Feely, ably supported by Jim Bannon and Joe Mahon, concentrated initially on the development of a two-crop system, in order to avoid overproduction in mid-season when cold house tomatoes were freely available. Later, as varieties and nutrition improved, a single long-season cropping system was adopted. The systems were further modified and refined as alternatives to soil-based cropping were explored.

Problems relating to the build-up of root diseases and the cost and difficulty of soil sterilisation led researchers to examine the feasibility and economics of isolated growing systems. This resulted in the development of tomato production systems involving peat modules and eventually to rockwool and full hydroponic systems where the crops were grown in a shallow re-circulating stream of nutrient solution. This work also laid the foundation for the commercial development of peat composts and growing media by developing specific fertiliser formulations for the various stages of crop growth.

Open day at Kinsealy.

Considerable work was also carried out in the 1960s and 1970s by Ronan Gormley and Tony Kenny on quality and nutritional aspects of tomatoes. Both of these scientists went on to play important roles in wider aspects of food research at Ashtown food research centre.

While the main emphasis was placed on tomatoes, production protocols were also developed for cucumbers, peppers and aubergines. Considerable work was also carried out on ornamental crops, initially on cut flowers but subsequently on flowering and foliage pot plants and species suitable for interior landscaping in offices and shopping centres.

As labour became an important cost to the sector, studies on efficient labour use and automation led to the development of a patented tomato training system. As production systems became increasingly more complex and pushed the boundaries of crop performance, the necessity for exact control of the internal climate of the glasshouse led to the development of computerised control systems. These again laid the foundation for current research on energy efficient closed glasshouse systems. Biological control of glasshouse pests, including red spider mite and whitefly, was studied and recommendations developed for what is now standard practice by food and ornamental growers.

Michael Boland cutting the first cucumbers of the year at Kinsealy in 1965.

Cathal Mac Canna, a leading member of the mushroom research team that developed the low-cost polythene tunnels.

World Class Mushroom Growing

New technology for mushroom growing ranks as one of the most outstanding achievements of research, not just in horticulture but across the entire AFT research programme, during the past 50 years. During the 1960s, mushroom growing was a very small business with a handful of farms producing for the home market using compost based on horse manure. Ground-breaking research at Kinsealy revolutionised production. It involved the development of new composts, based on straw and poultry manure, with mushrooms grown in polythene bags in insulated polythene tunnels. The world-leading research, undertaken by a team including Cathal Mac Canna, Liam Staunton and Jim Grant, led to the establishment of a major mushroom industry in Ireland that has a current output of €100 million per annum with 80 per cent exported to multiples in the UK. The system facilitated the concept of satellite growing and allowed vertical integration of the sector. Marketing companies manufactured and supplied compost to growers who in turn delivered high quality produce back to the companies for marketing. Removing the high capital costs of composting and the development of the much cheaper polythene tunnel system made mushroom growing a real and viable business option for many farmers. Grower numbers peaked at over 550 in the 1990s and, while the number of growers is now less than one-fifth of what it was a decade ago, a big increase in the size of units has resulted in overall output being maintained.

A study in 2003 by Professor Gerry Boyle, the current director of Teagasc, showed that the mushroom research programme gave a return on investment of almost 50 per cent. This is 10 times higher than the minimum rate advocated by the Department of Finance for public sector investment projects.

Following the development of the unique Kinsealy production system, the research team remained at the forefront of mushroom research for many years. An example of the level of innovation emanating from the programme was the use of spawned casing whereby some compost is mixed through the top layer of casing, leading to earlier and more uniform cropping. This is now used worldwide. Another example was research on environmental control and internal airflow in tunnels, which helped to achieve uniformity of cropping and maintenance of high quality.

Deirdre O'Donoghue working on mushroom cytogenetics.

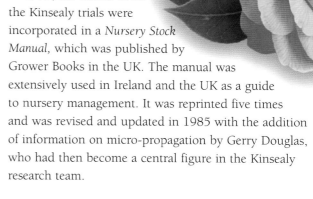

Taoiseach Séan Lemass at the official opening of Kinsealy in 1962 with from left: D C Lawlor, Bord na Móna; John Litton, AFT Chairman; J P Harman, Department of Finance; Cyril Cassidy, Kinsealy; General M J Costello, Irish Sugar Company and Senator Willie Ryan, AFT Council.

Emphasis on Nursery Stock

As far back as the 1950s, there was a tradition of high quality family nurseries in Ireland. Firms such as McGreedy's of Portadown, Co Armagh, Richardson's of Waterford, Slieve Donard in Newry, Co Down and Watsons in Killiney, Co Dublin were well known during the 1950s and 1960s. They combined breeding and plant production and specialised particularly in roses and narcissi where they achieved a worldwide reputation. Outside of these there had been little development of a modern sector. In the mid-1960s, a comprehensive research programme was undertaken at Kinsealy on the development of propagation, weaning and growing systems for a wide range of ornamental plants.

The nursery stock team, led by Keith Lamb and Jim Kelly, concentrated initially on high value shrubs such as rhododendron and camellia and a range of species that were required in large quantities for ground cover and mass planting schemes, with specific recommendations developed for each species. Lessons learned through the glasshouse programme on peat-based composts, nutrition, slow release fertiliser, liquid feeding, capillary beds and the use of plastic clad structures were modified and adapted for nursery stock use.

In 1975, the results of all the Kinsealy trials were incorporated in a *Nursery Stock Manual,* which was published by Grower Books in the UK. The manual was extensively used in Ireland and the UK as a guide to nursery management. It was reprinted five times and was revised and updated in 1985 with the addition of information on micro-propagation by Gerry Douglas, who had then become a central figure in the Kinsealy research team.

Transforming Strawberry Growing

Up to the time the soft fruit research station at Clonroche, Co Wexford was established in 1959, there was limited production in the south east of strawberries and blackcurrants for processing, but yields and quality were poor due to disease and weed problems. David Robinson, who had worked on chemical methods of weed control at Loughgall in Armagh before taking charge of the AFT horticultural research programme, led a research team that developed comprehensive weed control programmes in strawberries and these were adopted as standard practice by growers in Ireland and throughout western Europe. The team, which included Nick Rath, Pádraig Mac Giolla Rí, Finnáin Mac Naeidhe, Fionnbarr O'Ríordáin and Tim Callaghan, also produced research-based protocols on other key aspects of the growing of strawberries and other soft fruits. Selection of the best varieties of strawberries for processing and the fresh market was also an important element of the research programme with varieties for processing being bred at Clonroche.

Modern production of strawberries is dramatically different to that when the early production blueprints were developed. The original outdoor production systems confined the strawberry season to 4-6 weeks. Production in glasshouses and in polythene and tunnel systems now enables fresh strawberries to be produced for up to eight months of the year, giving much higher yields and more consistent quality than outdoor production. During the past decade, the Clonroche centre closed and research is now concentrated at Kinsealy where new technologies are offering the potential to deliver further dramatic increases in strawberry yields. Work on biological control as an alternative to chemicals in dealing with pests and diseases also offers the exciting prospect of enhancing strawberries and other soft fruits as natural products.

Research on beekeeping was also an important component of the work at Clonroche for many years and honey producers were provided with technical information that enabled big increases in productivity. Pest and disease control was a challenge for researchers and growers and still continues as a barrier to profitable production.

Support for Apple Growing

The establishment of AFT coincided with an effort to modernise apple production and marketing in the south east. In the late-1950s, a co-operative was set up in Dungarvan, Co. Waterford and a number of dessert and culinary orchards were planted in Waterford and surrounding counties. In order to give scientific support to the initiative, AFT opened a research station at Ballygagin, near Dungarvan.

Niall O'Kennedy with apple growers at the Ballygagin research centre.

The initial research, led by Niall O'Kennedy and Pat McDonnell, concentrated on systems of production for Golden Delicious, the predominant variety at the time. However, while the variety was capable of giving very good yields, it could not match imports from France in critical areas such as smoothness and skin finish.

As most apple varieties were produced abroad, priority was given to the screening of new varieties and rootstocks suited to Irish conditions. This work helped to identify varieties such as Johnagold, which is still prominent in orchards. Over a period of more than 20 years, the programme at Ballygagin developed management systems for different varieties and the recommendations on crop nutrition, weed, pest and disease control, growth regulators, pruning and storage helped greatly to enhance performance. The Ballygagin station fell victim to the first retrenchment in AFT and was closed in 1982.

Research was also carried out on other top fruits, including pears and plums, but the station was closed before the development of spanish tunnels, which would have added a new dimension to the research work. Successful trials were also undertaken on hop production for the brewing industry and a number of commercial hop gardens were established in Kilkenny.

Feed intake of the sow increased with age and also with the number of pigs being suckled.

CHAPTER 12

TECHNOLOGIES FOR WORLD CLASS PIG PRODUCTION

Brendan Lynch

Tipperary man Jim O'Grady was the second person to be appointed to the research staff at the fledgling Moorepark centre. Because of the close linkages between pigs and milk at farm level at that time, it was decided that pig research should be located on the same campus as the dairy research centre. O'Grady was given the task of developing from scratch the facilities and programme that would provide the vital technology for what was to become an internationally competitive pig production sector.

The industry he was asked to service in 1959 was dramatically different to that of today. There were around 120,000 pig producers in Ireland supplying a national output of well under a million pigs. Today, 450 commercial producers supply the national output of over three million pigs. An early survey showed that while sows produced a respectable average litter size of 11.4 pigs, mortality was high with an average of two pigs per litter dying by the time they were weaned at eight weeks of age. It also showed poor sow productivity resulting in an average output of just 15 pigs per sow per year, compared to 23 on many herds today.

While pigs were an important source of income on thousands of farms, the number of pigs per farm was very low. A report in 1968 by Brendan Kearney and John Heavey of the AFT rural economy division showed that the average number of pigs per farm was still only eight. That report, entitled *"Are Pig Units Too Small?"*, proposed that on a farm of under 80 acres a pig unit equivalent to at least five sows and fattening the progeny would be a necessary part of any plan to make optimum use of the resources on the farm. Such a pig unit could be expected to contribute an average of £200 to the annual family farm income at the time.

Jim O'Grady was joined by technicians Tom Gardiner and Sean Scanlon, and the trio formed the nucleus of the pig production research effort for much of the next decade. The first undertaking was to build a pig unit for 80 sows with farrowing pens and dry sow accommodation, which was on straw with individual feeders. The unit was stocked and a strategic programme was drawn up aimed at providing the technologies on housing, feeding and fertility that would revolutionise the Irish pig industry over the following decades.

Nutrition and Housing

Some of the first experiments concentrated on the feeding of sows in pregnancy and lactation. Jim O'Grady soon realised that the size of the herd in Moorepark was too small for statistically reliable studies on fertility or productivity traits and he linked up with several research centres in the United Kingdom. This was the beginning of a very satisfactory relationship during which co-ordinated trials were carried out on up to 10 research centres with the same diets and experimental design in all. Over the following decade, Jim O'Grady became world famous as an expert on sow nutrition and management.

A major experiment was undertaken on pig housing. Three different houses for finishing pigs – *the Jordan, the Solari and the Danish* – were compared. The cheapest of these was *the Jordan,* an uninsulated concrete structure originally used in Northern Ireland, which later became known as the 'sweat box'. *The Solari* was a hayshed type structure with kennels, under which the pigs slept with straw stored on top. *The Danish* was the most expensive of the three and cost three times as much as the Jordan. It had a single feeding passageway through the centre and small pens on each side. The feeding trough was parallel to the passageway. In the other two houses, pigs were fed on the floor.

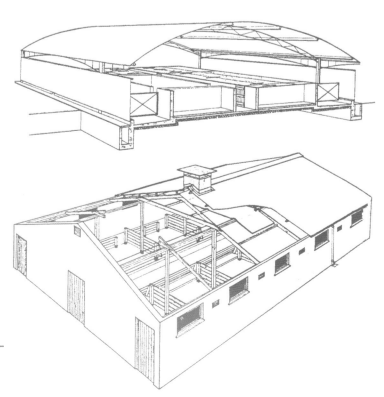

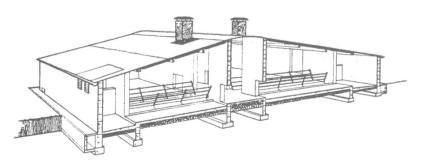

The Jordan, Solari and Danish pig houses were compared in Moorepark trials.

A comparison of environmental conditions and pig performance in the three houses, which lasted a number of years, showed that pigs in the Danish house grew fastest and utilised their feed more efficiently. However, the experiment showed that, overall, the Jordan house gave the most profitable system of production with the low incidence of respiratory diseases being one of its major strengths.

Housing for sows also got attention at Moorepark and in 1968 the centre was one of the first units in the country to fit individual stalls for pregnant sows. Slightly later, the use of tethers in farrowing crates became commonplace and these tether crates made working conditions much easier for the stock person than the old fully-enclosed farrowing crate. These are some early examples of usable research generated by Moorepark that brought real benefits to pig producers and was vital in underpinning the development of a highly commercial pig sector.

The Early Adopters

Buddy Kiernan, Benny Maguire and the Hanleys, all of whom went on to establish large units in the midlands and north east, were among the early adopters of the new technologies emanating from the AFT research programme. Other early adopters included Maurice Tierney and Eddie Cunningham in Waterford, the O'Briens and O'Keeffes in Mitchelstown as well as Ken Walsh and Bill Carroll in Tipperary.

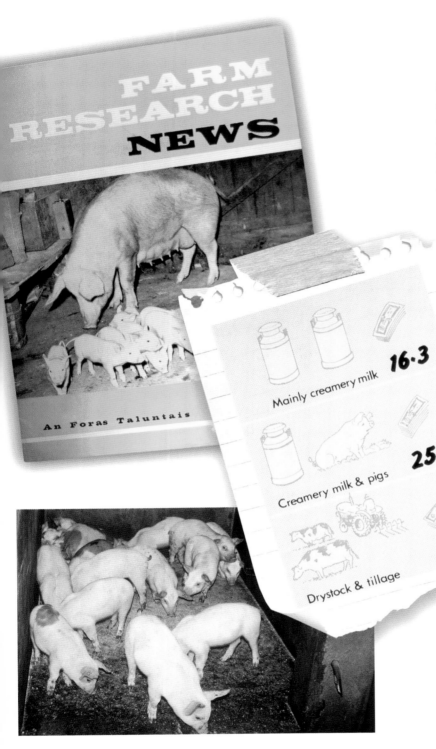

Dramatic Improvements

Another example of ground-breaking research in housing was work carried out in the early-1970s on the effect of room temperature on feed intake by lactating sows. This involved the installation of climate control rooms at Moorepark. The information generated on the relationship between room temperature, sow feed intake and subsequent fertility is classic in its category even to this day.

From the late-1960s, the research team was substantially strengthened with the recruitment of two new scientists, Tom Hanrahan and Brendan Lynch. This enhanced expertise led to a massive expansion in the research programme and the generation of a bank of information, particularly in the area of feeding and nutrition, that led to dramatic improvements in the efficiency of pig production at farm level.

The earlier trials convinced the researchers that it was not possible to look at one stage of the sow's reproductive cycle in isolation. Feeding in pregnancy affected body condition of the sow at farrowing. This in turn affected feed intake during lactation, which ultimately affected the body condition of the sow at weaning. Sows in pregnancy were poorly managed on farms at that time and this resulted in high culling rates and long weaning to oestrus intervals. Once it became clear that proper feeding of the sow during lactation was necessary for her to return to oestrus quickly after weaning, the stage was set for dramatic increases in sow productivity. This technology was taken up very rapidly at farm level and by the mid-1970s Ireland was a world leader in sow productivity, being ahead of countries such as Denmark and France.

The Moorepark Diet

Work at Moorepark played a crucial role in the huge improvements that took place in feed conversion efficiency. In the early-1960s, it took about 4 kg of feed to produce 1 kg of live weight gain. The figure today is 2.5 kg. Feeds usually contained cereal by-products such as pollard and bran. Indeed, some years previously, the diet fed to finishing pigs would have been purely barley and skim milk. Fishmeal and meat and bone meal were often included. As well as providing protein, they were a source of essential minerals and some vitamins that might have been lacking in the other ingredients. Vitamin and mineral mixtures at the time were confined to limestone flour.

In the late-1960s, Tom Hanrahan, having spent some time in Illinois where he was impressed by the simplicity and excellent pig performance on maize-soyabean diets, supplemented with minerals and vitamins, came back to Moorepark and introduced the barley-soya bean meal diet. This "Moorepark Diet" became the standard diet for finishing pigs and, while improved by substitution of some of the barley by wheat, which has higher energy content, it remains the benchmark diet. In recent years, the use of synthetic amino acids has become more widespread for environmental reasons because low protein diets result in less nitrogen being excreted and therefore less nitrogen in the manure.

Since feed is the major cost component in pig production, feed quality is extremely important to profitability. Around 1970, the big issue was the quality of compound feed and there were tensions between AFT and the feed industry as research by Tom Hanrahan continued into this topic. In the early-1980s, a new feed mill was built at Moorepark, financed by funds from the dissolution of the Irish Grain Board and from the feed industry. This allowed work on pelleted feed and facilitated incorporation of a wider range of ingredients in feeds.

International Contacts

The quality of the research work at Moorepark and the collaboration with other research institutes led to the development of a wide network of international contacts during the 1960s and 1970s. Participation by Jim O'Grady in the British Society of Animal Production (BSAP) and the European Association for Animal Production (EAAP) opened several doors in Europe, North America and Australia. In recognition of his contribution, Jim later became President of BSAP and President of the Pig Committee of EAAP. International links were further enhanced with Tom Hanrahan and Brendan Lynch studying at the University of Illinois and Jim O'Grady spending a year at the University of Alberta.

New Technologies

Ireland is one of the few countries in Europe where all male pigs are reared as entire boars up to slaughter. The earliest comparisons of boars and castrated males were carried out at Moorepark in the late-1960s. At the time boar taint was a concern but, by the end of the 1970s, it became clear that when pigs were slaughtered at lighter weights the incidence of boar taint was relatively low. Within a very short period, the industry changed completely from castration to the rearing of boars. Boars are leaner and have better feed conversion efficiency so the producer benefits from both lower feed costs and a higher pig price.

Throughout the late-1960s, it became increasingly clear that the future was with large pig units. However, disease was a serious problem when large numbers of pigs were housed together. Blueprints developed by Moorepark on housing and hygiene gave producers the technologies and the confidence to handle large numbers of pigs without disastrous disease problems and this led to a number of producers developing large units.

Another initiative, undertaken by the Department of Agriculture, was the development of co-operatives where several small breeders would sell their weaned pigs at about 25-30 kgs live weight for finishing in a central unit. These small breeders were not in a position to finish the pigs themselves or to deliver a uniform product to the meat plants and the development of the centralised finishing units,

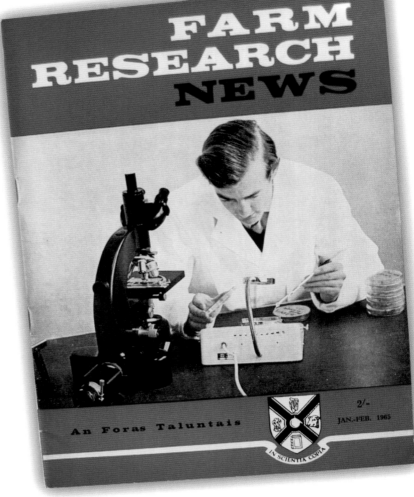

where quality of feed and stockmanship was superior, enabled the smaller breeders to share in the profit from finishing the pigs to slaughter.

However, it soon emerged that the mixing of pigs from several units in a single room resulted in the introduction of diseases that were present on all the supplying farms. This led to high mortality on the centralised finishing units and, over a period of 10 years, these units tended to gradually cease accepting pigs from producers, but some of them developed their own breeding herds. One of the first pig co-operatives to be set up was in the Glen of Aherlow, which was very successfully managed for several years by Tom Gardiner who had trained at Moorepark. It still operates today as an integrated pig unit.

The contribution of the Department of Agriculture to the pig industry over the last 50 years must be acknowledged. In particular, the importation of superior quality breeding stock of the Landrace and Large White breeds. Also, the operation of the progeny and performance testing stations over about 40 years was extremely important in improving carcass quality.

In later stages, the breeding industry developed independently and companies like Hermitage AI in Kilkenny have been extremely successful in this area and are now major exporters of breeding stock.

Overall, the scientists in the early decades of AFT and their successors in Teagasc played a leading role in the development of a modern, world-class pig industry. The technologies developed at Moorepark enabled the move towards larger herd sizes that resulted from the dramatic restructuring of the industry, particularly during the 1970s and 1980s. The trend towards larger herd sizes has been copied in other European countries where herd sizes are gradually edging upwards. The high animal productivity on Ireland's large pig farms has enabled the industry to survive against the disadvantages of high feed prices and expensive access to export markets. Of course, with the low price of pig meat today, the major beneficiary of high efficiency on pig farms has been the consumer.

Training the Pig Managers

The move towards bigger units created a big need for skilled managers and stock persons. This led to the development of a two-year course, which started at Mellows College, Athenry in 1969 and for over 30 years provided a steady supply of top class managers and senior stock persons. At its peak in the early-1990s, it was producing 20 graduates a year. As employment opportunities widened, the number of people opting for careers in pig production declined and, in 2003, Teagasc terminated the course because there were no applicants. Today, a significant number of people working on pig units come from Eastern Europe. There is a great need for continued education and upskilling of these people. There is also a gap in the training system for good quality senior stock persons and managers.

Advisers to the Fore

During the past 50 years, the advisory services operated by the Department of Agriculture, the county committees of agriculture, ACOT and Teagasc have played a major role in disseminating the technologies developed by the research service and in helping producers to adopt the best management systems. Among the people who made a major contribution at official level to the development of the pig industry though the 1960s and 1970s was Ned Hallihan in the department who was involved in the development of many of the large pig finishing units. In 1970, two young agricultural graduates, Pat Tuite and Michael Martin, were appointed specialist pig advisors by the department and had a major role in the development of the pig industry through the 1970s and 1980s.

In the early decades, advisers employed by county committees of agriculture tended to cover pigs as well as other enterprises on the farm. As the industry became more sophisticated, it became clear that specialisation in the advisory service was necessary in order to provide the expert advice needed by the emerging group of highly commercial producers. In some of the more intensive pig producing counties, a specialist pig advisor was designated and, soon after the formation of ACOT in 1980, a small national team of eight specialised pig advisors, led by Pat Tuite and Michael Martin, was established. This group was integrated into Teagasc in 1988 and in 2005 the advisory, research and training services within Teagasc were merged into a pig production development unit.

CHAPTER 13
A CENTURY OF ADVISORY SERVICES FOR FARMERS

T o m   K i r l e y

The earliest recorded advisory services to farm families go back to the late-1800s when 'itinerant instructors' were employed to promote the adoption of better farm practices through a programme of demonstration and training. The employment of the first instructors was promoted and supported by organisations such as the Royal Dublin Society (RDS), the Royal Agricultural Society (RAS), agricultural show societies and breed societies. Many of these bodies had strong linkages with larger farmers or landed gentry and were linked to similar organisations in Britain. The Irish Agricultural Organisation Society (IAOS), established in 1894 to promote and co-ordinate co-operatives, also employed advisers to assist in the adoption of better farm practices.

It was not until the establishment of the Department of Agriculture and Technical Instruction (DATI) in 1899 that the state got involved in the employment of advisers. Horace Plunkett, the first vice-president of the DATI, insisted that a separate fund be set aside for the employment of 'itinerant instructors' throughout the 32 counties to teach winter farm schools and conduct field demonstrations and experiments. As well as agriculture, instructors were also to be employed in horticulture and beekeeping, poultry and butter-making. The cost of the instructors was to be shared by the DATI and the county committees of agriculture, which had been established under the 1898 Local Government act.

The first instructor was appointed in Tyrone in October 1900, followed by Down and Antrim over the following two months. By 1903, an instructor was employed in 11 counties. As funding for the services was part dependent on contributions from the local agricultural rates, the pace at which instructors were employed varied between counties. There were also disagreements between county committees of agriculture and the DATI over who should be appointed. Another reason for the slow pace of recruitment, particularly of agricultural instructors, in the early years was the shortage of suitably qualified graduates. In spite of these impediments, there were still over 100 instructors employed in1906 and, by 1911, this had increased to 147 – 40 in agriculture, 39 in horticulture and beekeeping, 35 in poultry and 33 in butter-making.

Boom and Depression

Agriculture in Ireland boomed during World War I with big increases in prices for cattle, horses, butter and eggs but the industry went into serious decline in the early 1920s. Costs of production had risen dramatically and there was no agreement on trade or agriculture in the Anglo-Irish treaty of 1921. Despite dominion status, Irish produce was not competitive with Canadian, New Zealand or Australian on the British market.

The Commission on Agriculture, set up by the government during the height of the civil war in autumn 1922 and chaired by James Drew, professor of agriculture in the College of Science, highlighted the lack of competitiveness of Irish produce. However, with the exception of the attempted development of a tobacco industry and the establishment of a sugar industry, little was done to improve productivity, particularly in cattle production where stocking rates and grassland management were very poor.

The overriding priority was on cattle breeding, with support for the production of subsidised bulls (based on the dual purpose shorthorn breed) becoming an industry in itself. Agricultural incomes remained depressed during the Economic War with Britain in the 1930s and there was no appetite or money for advisory services. In 1938, there were 38 agricultural instructors employed in the 26 counties, two less than the number employed in the 32 counties in 1911. There were 35 horticultural instructors and 38 in poultry and butter-making.

The Commission on Agriculture had recommended that the secretaries of the county committees of agriculture should be graduates in agricultural science and this recommendation was implemented in the mid-1920s, with the establishment of the post of chief agricultural officer (CAO). The title of CAO as the manager of the advisory services in each county continued for the following 80 years until Teagasc introduced the position of area manager in 2007.

The method of recruiting instructors was also changed in the 1920s. Until then, recruitment was through the DATI and, from 1922, the new Department of Lands and Agriculture. From 1927, advisers were recruited through the local appointments commission, a system that remained until the establishment of ACOT in 1980. The Agricultural act of 1931, introduced by the Minister for Lands and Agriculture Patrick Hogan, reformed the structure and funding of the 27 county committees of agriculture (one in each county and two in Tipperary) and also brought about some improvement in the employment conditions of instructors

While farmers fared somewhat better than the rest of Irish society during World War II, the bulk of the advisory activity went into managing the compulsory tillage programme which, combined with the shortage of fertilisers, did serious damage to soil fertility during the following decade or more. By 1950, the number of agricultural instructors had increased to 83. There were 80 instructors in poultry/butter-making and 49 in horticulture.

The Beginnings of Change

Following compulsory tillage during the war years, a level of distrust had built up between the Department of Agriculture and farmers. Elements in the department had become inward looking and had lost touch with progressive international farming developments. There was huge emphasis on dual purpose breeding of cattle and a lack of emphasis on soil science and on the exploitation of intensive systems of grassland. However, a younger cohort of scientists was emerging in the department and they began to show what was possible in terms of increased yield through liming and fertiliser application.

The opening of the soil testing laboratory at Johnstown Castle in 1948 marked the beginning of a revitalisation of farming. Since joining the department in 1945, the 'Doc' (Dr Tom Walsh who was appointed director of AFT in 1958) had developed strong linkages with instructors, or advisers as they were now being called, and was convinced of their pivotal role in transferring new technology to farmers.

The soil test became the single most important tool for the advisory service in demonstrating the benefits of lime and fertiliser for grassland, tillage and horticulture crops and it marked the beginning of intensive contact between advisers and farmers that ultimately led to the transformation of agriculture.

In 1960, the number of soil samples sent to Johnstown Castle was over 100,000, the vast majority submitted by advisers. The number of agricultural advisers expanded rapidly during the 1950s, reaching 230 in 1960, a three-fold increase on the figure a decade earlier. While overall numbers had increased, there were still huge variations in the quality of the service provided by the 27 different county committees of agriculture. This would lead to intense debate over the following years.

Spreading the New Gospel

The leadership provided by AFT from the early-1960s in the development of new technologies tailor-made for Irish farming conditions heralded a new era for the advisory services. The two decades after the establishment of AFT were an exciting and satisfying time to be involved in advisory work. Advisers spread the new gospel with missionary zeal and played a major role in ensuring that new innovations in grazing management, silage making and animal management were adopted by farmers. Production blueprints for milk, beef and sheep production, developed at research centres and demonstrated on satellite demonstration farms on a scale that farmers could identify with, were enthusiastically promoted by advisers. The biggest and earliest impact was in milk production where advisers in the traditional dairy farming areas, working with ambitious young farmers, led the way in the adoption of improved management practices that transformed yields and incomes.

On the more traditional farms, the level of change needed to develop an efficient dairy herd was enormous and advisers had to work more slowly with this group in bringing about incremental improvements. As the systems of production became more refined and profitability improved, advisers in the non-traditional dairying areas embarked on an intensive campaign to establish specialist dairy enterprises. As a result, some of the most progressive and efficient dairy units began appearing in counties like Laois, Kilkenny, Wexford and Offaly - areas not previously identified with intensive dairying. Enthusiastic advisers, with the active support of researchers and specialists, played a huge part in helping to make this happen.

While the development of an integrated and profitable system of production gave a tremendous impetus to intensification, getting the key components right was critical. Prime examples were the pioneering work carried out at Moorepark on setting standards for milking machine components, cleaning equipment and refrigerated tanks, all of which were promoted by advisers. In a similar vein, the new technologies from Oak Park that revolutionised tillage farming were seized on and transferred to farmers. Other examples were the transmission by advisers of solutions from research to problems of mineral and trace element deficiencies in animals and crops.

Advisers worked hand-in-hand with research scientists in ensuring that the recipes for better farming were packaged in a user-friendly way and the scientists were extraordinarily generous with their time in attending meetings and in welcoming advisers and groups of farmers to the various research centers. In 1965, the Department of Agriculture established a specialist advisory service to provide leadership and in-service training to advisers and to act as the crucial link between the county advisers and the AFT research staff.

Specialists were appointed in all key areas of agriculture and horticulture as well as farm management and, under the direction of Ned Keating, they had the task of ensuring that advisers were up to date with research findings and had the confidence to promote them to farmers. The specialists also developed their own advisory innovations. One very simple and practical example was the introduction by Joe Prendergast of the frame fence for paddock grazing. Modeled on a system used in Victoria, Australia, it involved the use of simple materials and construction methods and rapidly became the standard throughout the country.

The Frame Fence

advisory service on the emerging intensive production sector was never the same as that on the earlier farmyard-based industry.

Advice on home butter-making was also seen as important by the DATI and, in the early-1900s, were appointed in this area. However, as the dairy co-ops developed, home butter-making became less important and the need for advice diminished. In 1911, there were 35 instructors in poultry and 33 in butter-making. By 1938, the roles were merged and there were 38 instructors in poultry and butter-making, with poultry the dominant feature of their work. Advice on home cheese production was also part of their brief but demand was low. All of the advisers were trained at the Munster Institute in Cork.

The number of poultry instructors (or advisers) peaked at 80 in 1950. Numbers declined steadily from the 1960s onwards and some were re-skilled for employment in the new farm home advisory service. As the demand for free range eggs and poultry emerged in the 1980's, interest in farmyard enterprises increased again and was supported by the remaining advisers. However, since there was no source of new graduates in poultry in Ireland (training of poultry advisers at the Munster Institute ended in 1975), the service continued to decline. In 2008, there is just one specialist poultry adviser working in the Teagasc rural development advisory service.

Emphasis on Poultry and Butter

Instructors in poultry and butter-making were among the earliest appointments by the Department of Agriculture and Technical Instruction (DATI) from 1900 onwards. The department established poultry stations from which sittings of eggs were provided to local farmers for hatching to produce birds for egg or poultry meat production. The stations were subsidised by the department and supervised by the poultry instructors who also advised on all aspects of production. The initiative led to a big increase in the national poultry flock and exports of eggs and poultry meat more than trebled between 1904 and 1917 – from under £3 million to over £9 million per annum – making poultry the second most important export item, after live cattle.

The industrialisation of poultry production spread from the US to Europe from the mid-1920s, leading to huge advances in breeding, nutrition, disease control and intensive housing. From the mid-1940s, the poultry stations began to give way to commercial hatcheries and the eventual vertical integration of the industry. Production at farm level declined rapidly and large units emerged, controlled either directly or indirectly by the processing industry. The influence of the poultry

Horticulture – A Chequered History

As part of the campaign of developing enterprises to generate increased income for farmers, the horticultural advisory service developed almost in parallel with the poultry service from the early-1900s onwards. As early as 1903, under the 'itinerant instructors' initiative established by the Department of Agriculture and Technical Instruction (DATI), eight counties had recruited instructors in horticulture and beekeeping. By 1911, the number of instructors had increased to 39 and remained at more or less the same level for the following two decades. By 1960, the number of instructors had increased to 62.

Activities during the first half of the 20th century concentrated on the growing of vegetables and fruit and the county committees of agriculture provided various incentives, including subsidising the cost of plants and trees. An early example of an initiative to promote horticulture was the planting in 1904 by the DATI of 20 acres of fruit at four centres, which were used by horticultural instructors for demonstration.

Another later example, in the 1940s, was the establishment by the government of over 60 glasshouses for tomato growing in Connemara under Scéim na d'Tithe Gloine (the Glasshouse Scheme). The experiment failed because of location and difficulties in marketing the produce.

The horticultural advisory service was expanded during the 1960s and 1970s when the number of advisers exceeded 80. However, in 1982, the newly established ACOT was instructed by the government to end the provision of advice on amenity horticulture. Over the following years, the number of advisers was more than halved through early retirement, recruitment embargoes and the retraining of some horticulturalists as tillage advisers. The service, which now consists of 10 advisers, is exclusively focused on commercial producers in mushrooms, fruit, nursery stock and vegetables.

Turf Wars Over Farm Home Advisers

In the early-1960s, attention switched to the training of farm women to enhance their home management skills and to enable them play a bigger role in running the farm business. The provision of advisory services that embraced both the home and farm had become well established in the US and some European countries and the Department of Agriculture set about establishing a similar service in Ireland and integrating it into the advisory services provided by the county committees of agriculture. However, the proposal met with stern opposition from the Department of Education, which insisted that the service should come under its control, as it was an extension of the home economics courses already conducted by vocational schools.

An interdepartmental committee, established by the Taoiseach Seán Lemass, ended in stalemate, with both departments refusing to give ground. The impasse was broken when the Second Programme for Economic Expansion, published in 1963, declared that the new service should be under the control of the Department of Agriculture.

A one-year pilot training course in farm home management had already started at the Munster Institute, involving 12 poultry advisers employed by the county committees of agriculture. Similar courses took place over the following years and, in 1965, a three-year diploma in farm home management was introduced. The course was later upgraded to degree status, with UCC as the awarding body. By 1966, there were 42 farm home advisers employed and in 1977 the number had increased to 84. The advisers played a major role in improving the skills of women in the management of the farm home and family finances. The training also enabled women to make an important contribution to the overall running and financial management of the farm. The service worked closely with the Irish Countrywomen's Association (ICA), which benefited from significant funding in the 1960s from the US Kellogg Foundation to promote training and personal development of women in farming.

The farm home advisory service fell victim to cutbacks in government funding for ACOT in the 1980s and was effectively disbanded. Advisers were retrained into new roles as socio-economic advisers and became involved in promoting and providing specialist advice on supplementary farm enterprises. In more recent years, the socio-economic service has been absorbed into the Teagasc rural development advisory service.

Experts in Farm Planning

The expertise of advisers in farm planning was demonstrated in the central role they played in the farm modernisation scheme, which was introduced following Ireland's entry into the EEC in 1973. The aim of the scheme was to bring incomes in farming up to the level of those enjoyed by non-agricultural workers and generous grants were provided to correct the low level of capital investment that had held farm development back for decades. It required an inordinate amount of advisory input and dominated the work of the advisory service throughout the 1970s and the early-1980s. It also resulted in a big increase in the number of advisers – from around 270 in 1966 to over 400 in 1977. Advisers got vital support in the areas of farm planning, farm management and account keeping from farm management specialists employed by the Department of Agriculture and later by ACOT.

Over 100,000 farmers participated in the farm modernisation scheme, which led to a significant increase in agricultural output. However, high interest rates and spiraling inflation resulted in participants failing to achieve the target income levels. The scheme gave farmers and advisers experience of working to a detailed plan, setting targets and assessing outcomes and clearly demonstrated the benefits of intensive advisory contact. Because of the huge amount of advisory time involved in meeting the administrative requirements of the scheme, it had the downside of making advisers desk bound, leading to a dilution of their role in technology transfer.

The Parish Plan

The 'parish plan' was the subject of much controversy and debate over a 10-year period between 1948 and 1958. Launched by Minister for Agriculture James Dillon in 1948, it involved assigning a parish agent to every three parishes in order to *"assist the farmers of the parish in obtaining maximum production from their holdings through improved farm practices and to encourage them to avail of the many schemes in operation for the improvement of agriculture"*. The concept was devised by Harry Spain, a contemporary of the 'Doc' in the Department of Agriculture, and had the enthusiastic support of Canon Hayes, founder of Muintir na Tíre and a very early leader in rural sociology. It was actively supported and promoted by Dillon.

The first parish agent was appointed in Bansha, Co Tipperary, the parish of Canon Hayes, in late-1948 and further appointments were made in Tydavnet in Monaghan and Ardee in Louth in 1949. The agents reported to the Department of Agriculture while other instructors in these counties were under the control of the county committees of agriculture. The initiative met with vehement opposition from the Agricultural Science Association (ASA), established in 1942 to represent the interests of agricultural graduates. The ASA objected to non-graduates being appointed as agents and was also opposed to the salary levels that were being paid. Fianna Fáil, which was now in opposition, was also opposed as was Macra na Feirme, which saw it as the centralisation of the advisory service within the Department of Agriculture. While the initial pilot scheme in the three parishes showed some evidence of success, the parish plan continued to be dogged in controversy and led to a fractious relationship between Dillon and the ASA. Ironically, the 'Doc' was president of the ASA during some of the more contentious exchanges with Dillon on the parish plan. However, this does not appear to have damaged the relationship between him and Dillon, who focused his opprobrium on the ASA as a body, describing is at one stage as *"the refuge for middle-aged incompetents"*.

When Fianna Fáil was returned to government after the 1951 general election, the parish plan was shelved. However, following the re-election of the inter-party government in 1954 and the return of Dillon as Minister for Agriculture, the plan was revived. The opposition from ASA continued and some parish agents were persuaded not to take up duty. The majority of the county committees of agriculture also refused to loan staff to work as parish agents. When Dillon left office in 1957, there were 24 parish agents employed and reporting to Harry Spain in the Department of Agriculture.

The First Programme for Economic Expansion, published in 1958, recommended that the initiative should be abandoned, stating that: *"…to allow two systems to develop, one centrally controlled by the state and the other under committees of agriculture, would inevitably lead to friction and confusion"*. That marked the end of the experiment. Many of the parish agents were absorbed into the inspectorate staff of the Department of Agriculture or joined the committees of agriculture while a few continued to operate in conjunction with the committees of agriculture while reporting to the district inspectors in the department.

The in-fighting and delays led to a loss of confidence in the state advisory services by progressive elements in the farming community and this resulted in at least three co-ops, in Cork and Wexford, appointing their own advisers. However, the parish plan concept had many good points, some of which were later adopted in the pilot areas in western counties and in the development of new methodologies for advisory work by county committees and later by ACOT.

The Long Road to ACOT

While the number of advisers increased rapidly during the 1950s, the service was still controlled by 27 county committees of agriculture, leading to poor national co-ordination. Also, because the costs of employing advisers were shared equally between the Department of Agriculture and the county committees, farmers in the poorer counties had access to fewer advisers. The number of farm holdings per adviser varied from 350 in Kildare to 1,500 in Donegal. To correct the imbalance, the government decided in 1962 to cover 75 per cent of the cost of advisers in the 12 western counties. While this led to an increase of 50 per cent in the number of advisers in these counties, the deficiencies in organisation and management persisted and these became more apparent with the success of AFT in developing new technologies.

In 1966, the Minister for Agriculture Charles Haughey commissioned W Emrys Jones and Albert J Davies, two senior executives from the advisory services in England and Wales, to carry out an independent appraisal of the services. The Jones/Davies report was presented to Haughey's successor, Neil Blaney, in 1967 and recommended the establishment of a unified national agricultural advisory service within the Department of Agriculture. No action was taken over the following four years and, in 1970, Blaney was sacked as minister by Taoiseach Jack Lynch during the crisis over the alleged importation of arms. Jim Gibbons was appointed Minister for Agriculture but the wheels of change in the advisory service continued to move slowly.

In January 1973, Gibbons circulated a memorandum that proposed the restructuring of the advisory service along the lines recommended in the Jones/Davies report. But the Dáil was dissolved before the government had an opportunity to discuss the proposal. The election resulted in a Fine Gael-Labour government with Mark Clinton as Minister for Agriculture. In April 1975, a White Paper published by the government proposed that the advisory and training services should be merged with AFT to form a national agricultural advisory, education and research authority. The proposal was subsequently incorporated into the National Agricultural Advisory, Education and Research Authority (NAAERA) bill, which was enacted in May 1977. As outlined elsewhere in this book, the new body, called the National Agricultural Authority (NAA), was vehemently opposed by Jim Gibbons, then opposition spokesman, who pledged to repeal the legislation when Fianna Fáil was returned to office.

National Structure

The June 1977 election saw the return of Fianna Fáil to government and Gibbons was re-appointed minister for agriculture. He proceeded to repeal the NAA legislation and, in 1978, introduced the Agriculture (An Comhairle Oiliúna Talmhaíochta) bill, which brought together the staff of the county committees of agriculture, the education staff in the agricultural colleges controlled by the Department of Agriculture and specialist advisory and education staff of the department into a single body.

The new body, called ACOT, was established in July 1980 with the 'Doc' (Dr Tom Walsh) as its first director. It marked the first restructuring of the advisory services, 80 years after the first 'instructor' was appointed.

The county committees of agriculture were retained, but with very limited functions, and AFT remained as a separate body for research.

ACOT was governed by a chairman and a 14-member board, drawn from the farming and rural organisations, the general council of committees of agriculture, staff and government appointees. With the objective of developing close linkages between advice and research, two members of the ACOT board would also sit on the AFT council. ACOT had three chairmen during its eight-year existence – James O'Keeffe, former president of the Irish Creamery Milk Suppliers Association (ICMSA), Paddy Donnelly, former CAO in Kildare and Matt Dempsey from the Irish Farmers Journal.

Framework for Technology Transfer

While ACOT was established at a period when both the national economy and agricultural profitability were in decline, the 'Doc' infused it with his enthusiasm for development and set about integrating 400 advisory staff from the county committees and some 30 specialist staff from the department. A regional structure was put in place to streamline management and to provide a specialist support structure for the county-based staff. With the introduction of a staff scheme in late 1983, the specialisation of advisory staff at local level became a reality. Under the direction of Liam Downey, who took over from the 'Doc' in January 1983, teams of national and regional enterprise specialists were established and specialised advisory staff put in place at county level. The framework for more effective transfer of technology from research centres to farms was now in place.

The introduction of milk quotas in 1984 put a huge constraint on the development of Irish agriculture, as expansion in dairying was by far the best development option for grassland farmers. Some dairy research staff understandably had difficulty facing up to the consequences of the milk quota and the need for dairy farmers to look at complementary alternative enterprises. ACOT specialists put tremendous effort into examining development options and produced an 'advisory casebook' of options for a range of farms at different stages of development.

This exercise gave direction at a time of great uncertainty and helped maintain a momentum for development in agriculture through expansion in ewe numbers, suckler cows and tillage.

The value of gross agricultural output declined in the two years following the introduction of the milk quota regime but increased subsequently until 1993. By that stage, however, with the MacSharry reforms in place, all avenues for expansion in the major enterprises were closed.

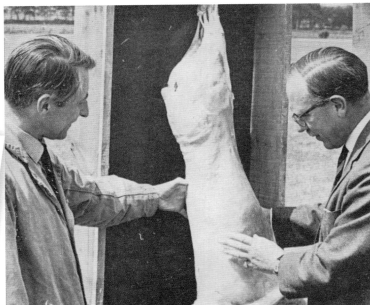

The establishment of Teagasc also saw the end of the county committees of agriculture, after 90 years in existence. They had been effectively reduced to talking shops on the formation of ACOT in 1980 and the 1988 Teagasc legislation provided for their disbandment, with surprisingly little opposition from the elected representatives in each of the 27 county structures.

The establishment of Teagasc was preceded by the introduction of charges for advisory services. Since 1900, all advisory services were free but, in September 1987, the government introduced legislation that required part of the cost of the service to be recovered from farmers. This was uncharted territory particularly for older advisers who had spent all of their working lives in a free service environment. Having examined the history of fee-paying services in other countries, ACOT decided on a system where all farmer clients would be asked to make some contribution to the cost of the service, with larger, commercial farmers paying higher fees to reflect the higher level of service provided. The objective was to maintain contact with the maximum number of farmers by keeping fees at a reasonable level.

Charges and Budget Cuts

The cut of 43 per cent in budget that accompanied the merging of ACOT and AFT to form Teagasc in 1988 led to a definite air of despondency across the new organisation. The advisory service was less damaged by the process as fewer advisers took early retirement and demand for advice and support from farmer clients remained strong, providing a boost in morale for advisers on the ground. Most damage was caused by the non-replacement of advisers as, in order to provide a level of service in areas that were short of staff, the specialisation of advisers unraveled to the detriment of the service. The number of agricultural advisers, which had peaked at 409 in 1977 and had dropped to 355 in 1986, fell to 256 in 1989.

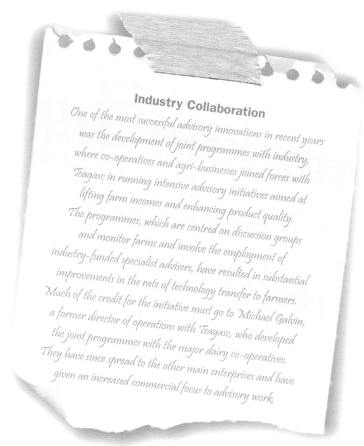

Industry Collaboration

One of the most successful advisory innovations in recent years was the development of joint programmes with industry, where co-operatives and agri-businesses joined forces with Teagasc in running intensive advisory initiatives aimed at lifting farm incomes and enhancing product quality. The programmes, which are centred on discussion groups and monitor farms and involve the employment of industry-funded specialist advisers, have resulted in substantial improvements in the rate of technology transfer to farmers. Much of the credit for the initiative must go to Michael Galvin, a former director of operations with Teagasc, who developed the joint programmes with the major dairy co-operatives. They have since spread to the other main enterprises and have given an increased commercial focus to advisory work.

The strategy worked and client contact was largely maintained over the first few years following the introduction of charges. When a whole range of new challenges began to emerge, in particular following the reform of the Common Agricultural Policy (CAP) in 1992, demand for services increased. The introduction of area aid payments to farmers and the onset of the rural environment protection scheme (REPS) in 1994 provided new opportunities for advisers to re-engage with their farmer clients and, very rapidly, demand for service exceeded the supply available. This resulted in a significant increase in the number of advisory staff for REPS planning and, in more recent years, to service other environmental protection and enhancement schemes.

The experience of charging for services in Ireland was dramatically different to that in other countries, notably England and Wales where charges were introduced in the mid-1980s. The British opted for a full cost recovery system from a small group of highly commercial farmers, leading to the privatisation of the service and a situation where agriculture is no longer its main market.

The negative impact of the lack of an advisory network, trusted by and in contact with the farming community, was clearly demonstrated in England and Wales in 2001 with the serious difficulties experienced in controlling the outbreak of foot and mouth disease.

The policy on charging for advisory services has now evolved to the stage where Teagasc competes with private sector operators in areas such as REPS planning and fees are based on full cost recovery, while technology transfer and public goods services are supported from the annual grant-in-aid from the government. EU and national support for advisory services has turned full circle and it is now an EU requirement that each state must have a 'Farm Advisory System' in place to assist farmers with the requirements of cross compliance, following the most recent reform of the CAP.

New Structures and Services

There are almost 500 advisers employed by Teagasc in 2008, one-third higher than the number employed following the merger of AFT and ACOT 20 years ago. The expansion in numbers has stemmed from the increased emphasis since the mid-1990s on protecting and enhancing the rural environment. One-third of all advisers are now involved in providing professional services for participants in the rural environment protection scheme (REPS) and in preparing nutrient management plans for farmers seeking derogations under the nitrates regulations.

All of these advisers operate on the basis of full recovery of the cost of the service. Some 140 business and technology advisers provide consultancy and technology-transfer services to commercial milk, beef, sheep, tillage, pig and horticultural producers, using leading-edge advisory and business management technologies. Less intensive and part-time farmers are assisted by the good farm practice service, which involves some 120 advisers and is focused on maximising income through a combination of farming, income support schemes and off-farm income.

With support payments from the EU and national exchequer constituting a significant proportion of farm income, helping farmers to comply with the myriad of regulations is a key component of the good farm practice service. Advisers in both services are supported by a corps of national and regional specialists, who provide technological and programme leadership and ensure that the results of research are transferred to frontline advisers.

A separate team of 24 specialists and advisers is involved in helping farmers to establish and run supplementary farm-based enterprises in tourism, food, horses, poultry and small animals and in supporting rural development initiatives and small business start-ups in rural areas. Reflecting the growth in farmer-owned forests during the past 15 years, a group of 10 professional foresters provide advice on all aspects of tree growing and harvesting.

From their establishment in 1900 until 2007, the advisory services were run on a county basis, with the chief agricultural officer (CAO) as manager. The services are now operated from 18 units, each under the control of an area manager and with a more uniform number of staff than existed under the rigid county system. This ensures a more effective delivery of advisory expertise in an ever-changing landscape for farming and food production.

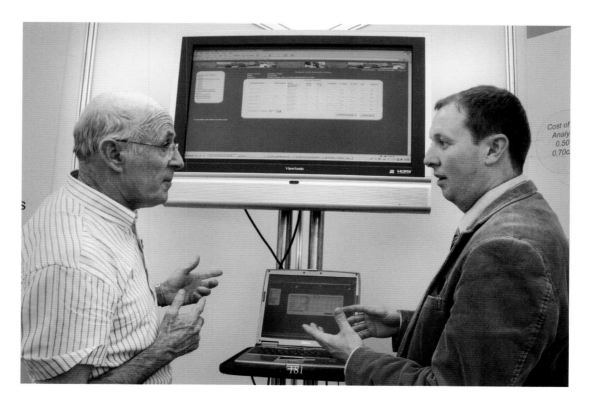

Tony Aylmer gives a demonstration to a group of students, Ballyhaise College, 1962.

Tony Foley demonstrates animal physiology, in Ballyhaise College, 1962.

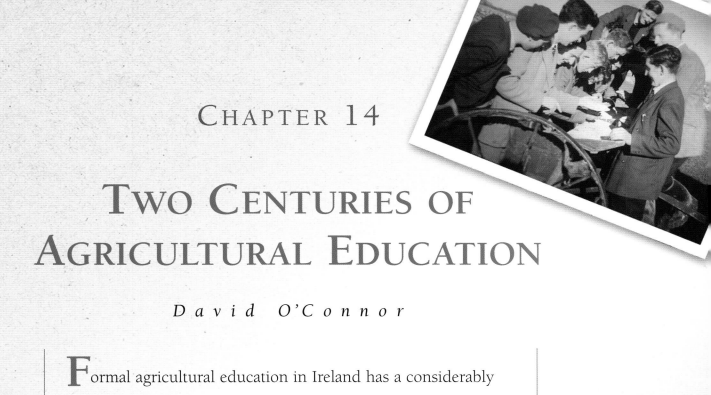

CHAPTER 14

TWO CENTURIES OF
AGRICULTURAL EDUCATION

David O'Connor

Formal agricultural education in Ireland has a considerably longer history than formal agricultural research. It has also had a much bumpier ride, structurally and financially, than research. Agricultural education has been exposed to the "market economy" to a much greater extent than the relatively cosseted institutional research, competing for students initially against inertia and the labour market and more recently against other disciplines and institutions. Throughout most of its existence, it has been chronically under-funded.

Mechanical grading of potatoes, Ballyhaise College, spring, 1962.

Model Schools

In the 19th century, a number of Model Schools were established, some by the Board of Education and some by local landlords. The first of these was set up in 1838 at Glasnevin, Dublin and later became the Albert College. In its early years, it was used to train teachers for rural primary schools who were then required to teach the principles of agricultural science to their pupils. By the early-1850s, there were 17 Model Agricultural Schools in the country, all of which were considerably smaller than the school in Glasnevin. By this time, there were also 37 Ordinary Agricultural Schools, primary schools in rural areas with a small plot of land where basic agriculture was taught.

Over the following decades, the Model Agricultural Schools died through lack of money so that by the 1880s only the Albert College in Dublin and the Munster Institute in Cork remained. The number of Ordinary Agricultural Schools continued to increase up to the end of the 1800s when the government decided to phase them out as the primary school was deemed not to be the appropriate place to teach agriculture.

The Department of Agriculture and Technical Instruction, the first Irish government department, was set up in 1899. Part of its remit was to provide agricultural education for farmers and future farmers. Horace Plunkett, the first vice-president of the department, equivalent to the Minister today, and its principal thinker on agricultural education, articulated the department's policy on this.

His memorandum, *Agricultural Education for Ireland,* in 1900, formed the basis of state policy on agricultural education for many years. He wrote that *"A thoroughly sound and modern system of agricultural education must precede any considerable or rapid progress towards a high state of efficiency in this our chief industry."*

Agricultural Colleges

On its establishment, the Department of Agriculture and Technical Instruction took over the running of the Albert College, where it offered courses in agriculture for men, and the Munster Institute, where it offered courses in poultry-keeping and butter-making for women.

It was instrumental in establishing a Faculty of Agriculture in the Royal College of Science in Merrion Street, Dublin in 1900. In 1904, the Franciscan Brothers in Mountbellew, Co Galway opened the first of the modern agricultural colleges, with financial assistance from the Department

Teacher John Murphy has the full attention of the well-dressed class of 35 at Ballyhaise.

James Moloney former vice-principal of Clonakilty College and Jim Flanagan, Teagasc director, at the college centenary celebrations in 2005.

The deployment of itinerant instructors was the other main plank of Plunkett's framework for the education and training of farmers. They were given the task of teaching part-time winter schools to practising farmers and carrying out field demonstrations and experiments. The first instructor was employed in 1900 and by 1908 a total of 34 had been deployed in 27 counties.

In 1920, nearly 20 years after the opening of the first private agricultural college at Mountbellew, the Salesian Order set up a college at Pallaskenry, Co Limerick. It enjoyed the same relationship with the department as did Mountbellew. Three years later, the Salesian Order opened another agricultural college at Warrenstown in Meath. The Department of Lands and Agriculture was then in place under the new Free State government with Patrick Hogan as Minister. In 1926, the department agreed to provide financial assistance to the new college at Warrenstown. In 1943, the Catholic diocese of Clougher set up the fourth privately owned agricultural college beside Monaghan town.

All of these colleges were for male students only. However, in 1947, the Methodist Church in Ireland set up Gurteen College as the first residential, co-educational agricultural college in the state. This was located at Ballingarry, Roscrea, Co Tipperary. It also opened a school of rural domestic economy there. In 1956, the Franciscan Order opened an agricultural college at Multyfarnham in Westmeath and, two years later, the Salesians added a horticultural college on the same campus as their agricultural college at Warrenstown.

of Agriculture and Technical Instruction. The department also set about establishing "Agricultural Stations" at strategic locations throughout the country. These were to serve as propagation and distribution centres for improved crops and livestock and agricultural inputs as well as providing agricultural education and training. In the period 1905 to 1914, it acquired relatively large farms for these purposes, at Athenry in Galway, Ballyhaise in Cavan, Clonakilty in Cork, Cookstown and Strabane in Tyrone and near Antrim town. During the first decade and a half of its existence, the department established an agricultural college at each of these locations.

Increased Focus

Following the flurry of activity in establishing state owned colleges by the British administration in the early-1900s, it was almost 50 years before the next state college was set up. The one small exception was the establishment of a horticultural college at the Johnstown Castle estate following the handing over of the estate to the Department of Agriculture in 1945. The college, which had an annual intake of only around 10 students, ceased operation in the late-1950s when AFT took over Johnstown Castle.

Over the next decade or so, student capacity was increased substantially through the establishment and modernisation of state and private colleges. In 1959, the Department opened the non-residential College of Amenity Horticulture at the National Botanic Gardens in Glasnevin, Dublin and a few years later two new state-owned agricultural colleges at Clonakilty and Athenry were built to replace the original colleges constructed 60 years earlier.

The Third Programme for Economic and Social Development, published in 1969 promised that: *"...about 300 extra student places will be provided in agricultural colleges before 1972."* Some of the steps taken to meet this commitment were the approval in 1969 of a new agricultural college, run by the Holy Ghost Order at Rockwell College, near Cashel in Tipperary, and the establishment by the Department of Agriculture of Kildalton Agricultural and Horticultural College at Piltown, Co Kilkenny in 1971.

Also, in the early-1970s, the department approved an expansion of Mountbellew College. Capacity for horticultural students was also increased with the establishment, in 1969, by the Irish Countrywomens Association of a college for girls at An Grianán, Termonfeckin, Co Louth. The last residential agricultural college to be set up in the state was at Ballinafad, near Balla in Mayo, which was established by Balla Co-operative Mart in 1980. It was also the shortest lived, closing down in 1989.

National Standards

As more agricultural colleges opened, the Department of Agriculture became more active in standardising the courses offered and, in the early-1960s, it revised the curriculum and introduced a national standard examination leading to the Certificate in Agriculture. While the one-year course in general agriculture was offered at all colleges and accounted for the vast majority of students, a number of enterprise specific second year courses were developed in some colleges.

Up to the 1960s, the majority of students at the agricultural colleges did not return to farming but sought employment in the off-farm agricultural industry. Also, many university students attended the colleges because, for a period, completing a year at an agricultural college was almost a prerequisite for doing a degree in agriculture at UCD. However, as farming became more commercial, an increasing proportion of farm inheritors did attend agricultural colleges. The founding of Macra na Feirme in 1944 had a very positive impact on attitudes of young farmers to education. In co-operation with local agricultural advisers, quite a lot of informal education took place through lectures, meetings and field evenings.

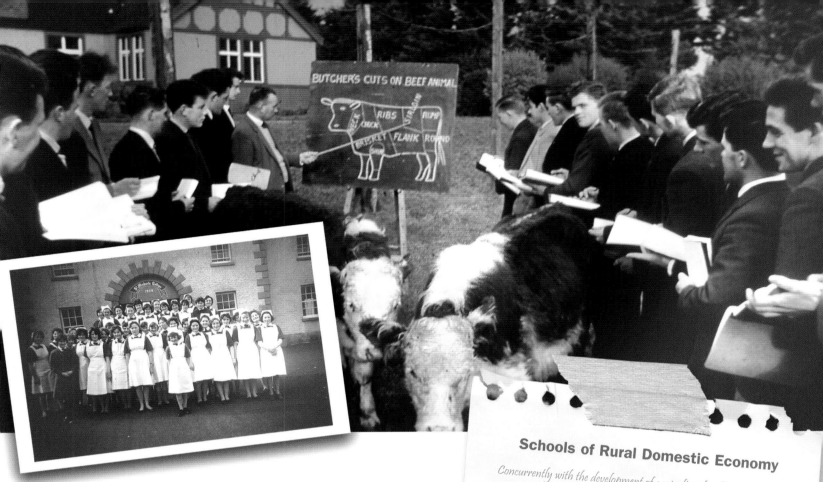

The Farm Apprenticeship Board was established in 1964 to provide a significant 'on the job' training component to the education of farm managers. A cohort of good farmers was identified who acted as Master Farmers to train the apprentices who had already completed a year at an agricultural college and who also attended block release courses during their apprenticeship. Some of the best farmers in Ireland today came through the Farm Apprenticeship Scheme.

Local Education and Training Initiatives

As well as the substantial expansion in college activity, there was also an extension of the training of young farmers at local centres. The most significant initiative occurred in 1959 with the establishment of the Winter Farm School. This was in response to the First Programme for Economic Expansion, published by the government in 1958. It was intended that the courses would be offered during the day, over two years, on a part-time basis. The courses were to be provided mainly by advisers employed by the county committees of agriculture with assistance from the vocational schools where many of the courses would be held. Initially, the Winter Farm Schools attracted large numbers of young farmers, an average of about 600 per year for the first 10 years. However, by the late-1960s, the vocational schools were under pressure to provide for second level students and they gradually withdrew from the programme. Eventually many of the courses contracted to one year and, increasingly, were offered at night.

Schools of Rural Domestic Economy

Concurrently with the development of agricultural colleges, a number of private colleges for girls from rural areas were established and attracted some financial assistance from the department. These were called Schools of Rural Domestic Economy and were all operated by catholic nuns. By 1908, there were schools at Portumna and Clifden in Galway, Westport, Swinford and Claremorris in Mayo, Loughglynn in Roscommon, Killeshandra in Cavan and Ramsgrange in Wexford.

Several more were established in later years including those at Navan in Meath, Ardagh in Longford, at Dunmanway and Millstreet in Cork and, as noted earlier, at Gurteen in Tipperary. Typically, these schools taught domestic science subjects as well as poultry keeping and butter making.

In the 1970s, the Schools of Rural Domestic Economy were re-titled Rural Home Economics Colleges to better reflect their course offerings. However, they were not to enjoy their new titles for very long. Changing aspirations of young women from farms as well as the increased availability of second and third level education and the opening of all agricultural colleges to women students had a serious impact on demand for places in these colleges. By 1980/81, the number of colleges had reduced to six which had a total of 262 students enrolled. In 1982, ACOT was instructed by the Department of Agriculture to cease funding the colleges and thus they were compelled to terminate their operations as Rural Home Economics Colleges. Most of them diversified into other educational activities.

New teaching facilities at Clonakilty, built in 2001.

Impact of AFT

The establishment of AFT in 1958 did not impinge directly on the agricultural education programme. However, the research conducted was eagerly absorbed and transmitted to students by the college teachers. The research bulletins were a welcome addition to the meagre supply of resource material in the colleges. Also, at that time there was a considerable turnover of teachers in colleges, mainly because of inferior pay and conditions, and several of the young teachers were personally acquainted with the new young researchers. Many of the researchers were generous with their time in giving lectures on their research findings at local colleges. The college students were eager attendees at open days held at the research centres.

New Structures and New Times

The new opportunities for farmers on joining the EEC in 1973 gave a considerable fillip to agricultural education. In particular, a network of local training centres was built around the country. These incorporated offices for the advisory services and classrooms and training kitchens for the farming community. The establishment of ACOT in 1980 brought the education and training services of the Department of Agriculture and the advisory and training services of the county committees of agriculture into a single national organisation. This led to a radical refocusing and expansion of agricultural education and training.

One of the first actions of the new ACOT director, Dr Tom Walsh, was to set up an expert group to recommend on the future provision of agricultural education. The most important recommendation of this group was that a training programme leading to a Certificate in Farming should be set up. In 1982, ACOT set up this three-year programme comprising formal course work and work experience. It could be followed in one of two ways - the College Option, where the student completed the one year course at an agricultural college followed by two years part time at a local ACOT training centre, or the Local Option, where the student completed three years course work part time at the local ACOT training centre. All participants were required to do work experience on what were called 'host farms'.

The launch of the new programme was accompanied by a substantial increase in the number of ACOT staff involved in education and training. In addition to a cohort of teachers in the 12 agricultural colleges and the four horticultural colleges that existed in the mid-1980s, over 60 full-time local education officers were designated by ACOT to deliver the Certificate in Farming. However, investment in facilities was paltry and many of the colleges were starved of capital funding and this was to remain for at least another decade.

The Certificate in Farming rapidly came to be recognised as the standard educational qualification for entry to farming and it became a required qualification for many of the financial aids available to young farmers. The availability of funding from The Youth Employment Agency initially and later from the European Social Fund was a great buffer for the programme at a time of severe constraints on ACOT's budget from the national exchequer. By 1994, the number of students participating in courses in colleges and local training centres had reached an all-time high of almost 1800, of which 650 were studying the local option of the Certificate in Farming.

In the meantime, the advisory, research and training services were merged into Teagasc in 1988 and education and training programmes were confronted with serious funding problems, starting with the 43 per cent cut in funding in the year the new body was established. In 1991, Teagasc set up a curriculum development unit, which updated the curriculum on an ongoing basis, introduced modularisation, made provision for student choice of subjects studied and produced a huge resource of staff manuals and student workbooks. In the mid-1990s, the Certificate in Rural Enterprise was introduced as a variation of the Certificate in Farming. This programme aimed to introduce participants to skills for off-farm employment as well as for farming, reflecting the growing shift towards part-time farming.

The shift to part-time farming was also one of the contributors behind the development, in recent years, of an e-college. The college has become a popular option for farm inheritors with jobs outside of farming who need the essential skills in production and management and who also require a minimum level of training in order to qualify for stamp duty relief and grants for farm development. It also has huge potential for providing updating courses on all aspects of farming and for executives and operatives in the food industry where the Teagasc food centres continue to have a vital training role.

National Accreditation

Up until the 1990s, first the Department of Agriculture and then ACOT and Teagasc, had the responsibility for accrediting and certifying the courses and training programmes that they provided.

In the late-1990s, moves were made to acquire external certification from the national certifying bodies. To facilitate this, courses were re-titled to fit into the national framework of course titles and six agricultural colleges and three horticultural colleges formed partnerships with adjacent institutes of technology to offer national certificate courses. Recipients of these certificates could progress to national diploma and degree courses. Recruitment to these courses would be through the Central Applications Office (CAO) and certificates would be awarded by the Higher Education and Training Awards Council (HETAC). All the other courses previously provided by Teagasc would lead to vocational or advanced certificates with the Further Education and Training Awards Council (FETAC) acting as the awarding body.

The new HETAC and FETAC courses were established in 2000. For the first time, agricultural training was brought into the mainstream education system and the potential for students to progress to degree level offered exciting opportunities. The availability of EU structural funds and the growth in the national economy from the mid-1990s onwards led to a better climate as far as funding was concerned. A major investment programme was initiated, particularly in the colleges that had formed partnerships with institutes of technology to provide third level courses. This investment brought facilities in many of these colleges up to the standards that existed in the institutes of technology.

Students at Kildalton College pictured in 2008.

Contraction

The national story of agricultural education for most of the 20th century was one of enormous expansion. However, a number of factors combined to dramatically decrease demand for agricultural education in the last decade or more. The number of farmers had been declining for decades. In the period between 1991 and 2002 the proportion of the workforce employed in agriculture fell from 14 per cent to 5 per cent with a 17 per cent decline in the number of farmers.

Level and survey exercise, 1962.

The national birth rate declined by one-third between 1980 and 1995. Farm incomes dropped and employment opportunities for young people outside of farming mushroomed in the late-1990s. This resulted in an increasing number of younger farmers having an off-farm job. There was also an enormous expansion in the number and variety of courses offered by the third level institutions, which attracted young people who in earlier years would have gone to agricultural colleges.

Two reports commissioned by Teagasc from the Economic and Social Research Institute, in 1995 and 2000, showed that demand for agricultural college places was almost certain to decline significantly. Numbers of students entering colleges peaked in 1996, at 1,150. By 2006, the number had fallen to 620 of whom two-thirds were participating in vocational courses and one-third in higher level courses.

Because of falling student numbers, several colleges were forced to close. Since 1998, five agricultural colleges, Monaghan, Athenry, Rockwell, Warrenstown and Multyfarnham have closed. The horticultural college at Termonfeckin, Co Louth also closed. Participation of young people attending courses at local training centres also dropped sharply. As noted earlier, the number of participants in the local option of the Certificate in Farming peaked in 1994, at 650, but it declined sharply to around 100 a decade later. Therefore, the total number of young people participating in formal training for careers in farming and related activities more than halved between the mid-1990s and the mid-2000s.

However, there is cause for some optimism. In 2007, enrolment in colleges increased by 25 per cent to 775, a figure not seen since 2003. The improvement in the fortunes of farmers, particularly those involved in dairying and tillage crops, and the brighter prospects for farming were clearly contributors to this increase. While many of the factors that have caused the contraction in numbers seeking agricultural education continue to exert an influence, the continuing downward trend in numbers during the past decade or more may have been halted. In any event, those who decide to pursue careers in farming have now the courses and the facilities that will equip them for the task.

CHAPTER 15

A FUTURE DRIVEN BY KNOWLEDGE AND INNOVATION

Gerry Boyle

Much has changed in the Irish agriculture and food sector since the establishment of An Foras Talúntais (AFT). Productivity has grown substantially, aided by the constant technological innovation and a continued outflow of labour from the primary sector. Better product prices in the wake of EEC entry, combined with improved productivity and an increase in the size of farms all in turn significantly lifted agricultural incomes. Consolidation in processing and the emergence of the plc model in the 1980s also improved efficiency and a number of key processing companies have become global players.

This chapter draws to a substantial extent on the recently published Teagasc Foresight Report, Towards 2030: Teagasc's Role in Transforming Ireland's Agri-Food Sector and the Wider Bioeconomy, May 2008.

Professor Gerry Boyle and Gale Buchanan, Under Secretary at the United States Department of Agriculture, keynote speaker at the Teagasc 2030 Foresight Conference, Dublin 2008

Membership of the EEC and latterly the EU utterly dominated the policy landscape of the agri-food sector for 35 of the last 50 years. The initial boost to prices gave way to a long and protracted reform process. While price support was attenuated and replaced by 'direct payments', the introduction of the milk quota in 1984 was perhaps the single biggest change. Following EEC entry, Irish milk production grew at an annual average rate of in excess of 5 per cent. The quota system halted this expansion. This policy has overshadowed the dynamic potential of the entire sector owing to the fact that dairying has consistently given the highest returns of all enterprises.

We are now again entering a unique era. Price support will at best be used as a safety net and the market place will be pre-eminent. An exporting nation like ours is a price taker and advances in incomes will be dependent on the capacity of the sector to improve productivity and to enhance the scale of production. The impending alleviation of the quota in a short seven years from now should unleash the latent growth potential of the sector and provide immense encouragement, especially for those young farmers who want to provide a better life for themselves and their families.

Investing in Knowledge

The dominance of a highly interventionist policy system in the agri-food sector for three decades or more also generated, as a consequence, a comparative neglect among policy makers and stakeholders alike of the critical role of knowledge creation and its transfer in the drive to improve farm incomes. Agriculture's requirement to become more self-reliant in the years ahead presages a central role again for the investment in and deployment of 'knowledge capital'.

The 1960s were a heady period of investment in 'knowledge capital' as the previous chapters in this publication amply demonstrate. A young AFT, supported by dynamic advisers and backed up by a commitment to farmer education, relentlessly pushed out the boundaries of what investment in useable knowledge could mean in real practical terms. A similar vibrancy beckons again.

The huge potential of the biotechnological revolution to transform the productivity of our agri-food sector is only partially grasped at present. But, unlike the 1960s, the receptivity, within Europe at least, to some aspects of these

technologies is lukewarm. Technologies such as GM, with their power to boost yields and drastically reduce costs, have the potential to address the current food security challenge and to make a real contribution to the problem of world hunger. Investment in knowledge is needed not alone to exploit this potential, but, faced with sceptical consumers, the knowledge of the safety and environmental impact of these technologies is, if anything, even more critical.

Investment in knowledge is also needed to ensure that the production and processing of food is environmentally sustainable, safe and traceable. Farmers have an instinctive appreciation of the value of sustainability. They want to hand on their farms to future generations in a manner that will generate a continuous flow of benefits. The targets adopted to reduce the sector's production of carbon by 2020 are challenging in the extreme and, if not modulated, will severely restrict capacity for expansion. Solutions' focused research will be required to overcome this dilemma. The challenges posed by the implementation of the EU Water Framework Directive and the impending directives that will address biodiversity and soils will also require creative research responses.

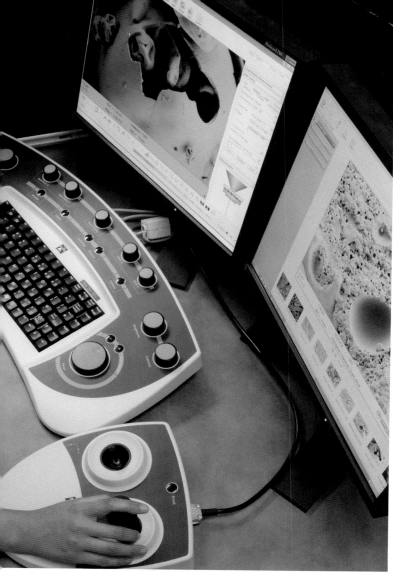

Vivian Gee obtaining images on the Field Emission-Scanning Electron Microscope on milk powder formulations at Moorepark.

Through a large network of farm advisory offices throughout the country, nearly 500 professional advisory staff work daily to transmit knowledge to some 45,000 farm families. Teagasc is also actively engaged in education and training, with close on 100 professionals employed in our network of colleges of further and higher education and local advisory and training centres.

This network is responsible for almost 700 students pursuing post-Leaving Certificate qualifications in professional agriculture, horticulture and equine courses. In addition, some 400 students are pursuing degree-level courses through joint programmes with a large number of institutes of technology throughout the country.

We have over 10,000 adults engaged annually – and the number is growing every year – in education and training activity through our newly established e-college and at virtually all of our 100 or so advisory and training centres. Teagasc is also a major participant in Ireland's fourth-level education system, mainly through its innovative Walsh Fellowship scheme, which was established in honour of Dr Tom Walsh. Currently, about 175 students are pursuing PhD programmes through the scheme in joint arrangements with all of Ireland's universities.

A Full Agenda

The agenda for an organisation like Teagasc thus appears more than full for the coming decades. The structure of Teagasc today, embracing as it does the functions of research, extension and education, is potentially better equipped than the fledgling AFT was to rise to the challenges of its era.

Teagasc today is a highly significant player in the development of Ireland's 'knowledge economy' and carries a particular leadership role in the agri-food sector and increasingly in the emerging wider bio-economy. Currently, it commands about seven per cent of public national research and development expenditure. It employs over 200 highly trained scientists across a range of cutting-edge disciplines.

195

The Knowledge Economy

For Ireland's agri-food and wider bio-economy to thrive in the future, its activities have to become fully integrated into the 'knowledge economy'. The 'knowledge economy' refers to the emphasis on investment in 'knowledge capital' as the means to meeting the economy's long-term rate of economic growth.

In order for living standards to grow in all economies, a constant level of capital investment is required. Capital can take on many forms - physical capital in the form of plant and machinery; public capital in the form of infrastructure; human capital in the form of education, training and work experience embedded in a country's labour force; and 'knowledge capital' which refers to the accumulation of ideas that enable new products and services to be developed, or, which outline new and more cost effective production systems.

The focus on 'knowledge capital' in recent years derives from the realisation that, due to its unique attributes, much higher rates of return can be generated from investment in this type of capital. Once a piece of knowledge is generated and made available publicly, for example, as a published scientific paper or a patent, it can then be used in a potentially infinite number of places at the same time. Moreover, the marginal cost of using this knowledge over and over again in different circumstances is virtually zero. No other form of capital shares these attributes.

The returns to investment in the creation of 'knowledge capital' are exceptionally high in circumstances where the knowledge is publicly available. But this also implies that the private sector will tend to under-invest in this form of capital because, in general, it is difficult for it to fully appropriate the benefits. As a consequence, the state will need to invest in 'knowledge capital', either on its own or in the form of public-private partnerships, to ensure that the economy-wide returns that can potentially accrue to investment of this type are maximised. This was the rationale for the establishment of AFT. The vision that led to that decision was clearly years ahead of conventional thinking regarding the role of publicly-funded research in promoting national economic development.

In recent years, government policy has recognised that investment in 'knowledge capital' has to be a central plank of national policy regarding economic development. This appreciation has led to innovative developments such as the establishment of Science Foundation Ireland (SFI) and the Programme for Research at Third Level Institutions (PRTLI). These initiatives in turn have led to the creation of many dedicated, multi-disciplinary research institutes within the third-level sector that have mirrored in many key respects the structures that were established by AFT and developed over the intervening years.

Conflicting Challenges

The application of useable knowledge will be even more important in underpinning the prosperity of our agricultural and food industries over the next 50 years than it has been for the past 50. There are several challenges but also immense opportunities. Challenges include the twin securities of food and energy. Related issues concern climate change and environmental sustainability. These challenges are conflicting to a considerable extent. On the one hand, the sector has the potential to significantly increase output and exports, especially in milk, and thereby contribute to easing global food security. Yet, the requirement to ensure environmental sustainability and at the same time alleviate the sector's contribution to the production of greenhouse gases places clear constraints on its capacity to respond to the challenge of food security. The role of research and knowledge transfer will play a central role in resolving these conflicting pressures.

The likely continuation of reform of agricultural policy driven by EU and global trade developments, will force changes in the structure of agricultural production with consequential implications for the processing sectors. Suckler beef production will be especially challenged in these circumstances. While the relative prices of many commodities over the medium term are likely to remain above the levels of recent decades, they are also likely to become much more volatile. Producers will thus have to adapt to greater risk.

The maintenance of competitiveness will also require a significant improvement in the capacity of our primary and processing sectors to absorb new technology. The capacity of the dairy sector to expand will also clearly require a concommitant enhancement of processing capacity. Against a backdrop of several years of relatively poor commodity prices and much uncertainty on the policy and market fronts, many young people have turned their backs on a career in farming. The motivation of the next generation of dynamic producers will be an overriding challenge.

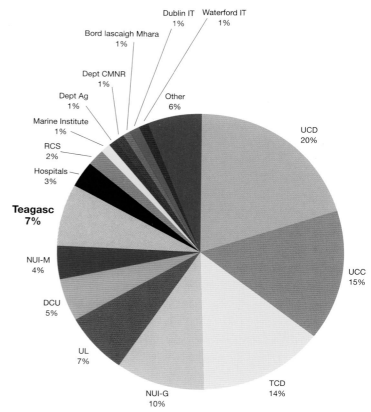

Source: Professor Paddy Cunningham

Research Performers 2006 (€633m)

Focus on the Bio-Economy

While there are clear and substantial challenges in the offing, there are even greater opportunities. The international markets for food production are growing, thanks to population and income growth in the huge economies of China and India. These trends, underpinned by a likely continuation of demand for bio-fuels, will assure an era of relatively firm prices for the foreseeable future. Strong global commodity prices are underpinned by the global cereals market. Ireland's comparative advantage in the production of livestock products from grass is poised to come to the fore.

The expected abolition of the dairy quota in 2015 carries the prospect of a substantial expansion in dairy output. There is huge scope for an expansion in production through the use of technological innovations in animal breeding and nutrition and especially through the efficient production and utilisation of grass.

The onset of 'peak oil' that is predicted by some experts to occur within the next 10-20 years will place the spotlight on the potential for biomass-based substitutes. The competitiveness of the food sector is also likely to be buttressed by profound shifts in consumer food preferences.

Food is no longer being consumed and valued for its energy and taste attributes. Consumers are increasingly concerned about the health and lifestyle benefits associated with particular food characteristics. More importantly for primary producers, consumers are prepared to pay for these characteristics as long as quality can be guaranteed and the health benefits scientifically verified. Consumers are also demonstrating a preference for foods of local origin and so-called artisan foods. They also are attaching a value to the rural environment and landscapes.

It is therefore reasonable to anticipate that traditional agricultural and food products will enjoy a sustained recovery in relative process over the medium term. At the same time, the scope of the sector to generate value will be considerably enhanced. The value-conversion capacity of our land resources has the scope for considerable expansion into the future. The focus will no longer be on the agri-food economy but on the bio-economy, which embraces the latter but also encompasses the production of bio-fuels and a potentially large range of non-fuel bio-products. The key resource in realising the potential of this new bio-economy will be the capacity within this new economy to create, transfer and deploy useable knowledge so as to underpin profitability, competitiveness and sustainability.

Farming and Processing Landscape

Given the nature of the challenges and opportunities for the bio-economy, clear demands will be placed on the farmers and processors of the future if they are to thrive. Farming will be much more knowledge-intensive than in the past and will need to be sustainable in both environmental and economic terms. Farmers will need to be highly educated and open to new models of doing business. They will have to cope with greater degrees of risk, especially in regard to prices. They will be producers of a range of products from food and animal feed to fuel and fibre. They will need to embrace new methods of doing business, including the adoption of more specialised production systems and partnership arrangements. Many more farmers than today will be actively engaged in investment in overseas farming businesses.

Processing entities of the future will also require re-configuration to prosper under the challenges and opportunities that lie ahead. Like farming, processing will also become a much more knowledge-intensive activity and processing operatives will be required to be more highly educated and trained. Sustainability will also be a core concern of these businesses. Their portfolio of products will need to be extended to embrace not only commodity products but also functional foods and foods for health. Artisan and foods of local origin will also achieve a significant market niche and offer greater opportunities for diversification both on and off farms. The processing of bio-products and the delivery of services in related markets is also likely to assume a certain market prominence.

The 'Open Innovation' Environment

The profitability of farms and processing firms and hence their competitiveness is driven by a combination of developments in productivity and relative product and input prices. Neither farms or firms can influence prices, which are driven by external factors. Therefore, the ultimate driver of competitiveness is the capacity of farms and firms to constantly improve productivity, which in turn is driven by the application of useable knowledge, or, in other words, by innovation.

Teagasc today is focused on science-based innovation support for its client sectors to a greater extent than ever was the case in the past. Innovation support requires the integrated delivery of research, advisory and education and training services. From the foundation of AFT until the establishment of Teagasc, these key elements of innovation operated under separate organisations but with significant collaboration between each element. Since 1988, these functions operate within a single organisational structure, which is unique in a European and probably global context, offering substantial potential to deliver a more effective innovation support service. It is fair to say, however, that this potential has not as yet been fully realised. It remains a major challenge for the future.

Innovation has been characterised as converting 'knowledge into money', unlike research, which converts 'money into knowledge'. Research focuses on 'producing knowledge' whereas innovation stresses the need to 'access knowledge'. A focus on research activity tends to be dominated by an emphasis on the scientific discipline and the pursuit of scientific curiosity. Innovation, on the other hand, is problem and solution focused. It thus tends to require a multi-disciplinary and team focus. Increasingly, this imperative will affect the nature of how Teagasc responds to the challenge of supporting our client sectors in an effective and relevant manner in face of their need to maintain and enhance competitiveness.

The nature of how our clients access useable knowledge has changed substantially since the foundation of AFT. For much of Teagasc's history, the application of knowledge could be characterised as following a 'gatekeeper model'. In other words, specialist researchers produced knowledge that was then transferred by advisers, and in some cases directly by researchers, through to farmers and processing firms. An educated farm and processing sector facilitated the absorption of this knowledge. That model is no longer relevant and will undergo further and radical evolution into the future.

Useable knowledge is acquired today in a much more 'open innovation' environment. Increasingly, more highly educated and trained farmers and processing-sector managers will acquire knowledge directly themselves in a global knowledge market place. They will have less need to rely on a 'gatekeeper' to filter the relevance and value of the knowledge that is available. Processing and input supply firms will perform a more interventionist role in delivering knowledge through to farmers. Large multi-national companies will engage in joint ventures with Irish companies and transfer knowledge through these arrangements.

What this implies for Teagasc is that we cannot take our relevance as knowledge brokers for granted. To retain our relevance we will need to be capable of and be seen to add value in an open innovation world. Organisational developments in recent years and planned changes in the future will be focused on ensuring this outcome.

The Need to Evolve

Ireland's agri-food and other bio-economy sectors of the future will need to be constantly innovative to ensure their competitiveness. In turn, Teagasc will need to innovate and evolve to provide the required science-based innovation support.

Within the livestock sectors, a concentration on reducing costs through better nutrition, improved animal health, greater utilisation of better quality grass and the breeding of animals with characteristics that maximise revenue will continue to receive priority. In tillage and energy crops, a similar focus will be placed on maximising yields and minimising costs through improved yield and disease-resistant varieties. At a more general level, the need to support the substantial potential expansion in the dairy sector in the wake of the abolition of quotas will require a particular focus from our research and advisory services.

The identification of efficiencies in labour use and the development of new optimal production systems will also demand particular attention. The suckler beef sector faces a huge challenge. Currently, only about 6 per cent of sucker-beef producers earn a derisory positive return from the market place. The future of beef production from this activity, especially as dairy quotas are abolished and direct payments are 'modulated', is under evident threat. Agriculture faces potential major restrictions from climate change and sustainability policies. The need for science-based innovation support to chart a path that will allow commercial farming to thrive while minimising its environmental impact will assume immense importance within the next decade. For Teagasc, its environmental research and development programme is and will increasingly need to become even more centred on solutions.

Innovation in the food sector will be concentrated on the development of high value-added products. Teagasc has developed an international expertise at the cutting edge of research in functional foods and nutraceuticals. The development of partnerships with other knowledge-providers in the universities and industry will help to ensure the rapid transfer of relevant and useable knowledge. Teagasc has the ambition to be the lead national player in this activity. We will need, however, to develop a more effective knowledge-transfer service for SME food companies in particular and to assist the enhancement of their capacity to absorb the kind of knowledge that will be generated.

Emphasis on Excellence

While I have given a high-level sketch of the likely research and development needs of the agri-food and wider bio-economy sectors over the next few years, it is impossible to identify in any comprehensive way the challenges that will need to be addressed. What is required, however, is that Teagasc ensures that 'it is fit for purpose' in both anticipating and responding to the innovation-support needs of our client sectors. Four requirements in this regard will be essential.

First, an emphasis on excellence, benchmarked against international norms, will need to be the hallmark of our core functions of 'knowledge creation', 'knowledge transfer' and 'knowledge absorption'. Second, Teagasc through its 'Vision' programme has embarked on a major investment in bio-science capability. The balance of recruitment has shifted from the exclusive traditional emphasis on the agricultural science graduate towards the recruitment of a range of specialist bio-scientists. These new staff and the associated capital investment will complement the existing corps of applied scientists in the animal, crops and food sectors.

The changed emphasis in terms of scientific capacity and skills will, of course, not alter Teagasc's mission of science-based innovation-support through the transfer of useable knowledge to our client sectors. However, we will now be equipped to effect potentially greater productivity enhancement and new product development for the benefit of these sectors. While the focus of the research activity will be unlikely to change appreciably, we can look forward with confidence to a much more rapid discovery process in areas such as animal and plant breeding as well as new product development in food and other bio-products.

Third, our commitment to 'knowledge transfer' and to the enhancement of 'knowledge absorption' will require a no lesser focus on international excellence. A commitment to ensure that Teagasc passes muster in respect of best international practice will be paramount.

Harnessing Resources

AFT and its successor Teagasc have been immensely fortified in their ability to service the needs of the agriculture and food sectors through an incredibly strong 'esprit de corps' throughout the organisation. In no small part, the durability of this ethos has been due to the strength of its internal structures. In AFT, the creation of substantially autonomous research centres ensured a commitment to excellence and a healthy competitive rivalry that helped to spur on constant innovation and a zest to achieve the best. The establishment of Teagasc added equally strong structures in the form of the county advisory system, which has recently been restructured into the area-management system, the specialist advisory corps and the network of advisory centres. These structures have served the industry well but we cannot stand still.

The fourth requirement stems from a recognition that excellence in the delivery of our core services is a necessary but not sufficient condition to ensure that the needs of our target sectors are adequately addressed. A commitment to working closely with our stakeholders in developing and reviewing all of our programmes on a partnership basis will also be required.

In this regard, much has changed in recent years and today we work closely through a number of highly effective 'commodity groups' comprised of key stakeholders. The effectiveness of these structures will be constantly reviewed and their role and contribution is likely to grow appreciably into the future.

The challenges faced by our agricultural and food sectors can no longer be easily boxed into neat commodity-specific categories. The challenges are increasingly becoming multi dimensional in scope. A good example of such a challenge is presented in the environmental area. It transcends all commodity areas and requires a multi-disciplinary response to devise effective solutions. Similarly, if we are to realise the opportunity presented in the current era of relatively high cereal prices to exploit our comparative advantage in grass, we will need to devise structures that embrace all livestock sectors and an eclectic mix of disciplines. Also, our investment in developing our capability in bio-sciences concerning animals, plants and foods requires innovative organisational structures to ensure the required critical mass and the necessary commodity focus.

Our knowledge transfer capacity can and will need to be enhanced by a deeper co-ordination between our applied research centres and our specialist advisory services. Likewise, the huge resource of our agricultural colleges must be harnessed to a more effective extent through the forging of linkages with our research and advisory activities. The challenge will be to conserve the best features of our traditional structures while, at the same time, superimposing an innovative organisational layer that will facilitate greater cross-disciplinary and cross-functional collaboration. This process would be greatly facilitated by the establishment within Teagasc of a single recruitment grade. This would enable people to move between the various functional areas of the organisation and to experience different roles throughout their careers.

The complexity of the challenges facing the agri-food and wider bio-economy sectors and the acknowledged rapid pace of change has meant that no organisation can validly claim to possess the required capacity to support the innovation needs of the overall sector.

Teagasc has a clear and well-defined capacity, which will evolve into the future but, if we are to be fully effective, we will need to devise and engage in partnerships with other knowledge providers on both a national and international basis. These partnerships across the spectrum of science-based innovation needs of the bio-economy will assist in devising an appropriate innovation-support agenda as well as the actors best equipped to deliver that agenda.

Stakeholder Confidence

For most of its existence AFT blazed a trail for what is today commonly referred to as the 'knowledge economy'. The modern Teagasc and its ambitious future agenda will assure that the agri-food and wider bio-sector plays a central role in that 'knowledge economy'. A continued commitment from the state to fund its activities will be rightly determined by the value that can be generated from that public investment. The continuation of public investment will be justified as long as Teagasc's activities are focused on addressing clear market failures, or, activities that privately-funded agencies would not care to support despite potentially high social returns.

Teagasc also needs to ensure that it continues to attract the confidence of its stakeholders. That confidence will be forthcoming as long as its programme of activities is relevant to their needs. Properly managed innovation-support systems have demonstrated time and time again that they repay the public investment involved handsomely. The evidence since AFT's foundation 50 years ago, as set out in the preceding chapters, strongly supports this proposition.

Teagasc Offices and Centres

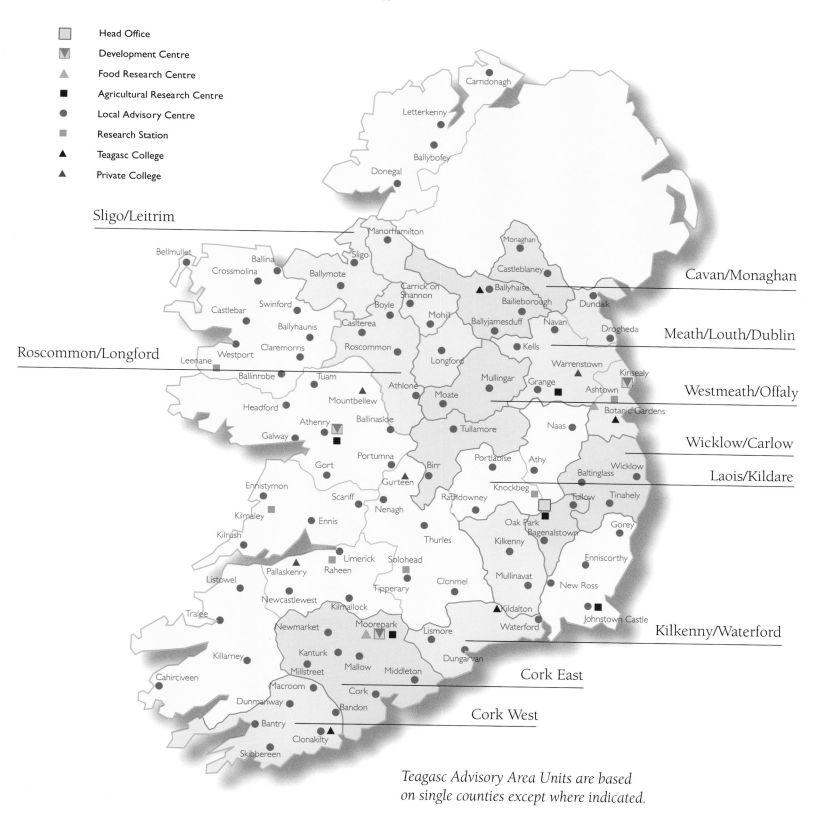

Head Office

Development Centre

Food Research Centre

Agricultural Research Centre

Local Advisory Centre

Research Station

Teagasc College

Private College

Sligo/Leitrim

Cavan/Monaghan

Meath/Louth/Dublin

Roscommon/Longford

Westmeath/Offaly

Wicklow/Carlow

Laois/Kildare

Kilkenny/Waterford

Cork East

Cork West

Carndonagh

Letterkenny

Ballybofey

Donegal

Manorhamilton

Monaghan

Bellmullet

Ballina

Sligo

Castleblaney

Crossmolina

Ballymote

Carrick on Shannon

Ballyhaise

Bailieborough

Dundalk

Castlebar

Swinford

Boyle

Mohil

Ballyjamesduff

Navan

Drogheda

Ballyhaunis

Caslterea

Roscommon

Kells

Claremorris

Longford

Warrenstown

Kinsealy

Leenane

Westport

Tuam

Mullingar

Grange

Ashtown

Ballinrobe

Athlone

Moate

Botanic Gardens

Headford

Mountbellew

Naas

Athenry

Ballinasloe

Tullamore

Galway

Portumna

Birr

Portlaoise

Athy

Wicklow

Gort

Gurteen

Baltinglass

Tullow

Tinahely

Ennistymon

Scariff

Nenagh

Rathdowney

Knockbeg

Gorey

Kilmaley

Ennis

Thurles

Oak Park

Bagenalstown

Enniscorthy

Kilrush

Kilkenny

Limerick

Solohead

Mullinavat

Kilruish

Pallaskenry

Raheen

Tipperary

Clonmel

New Ross

Listowel

Newcastlewest

Kilmallock

Kildalton

Tralee

Newmarket

Moorepark

Lismore

Waterford

Johnstown Castle

Killarney

Kanturk

Mallow

Middleton

Dungarvan

Cahirciveen

Millstreet

Macroom

Cork

Dunmanway

Bandon

Bantry

Clonakilty

Skibbereen

Teagasc Advisory Area Units are based on single counties except where indicated.

COUNCIL AND AUTHORITY MEMBERS

An Foras Talúntais: (1958-1988)
Teagasc: (1988-2008)

August 1958 – July 1961

John Litton – Chairman

George Mitchell
Matthew J Lyons
Seamus O'Donohoe
Patrick O'Loan
Jeremiah Buttimer
Professor Joseph Lyons
Professor John Carroll
Professor Connell Boyle
Patrick Bernard Connolly
John G Hill
James J Kennedy
James Mitchell

August 1964 – July 1967

John Litton – Chairman

Michael J Barry
Jeremiah Buttimer
Seamus O'Donohoe
Patrick J Finn
Vincent P Keeling
Fr Diarmuid Linehan
Matthew J Lyons
Professor James Mitchell
Professor James T Baxter
Fr Patrick Collins
Professor Desmond M McAleese
Professor Gerald T Pyne

August 1961 – July 1964

John Litton – Chairman

Michael J Barry
Nora Burton
Fr Patrick Collins
Michael T Connolly
Patrick Bernard Connolly
George Mitchell
Professor James Mitchell
John Phelan
Senator Michael A Prendergast
Professor James B Ruane
William Ryan
Professor Connell Boyle

September 1967 – July 1970

Dr Tadhg Ó'Tuama – Chairman

Matthew Joseph Bruton
Professor James T Baxter
Professor John Carroll (Sept 1968)
Michael Collins
Patrick Joseph Finn
James J Gallen
Martin O'Doherty
Joe Rea
John Richards Orpen
Professor Colm Ó hEocha
Dr Harry Spain
Professor Oliver M Roberts
Professor Thomas Clear (Dec 1968)

September 1970 – July 1973

Dr Tadhg Ó'Tuama – Chairman

Oonagh Corbett

Professor Thomas Clear

Patrick Joseph Finn

James J Gallen

Michael Grant

Michael Hassett

Professor Brendan S Mac Aodha

David O'Connor

Martin O'Doherty

Professor Timothy O'Mullane

Professor William A Watts

Dr Harry Spain

Professor Brian Spencer (March 1972)

September 1973 – July 1976

Paddy O'Keeffe – Chairman

Brendan L Brophy

Jerome Buttimer

Donal Cashman

Professor Edward J Clarke

Professor John Foley

Patrick Joseph Finn

Professor Patrick Fottrell

James J Gallen

Daniel Mullane

Martin O'Doherty

Edward Sheehy

Professor Brian Spencer

September 1976 – July 1979

Paddy O'Keeffe – Chairman

Donal Cashman

Professor Edward J Clarke

Professor John Foley

Patrick Joseph Finn

Professor Patrick Fottrell

James J Gallen

Daniel Mullane

Martin O'Doherty (retired December 1977)

Edward Sheehy

Professor Brian Spencer (retired March 1978)

Peter Coghill

Michael Gibbons

Eugene Harrington (December 1977)

Professor J V McLoughlin (March 1978)

Members of the Council of AFT pictured in September 1964, Seated (from left): Matthew J Lyons, Fr Diarmuid Linehan, John Litton, Chairman, Fr Patrick Collins, Professor Desmond M McAleese. Standing (from left): Dr Tom Walsh, Director, Professor Gerald T Pyne, Vincent P Keeling, Michael J Barry, Professor James Mitchell, Jeremiah Buttimer, Professor James T Baxter, Patrick J Finn and Seamus O'Donohoe.

September 1979 – July 1985

Rory Murphy – Chairman

Patrick Brennan (retired July 1982)

Redmond Brennan

William Carroll

Peter J Coghill

Sean Finlay (retired May 1980)

Patrick J Finn

Professor Patrick Fottrell

Eugene Harrington (retired June 1981)

Dr John McCarthy (retired September 1982)

Professor John V McLoughlin

Professor Thomas F Raftery

Liam Whyte

Anthony Byrne
(April 1980 – February 1983)

James J Gallen
(Retired February 1983)

Hugh Ryan (October 1980)

Joseph S Rowan
(October 1981 – July 1983)

Dermot McNamara
(September 1982 – March 1985)

Professor Eamonn J Gallagher
(September 1982)

Dan Leahy (May 1983)

Michael Broderick (May 1983)

Dr Patrick Power (September 1983)

Eamonn Gannon (May 1985)

December 1985 – July 1988

Matt Dempsey – Chairman

Michael Broderick

William Carroll

Con Scully

Gerard Murray

James J Sullivan

John Barry

Professor Patrick Fottrell

Professor John V McLoughlin

Hugh Ryan

Professor Eamonn J Gallagher

Dan Leahy

Dr Patrick Power

Eamonn Gannon

Professor John Foley

September 1988 – August 1993

Joe Rea – Chairman

Thomas Butler

Maurice Harvey

Professor Patrick Fottrell

Donal McDaid

Mary Walsh

Michael O'Dwyer

Padraig Walshe

Patrick Joseph Woulfe

Helen O'Dowd

Dr Patrick Power

John Donnelly (April 1991)

Professor Charles Daly (March 1992)

September 1993 – September 1998

Dan Browne - Chairman

William Gleeson

Professor Charles Daly (retired February 1997)

John Donnelly (retired December 1994)

Helen O'Dowd

Maurice Harvey

Mary Walsh (retired February 1997)

Dr Patrick Power (retired July 1996)

Michael O'Dwyer

Professor Patrick Fottrell

Tom Neville (May 1994)

Michael Slattery (January 1995 – March 1998)

Jim Beecher (September 1996)

Dan McSweeney (May 1997)

Carmel Fox (April 1997)

John Dillon (March 1998)

Eva Coyle

October 1998 – September 2003

Dr Tom O'Dwyer - Chairman

John Dillon (retired May 2002)

Maurice Harvey (retired September 2001)

Peter Kiely

Dan McSweeney (retired March 2002)

Carmel Fox (retired March 2002)

Jim Beecher

Professor Patrick Fottrell

Tom Neville (retired April 1999)

Michael O'Dwyer

Tom Gill (June 1999)

Joe Fitzgerald (November 2001)

James Brett (May 2002)

Anna May McHugh (May 2002)

Ruaidhri Deasy (June 2002)

October 2003 – September 2008

Dr Tom O'Dwyer – Chairman

Professor Patrick Fottrell

Margaret Sweeney (May 2007)

Joe Fitzgerald

James Brett

Stephen Flynn

Michael O'Dwyer

Martin Heraghty (October 2007)

Derek Deane (May 2006)

Patrick Kelly

Jerry Henchy

Jim Beecher (retired September 2007)

Anna May McHugh (retired April 2007)

Ruaidhri Deasy (retired June 2006)

Members of the AFT Senior Management Team pictured in 1971. Standing from left: John Kilroy, David Robinson, Michael Mulcahy, Vivian Timon, P J O'Hare and Larry O'Moore. Seated from left: Simon Curran, Tomás Breathnach, Dr Tom Walsh, Pierce Ryan, Bernard Crombie, Pat Ryan and Michael O'Sullivan.

1.

Farmers and instructors came in their thousands to An Foras Talúntais Open Days in recent weeks. Our pictures show: 1. Dr. Michael Neenan at Oakpark, talking to Instructors about trials on a straw-dwarfing hormone for cereals. 2. Gathering of growers and instructors at the Glasshouse Crops Open Day at Kinsealy. 3. Mr. Bernard Rice outlining his research work on sprayers in the Engineering Department, Oakpark. 4. Dr. Vivian M. Timon explaining sheep breeding work at Creagh. 5. Dr. Nigel Downey outlines research on hoose in relation to calf-rearing research at Grange. 6. Group at Moorepark discussing with Mr. D. Browne his work on nitrogen on pasture in terms of animal production. 7. Farmers take time off from discussions to inspect livestock on the Ballyderown farm, Moorepark

4.

6.

5.

This spread is reproduced from the AFT publication 'Farm Research News'.

research centres

2.

3.